Blazor WebAssembly By Example

Second Edition

Use practical projects to start building web apps with
.NET 7, Blazor WebAssembly, and C#

Toi B. Wright

BIRMINGHAM—MUMBAI

Blazor WebAssembly By Example
Second Edition

Copyright © 2023 Packt Publishing

Senior Publishing Product Manager: Suman Sen

Acquisition Editor – Peer Reviews: Saby Dsilva

Project Editor: Amisha Vathare

Content Development Editor: Shazeen Iqbal

Copy Editor: Safis Editing

Technical Editor: Aneri Patel

Proofreader: Safis Editing

Indexer: Sejal Dsilva

Presentation Designer: Pranit Padwal

Developer Relations Marketing Executive: Priyadarshini Sharma

First published: June 2021

Second edition: February 2023

Production reference: 1210223

Published by Packt Publishing Ltd.
Livery Place
35 Livery Street
Birmingham
B3 2PB, UK.

ISBN 978-1-80324-185-2

www.packt.com

To my boys, for their never-ending patience and understanding. To my readers, for their ceaseless curiosity about new technologies.

– Toi B. Wright

Foreword

Hi, friends! I love a good second edition. It's an opportunity to update and add to something that's already great. You take feedback from the readers and the community, absorb the zeitgeist, and turn an A into an A+. Toi has taken **Blazor WebAssembly By Example** to the next level and now we welcome you all, readers old and new.

I have known Toi Wright for more than 17 years. I first met her at the Microsoft MVP Summit in Redmond back in 2005, if you can believe that. She is a brilliant technologist, community leader, and tech organizer, and we see each other every year at the annual Microsoft MVP Summit. I've had the opportunity to travel from my home in Portland to beautiful Dallas to speak in person at the Dallas ASP.NET User Group where she's the president and founder.

Toi has been very active in the ASP.NET community for many years. She brings energy and expertise to everything she does. She has written courseware for Microsoft on ASP.NET and this is her third book on the topic. She's a respected programmer, architect, and communicator.

In this book, she walks you step by step through the creation of 11 standalone projects that are built using the Blazor WebAssembly framework. You'll learn how to leverage your experience with the .NET ecosystem to complete many different types of projects. Blazor takes .NET – and your .NET skills – to the web in a new way, and this book is the key.

The second edition adds small updates everywhere, but also includes new chapters on debugging, deploying to Azure, and using tech like Azure Active Directory to secure a Blazor WebAssembly app.

In **Blazor WebAssembly By Example**, Toi shares her extensive knowledge and years of experience as a web developer and has created an easy-to-follow guide for you to quickly learn how to use the Blazor WebAssembly framework. Through her words, step-by-step instructions, copious screenshots, and code samples, you will get started running C# in your browser instead of JavaScript. Everything she'll show you, including .NET and Blazor itself, is all open source and based on open standards! I'm so glad that we both have a partner in Toi Wright to guide us in this powerful new web framework!

Scott Hanselman – hanselman.com

Partner Program Manager at Microsoft

Host of the Hanselminutes Fresh Tech Podcast

Contributors

About the author

Toi B. Wright has been obsessed with ASP.NET for over 20 years and has been recognized as a Microsoft MVP in ASP.NET for the past 18 years. Toi is a full-stack web developer on the Microsoft stack as well as a book author, courseware author, speaker, and community leader with over 25 years of experience with full life-cycle application development in a corporate environment. She has a BS in computer science and engineering from the Massachusetts Institute of Technology (MIT) and an MBA from Carnegie Mellon University (CMU).

Toi B. Wright currently works with an amazing team at First Command Financial Services, Inc.

You can reach her on Twitter at @misstoi.

I would like to thank my husband and our two sons for their unwavering patience and encouragement during the countless hours I spent typing away at my computer writing this book. I could not have done this without you.

About the reviewers

Michele Aponte has been a passionate programmer since 1993, and has worked as a Java, .NET, and JavaScript programmer for several Italian software houses and IT consultancy firms. In 2013, he founded the IT company Blexin, which helps its customers to migrate their old solutions to new technologies, offering them training, consulting, and development.

In 2020 he founded Ellycode to combine two great passions of his life, artificial intelligence and user experience, which led to the creation of a dashboarding and data visualization platform: Elly. Last but not least, his passion for teaching prompted Michele to found Improove; a startup that will redefine the concept of teaching online courses.

He has always believed in the value of sharing, which is why, in December 2008, he founded DotNetCampania, a Microsoft community for which he has organized many free regional conferences. Microsoft awarded him the MVP award for these activities. In 2020, he brought his passion to Blazor Developer Italiani, the Italian community on the Blazor framework, of which he is the founder and community manager. His love for digital pushed him, again in 2020, to join Fare Digitale, an association that promotes the enhancement of digital culture in Italy.

Michele also speaks at the most important Italian and international conferences on Microsoft and JavaScript technologies. He has written several technical books and defines himself as a community addict.

Vincent Baaij has been working as a developer/consultant/architect in the IT industry for over 25 years and is still learning new things every day. His focus has always been on the Microsoft and .NET stack. Since 1999, he has worked primarily with content management systems like Umbraco and Episerver (now Optimizely). The open-source tools he created when he was an Episerver employee are ranked among the most popular community-contributed packages.

At present, Vincent works as a Cloud Solution Architect at Microsoft where he helps customers to be successful on the Azure platform. He is also the maintainer of the official Microsoft Fluent UI Web Components for Blazor library, an open-source component package that wraps the Fluent UI Web Components for use with .NET 6.0 or higher Blazor applications.

Join our community on Discord

Join our community's Discord space for discussions with the author and other readers:

https://packt.link/BlazorWASM2e

Table of Contents

Chapter 10: Using Azure Active Directory to Secure a Blazor WebAssembly Application   287

Chapter 11: Building a Task Manager Using ASP.NET Web API   325

Chapter 12: Building an Expense Tracker Using the EditForm Component   353

Preface

Blazor WebAssembly is a framework that enables you to build single-page web applications that use C# on the client instead of JavaScript. It is built on the popular and robust ASP.NET framework. Blazor WebAssembly does not rely on plugins or add-ons for you to use C# in the browser. It only requires that the browser support WebAssembly, which *all* modern browsers do.

In this book, you will complete practical projects that will teach you the fundamentals of the Blazor WebAssembly framework. Each chapter includes a stand-alone project with detailed step-by-step instructions. Each project is designed to highlight one or more important concepts concerning Blazor WebAssembly.

By the end of the book, you will have experience with building both simple stand-alone web applications and hosted web applications with SQL Server backends.

This is the second edition of this book. In this edition, we have added chapters on debugging, deploying to Microsoft Azure, and securing your application using Microsoft Azure Active Directory. Also, all the projects in the book have been updated to use the latest version of the Blazor WebAssembly framework.

Who this book is for

This book is for experienced web developers who are tired of the constant parade of new JavaScript frameworks and want to leverage their experience with .NET and C# to build web applications that can run anywhere.

This book is for anyone who wants to learn Blazor WebAssembly quickly by emphasizing the practical over the theoretical. It uses complete, step-by-step sample projects that are easy to follow to teach you the concepts required to develop web apps using the Blazor WebAssembly framework.

You do not need to be a professional developer to benefit from the projects in this book, but you do need some experience with C# and HTML.

What this book covers

Chapter 1, Introduction to Blazor WebAssembly, introduces the Blazor WebAssembly framework. It explains the benefits of using the Blazor framework and describes the differences between the three hosting models: Blazor Server, Blazor Hybrid, and Blazor WebAssembly. After highlighting the advantages of using the Blazor WebAssembly framework, the goals and support options for WebAssembly are discussed. Finally, it guides you through the process of setting up your computer to complete the projects in this book. By the end of this chapter, you will be able to proceed to any of the other chapters in this book.

Chapter 2, Building Your First Blazor WebAssembly Application, introduces Razor components through the creation of a simple project. This chapter is divided into two sections. The first section explains Razor components, routing, Razor syntax, and how to use `Hot Reload` while developing an application. The second section walks you step by step through the process of creating your first Blazor WebAssembly application by using the Blazor WebAssembly App project template provided by Microsoft. By the end of this chapter, you will be able to create a demo Blazor WebAssembly project.

Chapter 3, Debugging and Deploying a Blazor WebAssembly App, teaches you how to debug and deploy a Blazor WebAssembly app through the creation of a simple project. This chapter is divided into two sections. The first section explains debugging, logging, handling exceptions, using **ahead-of-time (AOT)** compilation, and deploying an app to Microsoft Azure. The second section walks you step by step through the process of debugging and deploying a Blazor WebAssembly application. By the end of this chapter, you will be able to debug a simple Blazor WebAssembly app and deploy it to Microsoft Azure.

Chapter 4, Building a Modal Dialog Using Templated Components, provides you with an introduction to templated components through the creation of a modal dialog component. This chapter is divided into two sections. The first section explains `RenderFragment` parameters, `EventCallback` parameters, and CSS isolation. The second section walks you step by step through the process of creating a modal dialog component and moving it to your own custom Razor class library. By the end of this chapter, you will be able to create a modal dialog component and share it with multiple projects through a Razor class library.

Chapter 5, Building a Local Storage Service Using JavaScript Interoperability (JS Interop), teaches you how to use JavaScript with Blazor WebAssembly through the creation of a local storage service. This chapter is divided into two sections. The first section explains the reasons that you still need to occasionally use JavaScript and how to invoke a JavaScript function from .NET. For completeness, it also covers how to invoke a .NET method from JavaScript. Finally, it introduces the Web Storage API that is used by the project. In the second section, it walks you step by step through the process of creating and testing a service that writes and reads to the local storage of the browser. By the end of this chapter, you will be able to create a local storage service by using JS Interop to invoke JavaScript functions from a Blazor WebAssembly application.

Chapter 6, Building a Weather App as a Progressive Web App (PWA), provides you with an introduction to progressive web apps through the creation of a simple weather web app. This chapter is divided into two sections. The first section explains what a PWA is and how to create one. It covers both manifest files and the various types of service workers. Also, it describes how to use the CacheStorage API, the Geolocation API, and the OpenWeather One Call API that are required by the project in this chapter. The second section walks you step by step through the process of creating a 5-day weather forecast app and converting it into a PWA by adding a logo, a manifest file, and a service worker. Finally, it shows you how to install and uninstall the PWA. By the end of this chapter, you will be able to convert a Blazor WebAssembly app into a PWA by adding a logo, a manifest file, and a service worker.

Chapter 7, Building a Shopping Cart Using Application State, explains how to use application state through the creation of a shopping cart web app. This chapter is divided into two sections. The first section explains application state and dependency injection. The second section walks you step by step through the process of creating a shopping cart application. To maintain state in your application, you will create a service that you will register in the DI container and inject into your components. By the end of this chapter, you will be able to use dependency injection to maintain application state within a Blazor WebAssembly app.

Chapter 8, Building a Kanban Board Using Events, provides you with an introduction to event handling through the creation of a Kanban board web app. This chapter is divided into two sections. The first section discusses event handling, attribute splatting, and arbitrary parameters. The second section walks you step by step through the process of creating a Kanban board application that uses the `DragEventArgs` class to enable you to drag and drop tasks between the drop zones. By the end of this chapter, you will be able to handle events in your Blazor WebAssembly app and will be comfortable using both attribute splatting and arbitrary parameters.

Chapter 9, Uploading and Reading an Excel file, explains how to upload various types of files and how to use the **Open XML SDK** to read an Excel file. This chapter is divided into two sections. The first section explains uploading one or more files and resizing images. It also explains how to use virtualization to render data and how to read data from Excel files. The second section walks you step by step through the process of creating an application that can upload and read an Excel file and then use virtualization to render the data from the Excel file. By the end of this chapter, you will be able to upload a file into a Blazor WebAssembly app, use the Open XML SDK to read an Excel file, and render data using virtualization.

Chapter 10, Using Azure Active Directory to Secure a Blazor WebAssembly Application, teaches you how to secure a Blazor WebAssembly App through the creation of a simple application that displays the contents of a claim. This chapter is divided into two sections. The first section explains the difference between authentication and authorization. It also teaches you how to work with authentication and how to use both the Authorize attribute and the AuthorizeView component. The second section walks you step by step through the process of adding an application to Azure AD and using it for both authentication and authorization. By the end of this chapter, you will be able to secure a Blazor WebAssembly app using Azure AD.

Chapter 11, Building a Task Manager Using ASP.NET Web API, provides you with an introduction to hosted Blazor WebAssembly applications through the creation of a task manager web app. This is the first chapter to use SQL Server. It is divided into two sections. The first section describes the components of a hosted Blazor WebAssembly application. It also explains how to use the HttpClient service and the various JSON helper methods to manipulate data. The last section walks you step by step through the process of creating a task manager application that stores its data in a SQL Server database. You will create an API controller with actions, using Entity Framework. By the end of this chapter, you will be able to create a hosted Blazor WebAssembly app that uses ASP.NET Web API to update data in a SQL Server database.

Chapter 12, Building an Expense Tracker Using the EditForm Component, teaches you how to use the EditForm component through the creation of an expense tracker web app. This chapter uses SQL Server. It is divided into two sections. The first section introduces the EditForm component, the built-in input components, and the built-in validation components. It also explains how to use navigation locking to prevent the user from navigating to another page before they have saved their edits. The last section walks you step by step through the process of creating an expense tracker application that uses the EditForm component and some of the built-in components to add and edit expenses that are stored in a SQL Server database. By the end of this chapter, you will be able to use the EditForm component in conjunction with the built-in components to input and validate data that is stored in a SQL Server database.

To get the most out of this book

We recommend that you read the first two chapters of the book to understand how to set up your computer and how to use a Blazor WebAssembly project template. After that, you can complete the remaining chapters in any order. The projects in each chapter become more complex as you proceed through the book. The final two chapters require a SQL Server database to complete the projects. *Chapter 3* and *Chapter 10* require a Microsoft Azure subscription.

You will require the following software/hardware covered in the book:

- Visual Studio 2022 Community Edition
- SQL Server 2022 Express Edition
- Microsoft Azure

If you are using the digital version of this book, we advise you to type the code yourself or access the code via the GitHub repository (link available in the next section). Doing so will help you avoid any potential errors related to the copying and pasting of code.

This book assumes that you are an experienced web developer. You should have some experience with C# and HTML.

There are some projects that use JavaScript and CSS, but all the code is provided. Also, there are two projects that use Entity Framework, but once again, all the code is provided.

Download the example code files

You can download the example code files for this book from GitHub at `https://github.com/PacktPublishing/Blazor-WebAssembly-by-Example-Second-Edition`. In case there's an update to the code, it will be updated on the existing GitHub repository.

We also have other code bundles from our rich catalog of books and videos available at `https://github.com/PacktPublishing/`. Check them out!

Code in Action

Code in Action videos for this book can be viewed at (`https://packt.link/CodeinAction`).

Download the color images

We also provide a PDF file that has color images of the screenshots/diagrams used in this book. You can download it here: `https://packt.link/Q27px`.

Conventions used

There are several text conventions used throughout this book.

CodeInText: Indicates code words in text, database table names, folder names, filenames, file extensions, pathnames, dummy URLs, user input, and Twitter handles. Here is an example: "Add the DeleteProduct method to the @code block."

A block of code is set as follows:

```
private void DeleteProduct(Product product)
{
    cart.Remove(product);
    total -= product.Price;
}
```

When we wish to draw your attention to a particular part of a code block, the relevant lines or items are set in bold:

```
public class CartService : ICartService
{
    public IList<Product> Cart { get; private set; }
    public int Total { get; set; }

    public event Action OnChange;
}
```

Any command-line input or output is written as follows:

```
Add-Migration Init
Update-Database
```

Bold: Indicates a new term, an important word, or words that you see onscreen. For example, words in menus or dialog boxes appear in the text like this. For example: "From the **Build** menu, select the **Build Solution** option."

Warnings or important notes appear like this.

 Tips and tricks appear like this.

Get in touch

Feedback from our readers is always welcome.

General feedback: If you have questions about any aspect of this book, mention the book title in the subject of your message and email us at customercare@packtpub.com.

Errata: Although we have taken every care to ensure the accuracy of our content, mistakes do happen. If you have found a mistake in this book, we would be grateful if you would report this to us. Please visit www.packtpub.com/support/errata, selecting your book, clicking on the Errata Submission Form link, and entering the details.

Piracy: If you come across any illegal copies of our works in any form on the Internet, we would be grateful if you would provide us with the location address or website name. Please contact us at copyright@packt.com with a link to the material.

If you are interested in becoming an author: If there is a topic that you have expertise in and you are interested in either writing or contributing to a book, please visit authors.packtpub.com.

Share your thoughts

Once you've read *Blazor WebAssembly By Example, Second Edition*, we'd love to hear your thoughts! Scan the QR code below to go straight to the Amazon review page for this book and share your feedback.

https://packt.link/r/1803241853

Your review is important to us and the tech community and will help us make sure we're delivering excellent quality content.

Download a free PDF copy of this book

Thanks for purchasing this book!

Do you like to read on the go but are unable to carry your print books everywhere? Is your eBook purchase not compatible with the device of your choice?

Don't worry, now with every Packt book you get a DRM-free PDF version of that book at no cost.

Read anywhere, any place, on any device. Search, copy, and paste code from your favorite technical books directly into your application.

The perks don't stop there, you can get exclusive access to discounts, newsletters, and great free content in your inbox daily

Follow these simple steps to get the benefits:

1. Scan the QR code or visit the link below

https://packt.link/free-ebook/9781803241852

2. Submit your proof of purchase
3. That's it! We'll send your free PDF and other benefits to your email directly

1

Introduction to Blazor WebAssembly

Blazor WebAssembly is Microsoft's new **single-page application (SPA)** framework for building interactive web applications on **.NET Framework**. Since it is built on .NET Framework, Blazor WebAssembly allows you to run C# code on the client as well as the server. Therefore, instead of being forced to write **JavaScript** on the client, we can now use C# everywhere.

> *Blazor is red hot!*
>
> *Run C# on the client.*
>
> *Goodbye, JavaScript!*

In this chapter, we will explain the benefits of using the **Blazor** framework. We will introduce the three different Blazor hosting models and discuss both the advantages and disadvantages of each of them. Also, we will discuss the goals of **WebAssembly** and share where it is supported. Finally, we will guide you through the process of setting up your computer to complete the projects in this book.

In this chapter, we will cover the following topics:

- Benefits of using the Blazor framework

- Hosting models:

    - **Blazor Server**

    - **Blazor Hybrid**

    - Blazor WebAssembly

- Differences between the Blazor hosting models

- What is **WebAssembly**?

- Setting up your PC

Benefits of using the Blazor framework

Using the Blazor framework offers several benefits. For starters, it is a free and open-source framework built on Microsoft's robust and mature .NET Framework. Also, it is a SPA framework that uses **Razor** syntax and can be developed using Microsoft's exceptional tooling. Finally, Microsoft is actively supporting and updating the Blazor framework. Let's examine each of these benefits in detail in the following sections.

.NET Framework

The Blazor framework is built on .NET Framework. Therefore, anyone familiar with .NET Framework can quickly become productive using the Blazor framework. The Blazor framework leverages the robust ecosystem of .NET libraries and NuGet packages from .NET Framework. Also, since the code for both the client and server can be written in C#, the client and server can share code and libraries. For example, the client and server can share the application logic used for data validation.

Open source

The Blazor framework is open source. Since Blazor is a feature of the **ASP.NET** framework, all the source code for Blazor is available on GitHub as part of the dotnet/aspnetcore repository, which is owned by the **.NET Foundation**. The .NET Foundation is an independent, non-profit organization established to support the innovative, commercially friendly, open-source ecosystem around the .NET platform. The .NET platform has a strong community of over 100,000 contributions from more than 3,700 companies.

Since .NET Framework is free, this means that Blazor is also free. There are no fees or licensing costs associated with using Blazor, including for commercial use.

SPA framework

The Blazor framework is a SPA framework. As the name implies, a SPA is a web app that consists of a single page. The application dynamically rewrites the areas of the page that have changed instead of loading an entirely new page in response to each UI update. The goal is faster transitions that make the web app feel more like a native app.

When a page is rendered, Blazor creates a render tree that is a graph of the components on the page. It is like the **Document Object Model (DOM)** created by the browser. However, it is a virtual DOM. Updates to the UI are applied to the virtual DOM and only the differences between the DOM and the virtual DOM are rendered by the browser.

Razor syntax

Razor is the ASP.NET view engine used to create dynamic web pages with C#. Razor is a syntax for combining HTML markup with C# code that was designed for developer productivity. It allows the developer to use both HTML markup and C# in the same file.

Blazor web apps are built using **Razor components**. Razor components are reusable UI elements that contain C# code, markup, and other Razor components. Razor components are quite literally the building blocks of the Blazor framework. For more information on Razor components, refer to *Chapter 2, Building Your First Blazor WebAssembly Application*.

> **IMPORTANT NOTE**
>
> **Razor Pages** and **MVC** also use the Razor syntax. Unlike Razor Pages and MVC, which render the whole page, Razor components only render the DOM changes. One way to easily distinguish between them is that Razor components use the RAZOR file extension, while both MVC and Razor Pages use the CSHTML file extension.

The name of the Blazor framework has an interesting origin story. The term *Blazor* is a combination of the word *browser* and the word *razor*.

Awesome tooling

You can use either **Microsoft Visual Studio** or **Microsoft Visual Studio Code** to develop Blazor applications. Microsoft Visual Studio is an **integrated development environment (IDE)**, while Microsoft Visual Studio Code is a lightweight, yet powerful, editor. They are both incredible tools for building enterprise applications. As an added bonus, there are versions of both tools that are available for free.

Supported by Microsoft

Although the Blazor framework is open source, it is maintained by Microsoft. They continue to make large investments in the future of Blazor. The following list includes features that Microsoft is actively working on adding to Blazor:

- Hot reload improvements
- **Ahead-of-time (AOT)** compilation performance improvements
- Authentication improvements
- Additional built-in components
- Multithreading

There are many benefits associated with using the Blazor framework to develop web applications. Since it is built on .NET Framework, it enables developers to use the skills, such as C#, and the tools, such as Visual Studio, that they have already mastered. Also, since it is a SPA framework, Blazor web apps feel like native apps to the user. Finally, Microsoft is making a large investment in the future of Blazor.

Hosting models

As we mentioned earlier, Razor components are the building blocks of Blazor applications. Where those Razor components are hosted varies depending on the hosting model.

Blazor has three different hosting models:

- Blazor Server
- Blazor Hybrid
- Blazor WebAssembly

The first hosting model that Microsoft released was Blazor Server. In this hosting model, the Razor components are executed on the server. The second hosting model that Microsoft released, and the topic of this book, is Blazor WebAssembly. In this hosting model, the Razor components are executed on the browser using WebAssembly. The newest hosting model is Blazor Hybrid. Blazor Hybrid allows you to build native client apps by hosting the Razor components in an embedded Web View control.

Each hosting model has its own advantages and disadvantages. However, they all rely upon the same underlying architecture. Therefore, it is possible to write and test your code independently of the hosting model.

The major differences between the hosting models concern where the code executes, latency, security, payload size, and offline support. The one thing that all the hosting models have in common is the ability to execute at near native speed.

Blazor Server

As we just mentioned, the Blazor Server hosting model was the first hosting model released by Microsoft. It was released as part of the .NET Core 3 release in September 2019.

The following diagram illustrates the Blazor Server hosting model:

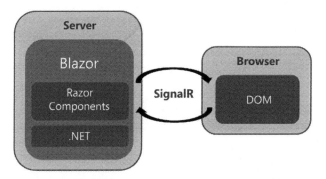

Figure 1.1: Blazor Server

In this hosting model, the web app is executed on the server and only updates to the UI are sent to the client's browser. The browser is treated as a thin client and all the processing occurs on the server. Therefore, this model requires a constant connection to the server. When using Blazor Server, UI updates, event handling, and JavaScript calls are all handled over an ASP.NET Core **SignalR** connection.

IMPORTANT NOTE

SignalR is a software library that allows the web server to push real-time notifications to the browser. Blazor Server uses it to send UI updates to the browser.

Advantages of Blazor Server

There are a few advantages of using Blazor Server versus using Blazor WebAssembly. However, the key advantage is that everything happens on the server. Since the web app runs on the server, it has access to everything on the server. As a result, security and data access are simplified. Also, since everything happens on the server, the assemblies (DLLs) that contain the web app's code remain on the server.

Another advantage of using Blazor Server is that it can run on thin clients and older browsers, such as Internet Explorer, that do not support WebAssembly.

Finally, the initial load time for the first use of a web app that is using Blazor Server can be much less than that of a web app that is using Blazor WebAssembly because there are much fewer files to download.

Disadvantages of Blazor Server

The Blazor Server hosting model has several disadvantages versus Blazor WebAssembly. The biggest disadvantage is that the browser must maintain a constant connection to the server. Since there is no offline support, every single user interaction requires a network roundtrip. As a result of all these roundtrips, Blazor Server web apps have higher latency than Blazor WebAssembly web apps and can feel sluggish. Also, network interruptions may cause a client to unexpectedly disconnect.

TIP

Latency is the time between the UI action and the time when the UI is updated.

Another disadvantage of using Blazor Server is that it relies on SignalR for every single UI update. Microsoft's support for SignalR has been improving, but it can be challenging to scale. When too many concurrent connections to the server are open, connection exhaustion can prevent other clients from establishing new connections.

Finally, a Blazor Server web app must be served from an **ASP.NET Core server**.

Blazor Hybrid

The Blazor Hybrid hosting model is the most recent hosting model released by Microsoft. It was released as part of the .NET 6 release in November 2021.

The following diagram illustrates the Blazor Hybrid hosting model:

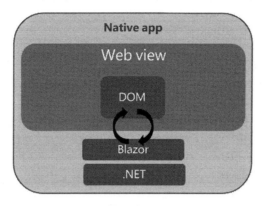

Figure 1.2: Blazor Hybrid

In this model, the Razor components run in an embedded Web View control. Blazor Hybrid apps include Windows Forms, WPF, and .NET MAUI apps. By using the Blazor Hybrid hosting model, your apps have full access to the native capabilities of the devices that you choose to target.

Advantages of Blazor Hybrid

The advantage of using this model versus Blazor WebAssembly is that it does not require WebAssembly. Also, since the component's C# code is executed in the host process, the Blazor Hybrid apps have access to the native capabilities of the device.

Disadvantages of Blazor Hybrid

The major disadvantage of using Blazor Hybrid is that they are hosted in a Web View component in the native app. So, the developer must know how to develop each type of native client app that they want to target. Another disadvantage is that they usually require a server to deliver the app. In contrast, a Blazor WebAssembly app can be downloaded as a set of static files.

Blazor WebAssembly

The Blazor WebAssembly hosting model is the topic of this book.

Blazor WebAssembly 3.2.0 was released in May 2020. **Blazor WebAssembly in .NET 5** was released as part of the **.NET 5.0** release in November 2020. **ASP.NET Core Blazor** was released as part of the .NET 6.0 release in November 2021, and it is a **long-term support (LTS)** release. The most recent release of Blazor WebAssembly was released as part of the .NET 7 release in November 2022 This book will be using **Blazor WebAssembly in .NET 7** for all the projects.

TIP

LTS releases are supported by Microsoft for at least 3 years after their initial release. Blazor WebAssembly in .NET 7 is a current release rather than an LTS release. Current releases get free support and patches for 18 months. We recommend that if you are starting a new project with Blazor WebAssembly, you should use the most recent release.

The following diagram illustrates the Blazor WebAssembly hosting model:

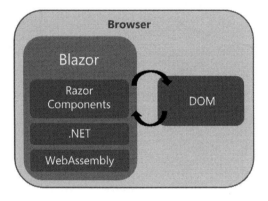

Figure 1.3: Blazor WebAssembly

In this hosting model, the web app is executed on the browser. For both the web app and the .NET runtime to run on the browser, the browser must support WebAssembly. WebAssembly is a web standard supported by all modern browsers, including mobile browsers. While Blazor WebAssembly itself does not require a server, the web app may require one for data access and authentication.

In the past, the only way to run C# code on the browser was to use a plugin, such as **Silverlight**. Silverlight was a free browser plugin provided by Microsoft. It was very popular until Apple decided to forbid the use of any browser plugins on iOS. As a result of Apple's decision, Silverlight was abandoned by Microsoft.

IMPORTANT NOTE

Blazor does not rely on plugins or recompiling the code into other languages. Instead, it is based on open web standards and is supported by all modern browsers, including mobile browsers.

Advantages of Blazor WebAssembly

Blazor WebAssembly has many advantages. First, since it runs on the browser, it relies on client resources instead of server resources. Therefore, the processing is offloaded to the client. Also, unlike Blazor Server, there is no latency due to each UI interaction requiring a roundtrip to the server.

Blazor WebAssembly can be used to create a **Progressive Web App** (**PWA**). A PWA is a web app that looks and feels like a native application. They provide offline functionality, background activity, native API layers, and push notifications. They can even be listed in the various app stores. By configuring your Blazor WebAssembly app as a PWA, your app can reach anyone, anywhere, on any device with a single code base. For more information on creating a PWA, refer to *Chapter 6, Building a Weather App as a Progressive Web App (PWA)*.

Finally, a Blazor WebAssembly web app does not rely on an ASP.NET Core server. In fact, it is possible to deploy a Blazor WebAssembly web app via a **Content Delivery Network** (**CDN**).

Disadvantages of Blazor WebAssembly

To be fair, there are some disadvantages when using Blazor WebAssembly that should be considered. For starters, when using Blazor WebAssembly, the .NET runtime, the dotnet.wasm file, and your assemblies need to be downloaded to the browser for your web app to work. Therefore, the first time you run a Blazor WebAssembly application it usually takes longer to initially load than an identical Blazor Server application. However, there are strategies that you can use to speed up the initial load time, such as deferring the loading of some of the assemblies until they are needed. Also, this is only an issue during the initial load since subsequent runs of the application will access the files from a local cache.

Another disadvantage of Blazor WebAssembly web apps is that they are only as powerful as the browser that they run on. Therefore, thin clients are not supported. Blazor WebAssembly can only run on a browser that supports WebAssembly. Luckily, due to a significant amount of coordination between the **World Wide Web Consortium** (**W3C**) and engineers from Apple, Google, Microsoft, and Mozilla, all modern browsers support WebAssembly.

Hosting model differences

The following table indicates the differences between the three models:

	Blazor WebAssembly	Blazor Hybrid	Blazor Server
Native execution speed	X	X	X
Executes on client	X	X	
Executes on server			X
Low latency after initial load time	X	X	
Fast initial load time			X
Offline support	X	X	
Does not require a server	X		
Requires constant connection to a server			X
Can build PWAs	X		
Assemblies sent to client	X	X	
Assembles remain on server			X
Can access native client features		X	
Requires WebAssembly	X		
Requires SignalR			X
Can run on thin clients			X

Table 1.1: Hosting model differences

The Blazor framework provides three different hosting models, Blazor Server, Blazor Hybrid, and Blazor WebAssembly. A Blazor Server web app runs on the server and uses SignalR to serve the HTML to the browser. A Blazor Hybrid web app runs in a Web View control in the native app. A Blazor WebAssembly web app runs directly in the browser using WebAssembly. They each have their advantages and disadvantages. However, if you want to create interactive, highly responsive, native-like web apps that can work offline, we recommend Blazor WebAssembly. Let's learn more about WebAssembly in the next section.

What is WebAssembly?

WebAssembly is a binary instruction format that allows code written in high-level languages, such as C#, to run on the browser at near-native speed. To run .NET binaries in a web browser, it uses a version of the .NET runtime that has been compiled to WebAssembly. You can think of it as executing natively compiled code in a browser.

WebAssembly is an open standard developed by a W3C Community Group. It was originally announced in 2015, and the first browser that supported it was released in 2017.

WebAssembly goals

When WebAssembly was originally being developed, there were four main design goals for the project. This is a list of the original goals for WebAssembly:

- Fast and efficient
- Safe
- Open
- Don't break the web

WebAssembly is fast and efficient. It is designed to allow developers to write code in any language that can then be compiled to run in the browser. Since the code is compiled, it is fast and performs at near-native speed.

WebAssembly is safe. It does not allow direct interaction with the browser's DOM. Instead, it runs in its own memory-safe, sandboxed execution environment. You must use JavaScript interop to interact with the DOM. The project in *Chapter 5*, *Building a Local Storage Service Using JavaScript Interoperability (JS interop)*, will teach you how to use JavaScript interop.

WebAssembly is open. Although it is a low-level assembly language, it can be edited and debugged by hand.

WebAssembly didn't break the web. It is a web standard that is designed to work with other web technologies. Also, WebAssembly modules can access the same Web APIs that are accessible from JavaScript.

Overall, WebAssembly was able to meet all of the original goals and rapidly gained support from all of the modern browsers.

WebAssembly support

As mentioned earlier, WebAssembly runs on all modern browsers, including mobile browsers. As you can see from the following table, all current versions of the most popular browsers are compatible with WebAssembly:

Browser	Version
Microsoft Edge	Current
Mozilla Firefox, including Android	Current
Google Chrome, including Android	Current
Safari, including iOS	Current
Opera, including Android	Current
Microsoft Internet Explorer	Not Supported

Table 1.2: WebAssembly browser compatibility

IMPORTANT NOTE

Microsoft Internet Explorer is no longer supported by Microsoft as of June 15, 2022. It does not support WebAssembly and will never support WebAssembly.

WebAssembly is a web standard that allows developers to run code written in any language in the browser. It is supported by all modern browsers.

Now that we have discussed the benefits of using the Blazor framework and compared the various hosting models, it's time to start developing using the Blazor WebAssembly framework. However, before we can get started, you need to set up your PC.

Setting up your PC

For the projects in this book, we use Microsoft Visual Studio Community 2022, .NET 7, Microsoft SQL Server 2022 Express Edition, and Microsoft Azure.

All the projects are built using **Microsoft Visual Studio Community 2022 (64-bit) – Current Version** 17.4.2 with the ASP.NET and Web Development workload. If you need to install Microsoft Visual Studio Community 2022, follow the directions in the *Installing Microsoft Visual Studio Community Edition* section later in this chapter.

TIP

Although we are using Microsoft Visual Studio Community 2022, any edition of Microsoft Visual Studio 2022 can be used to complete the projects in this book. Microsoft Visual Studio Code can also be used. However, all the screenshots are from Microsoft Visual Studio Community 2022.

Blazor WebAssembly in .NET 7 requires .NET 7.0. To determine the version of .NET that is running on your computer, open **Command Prompt** and enter the following command:

```
dotnet --version
```

If your computer is not running .NET 7.0 or higher, follow the directions in the *Installing .NET 7.0* section later in this chapter.

Chapters 3 and *10* use Microsoft Azure. *Chapter 3* uses Microsoft Azure to publish a Blazor WebAssembly application and *Chapter 10* uses Microsoft Azure Active Directory to secure a Blazor WebAssembly application.

The final two projects in this book use **Microsoft SQL Server 2022 Express Edition** as the backend database. If you need to install Microsoft SQL Server Express Edition, follow the directions in the *Installing Microsoft SQL Server Express* section later in this chapter.

TIP

Although we are using Microsoft SQL Server 2022 Express Edition, any year or edition of SQL Server can be used to complete the projects in this book.

Installing Microsoft Visual Studio Community Edition

Microsoft Visual Studio Community Edition is the free edition of Microsoft Visual Studio. To install Microsoft Visual Studio Community Edition, perform the following steps:

1. Download the **Visual Studio installer** from https://visualstudio.microsoft.com.

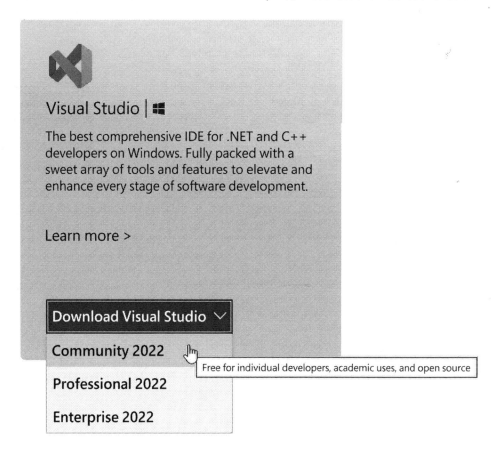

Figure 1.4: Download Visual Studio selector

2. Once the download is complete, run the installer to complete the installation.

3. During the first step in the installation process, the Visual Studio installer will check the system for existing versions of Visual Studio. Once the installer has finished checking for installed versions, it will open the following installation dialog:

Figure 1.5: The Visual Studio installer

4. Select the **ASP.NET and web development** workload and click the **Install** button to complete the installation.

Installing .NET 7.0

To install .NET 7.0, perform the following steps:

1. Download the **.NET 7.0** installer from `https://dotnet.microsoft.com/download/dotnet/7.0`. We are using the **Windows x64 SDK Installer**.

2. Once the download completes, run the installer to complete the installation of .NET 7.0 on your computer.

3. Open **Command Prompt** and enter the following command to verify that your computer is now running .NET 7.0:

```
dotnet --version
```

The following screenshot is from a computer that is running .NET 7.0:

Figure 1.6: .NET version

Installing Microsoft SQL Server Express

Microsoft SQL Server Express is the free edition of Microsoft SQL Server. To install Microsoft SQL Server Express, do the following:

1. Download the Microsoft SQL Server installer for **SQL Server Express** from `https://www.microsoft.com/en-us/sql-server/sql-server-downloads`.

2. After the download completes, run the SQL Server installer.

3. Select the **Basic** installation type:

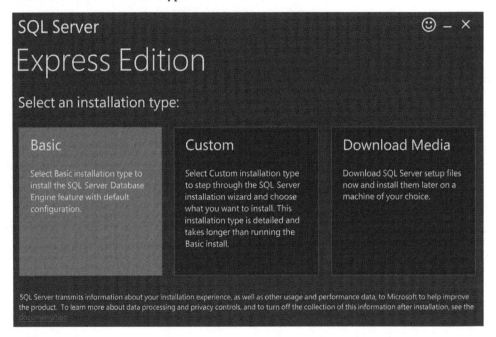

Figure 1.7: The SQL Server installer

4. Click the **Accept** button to accept the Microsoft SQL Server License Terms.

5. Click the **Install** button to complete the installation.

The following screenshot shows the dialog that appears after SQL Server Express has been successfully installed:

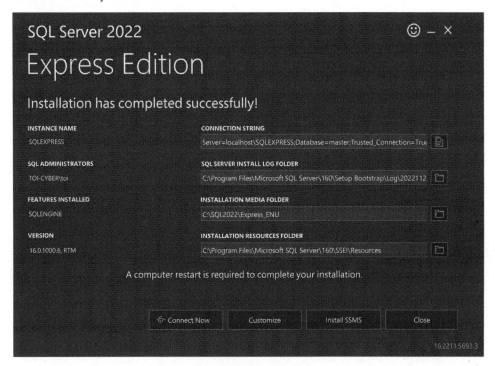

Figure 1.8: SQL Server Express Edition

Create a Microsoft Azure account

Microsoft Azure is Microsoft's cloud platform and it offers over 200 products and cloud services. You can use it to run and manage applications with the tools and frameworks of your choice.

If you do not already have a Microsoft Azure account, you can create a free account. Each free account comes with a generous $200 credit to get you started and over 55+ free services.

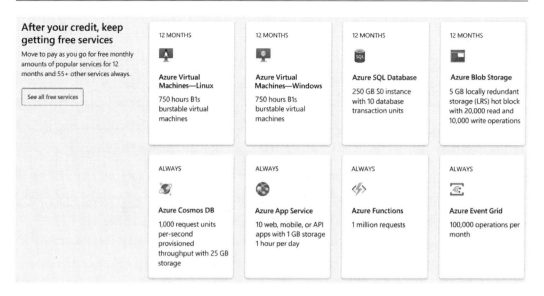

Figure 1.9: Microsoft Azure

To create a free Microsoft Azure account, do the following:

1. Navigate to the Microsoft Azure page, `https://azure.microsoft.com/`.

2. Click the **Free account** button.

3. Click the **Start free** button.

4. Complete the agreement and click the **Sign up** button.

To complete all the projects in this book, you will need a code editor, such as Microsoft Visual Studio Community 2022, .NET 7.0, Microsoft Azure, and Microsoft SQL Server. In this chapter, we showed you how to install Visual Studio 2022 Community Edition, .NET 7.0, and SQL Server 2022 Express Edition. We also showed you how to open a free Microsoft Azure account.

Summary

After completing this chapter, you should understand the benefits of using Blazor WebAssembly versus other Blazor hosting models and be prepared to complete the projects in this book.

In this chapter, we introduced the Blazor framework. The Blazor framework is built on .NET Framework and allows web developers to use C# on both the client and the server of a web app.

After that, we compared Blazor WebAssembly with both Blazor Server and Blazor Hybrid. All three hosting models are used to host Razor components. They each have their own advantages and disadvantages. We prefer Blazor WebAssembly.

In the last part of the chapter, we explained how to set up your computer with Microsoft Visual Studio Community Edition, .NET 7.0, and Microsoft SQL Server Express and how to open a Microsoft Azure account, all of which are required to complete the projects in this book.

Now that your computer is set up to complete the projects in this book, it is time to get started. In the next chapter, you will create your first Blazor WebAssembly web app.

Questions

The following questions are provided for your consideration:

1. Which of the following hosting models requires a constant connection to a server: Blazor WebAssembly, Blazor Server, or Blazor Hybrid?
2. Does using Blazor WebAssembly mean that you will never need to write JavaScript ever again?
3. Does Blazor WebAssembly require any plugins to be installed on the browser?
4. How much does it cost to get started developing with Blazor WebAssembly?

Further reading

The following resources provide more information concerning the topics in this chapter:

- For more information on Blazor, refer to `https://blazor.net`.
- For more information on the .NET Foundation, refer to `https://dotnetfoundation.org`.
- For more information on the ASP.NET repository on GitHub, refer to `https://github.com/dotnet/aspnetcore`.
- For general information on WebAssembly, refer to `https://webassembly.org`.
- For more information on browser compatibility with WebAssembly, refer to `https://caniuse.com/?search=wasm`.
- For more information on Razor Pages, refer to `https://learn.microsoft.com/en-us/aspnet/core/razor-pages`.

Join our community on Discord

Join our community's Discord space for discussions with the author and other readers:

https://packt.link/BlazorWASM2e

2

Building Your First Blazor WebAssembly Application

Razor components are the building blocks of Blazor WebAssembly applications. A Razor component is a chunk of user interface that can be shared, nested, and reused. Razor components are ordinary C# classes and can be placed anywhere in a project.

> *Razor components.*
>
> *Building blocks of Blazor apps.*
>
> *Nestable magic.*

In this chapter, we will learn about Razor components. We will learn how to use them, how to apply parameters, and how to create them. We will also become familiar with their life cycle and their structure. We will learn how to use the @page directive to define routing and we will learn how to use **Razor syntax** to combine C# code with HTML markup. Finally, we will introduce the **Hot Reload** experience.

The Blazor WebAssembly project in this chapter will be created by using the **Blazor WebAssembly App project template** provided by Microsoft. After we create the project, we will examine it to further familiarize ourselves with Razor components. We will learn how to use them, how to add parameters, how to apply routing, how to use Razor syntax, and how to separate the Razor markup and code into separate files. As we make edits to the code, we will use Hot Reload to automatically update the browser.

In this chapter, we will cover the following topics:

- Razor components
- Routing
- Razor syntax
- Hot Reload
- Creating the demo WebAssembly project

Creating the Demo Blazor WebAssembly Project Technical Requirements

To complete this project, you need to have Microsoft Visual Studio 2022 installed on your PC. For instructions on how to install the free community edition of Microsoft Visual Studio 2022, refer to *Chapter 1, Introduction to Blazor WebAssembly*.

The source code for this chapter is available in the following GitHub repository: `https://github.com/PacktPublishing/Blazor-WebAssembly-by-Example-Second-Edition/tree/main/Chapter02`.

The Code in Action video is available here: `https://packt.link/Ch2`.

Razor components

Blazor WebAssembly is a component-driven framework. Razor components are the fundamental building blocks of a Blazor WebAssembly application. They are classes that are implemented using a combination of C#, HTML, and Razor syntax. When the web app loads, the classes get downloaded into the browser as normal .NET assemblies (DLLs).

IMPORTANT NOTE

In this book, the terms Razor component and component are used interchangeably.

Using components

HTML element syntax is used to add one component to another component. The markup looks like an HTML tag where the name of the tag is the component type.

The following markup in the `Pages/Index.razor` file of the `Demo` project, which we will create later in this chapter, will render a `SurveyPrompt` instance:

```
<SurveyPrompt Title="How is Blazor working for you?" />
```

The preceding `SurveyPrompt` element includes an attribute parameter named `Title`.

Parameters

Component parameters are used to make components dynamic. Parameters are public properties of the component that are decorated with either the `Parameter` attribute or the `CascadingParameter` attribute. Parameters can be simple types, complex types, functions, **RenderFragments**, or event callbacks.

The following code for a component named `Hello` includes a parameter named `Text`:

Hello.razor

```
<h1>Hello @Text!</h1>

@code {
    [Parameter] public string? Text { get; set; }
}
```

To use the `Hello` component, include the following HTML syntax within another component:

```
<Hello Text="World" />
```

In the preceding example, the `Text` attribute of the `Hello` component is the source of the `Text` parameter. This screenshot shows the results of using the component as indicated:

Hello World!

Figure 2.1: The Hello component

A parameter's get and set accessors must not contain custom logic. They are only intended as a channel to allow information to flow to the child from the parent. Also, as mentioned earlier, they must be public.

IMPORTANT NOTE

The application will enter an infinite loop if a child component includes a parameter that causes rerendering of the parent component.

Required parameters

You can specify that a parameter is required by the editor by decorating it with the EditorRequired attribute. In the following version of the Hello2 component, the Text parameter is required:

Hello2.razor

```
<h1>Hello @Text!</h1>

@code {
    [Parameter]
    [EditorRequired]
    public string? Text { get; set; }
}
```

If we try to use Hello2 in a component and do not include the Text attribute, Visual Studio will display the following warning:

```
<Hello2 />
```

> BlazorApp1.Pages.Hello2
>
> RZ2012: Component 'Hello2' expects a value for the parameter 'Text', but a value may not have been provided.

Figure 2.2: Missing parameter warning

The preceding warning will not prevent the application from building, and it is not enforced at runtime. It is only used by the editor.

IMPORTANT NOTE

Decorating a parameter with the EditorRequired attribute does not guarantee that the parameter will have a value at runtime.

Query strings

A component can also receive parameters from the query string. A query string is used to assign values to the specified parameters. To indicate that the parameter can come from the query string, we decorate the parameter with the **SupplyParameterFromQuery** attribute.

In the following example, the `Increment` parameter has been decorated with the `SupplyParameterFromQuery` attribute:

```
[Parameter]
[SupplyParameterFromQuery]
public int? Increment { get; set; }
```

This is the code to set the value of Increment to 5:

```
https://localhost:7097/counter?increment=5
```

In the preceding example, everything after the question mark is the query string. The query string is not case sensitive. Also, the preceding example assumes that we are running our application locally on port 7097. Since the port that is used will vary by application, we will exclude the port in the rest of our examples.

> **TIP**
>
> The **applicationUrl** is defined in the `Properties/launchSettings.json` file. Each time we create a new Blazor project using a Microsoft project template, the `applicationUrl` will randomly reference a different port.

The parameters provided by the query string are restricted to the following types, arrays of the following types, and their nullable variants:

- `bool`
- `DateTime`
- `decimal`
- `double`
- `float`
- `Guid`
- `int`
- `long`
- `string`

They can also consist of arrays of the preceding types.

Naming components

The name of a Razor component must be in title case. Therefore, hello would not be a valid name for a Razor component since the h is not capitalized. Also, Razor components use the RAZOR extension rather than the CSHTML extension that is used by Razor Pages.

IMPORTANT NOTE

Razor components must start with a capital letter.

Component life cycle

Razor components inherit from the ComponentBase class. The ComponentBase class includes both asynchronous and synchronous methods that are used to manage the life cycle of a component. In this book, we will be using the asynchronous versions of the methods since they execute without blocking other operations. This is the order in which the methods in the life cycle of a component are invoked:

- **SetParametersAsync:** This method sets the parameters that are supplied by the component's parent in the render tree.

- **OnInitializedAsync:** This method is invoked after the parameters have been set and the component has been successfully initialized.

- **OnParametersSetAsync:** This method is invoked after the component initializes and each time the component rerenders. A component will rerender when the parent component rerenders and at least one parameter has changed. Also, a component will rerender when the **StateHasChanged** method of the component is called.

- **OnAfterRenderAsync:** This method is invoked after the component has finished rendering. This method is for working with JavaScript since JavaScript requires the **Document Object Model (DOM)** elements to be rendered before they can do any work.

Component structure

The following diagram shows code from the Counter component of the Demo project that we will create in this chapter:

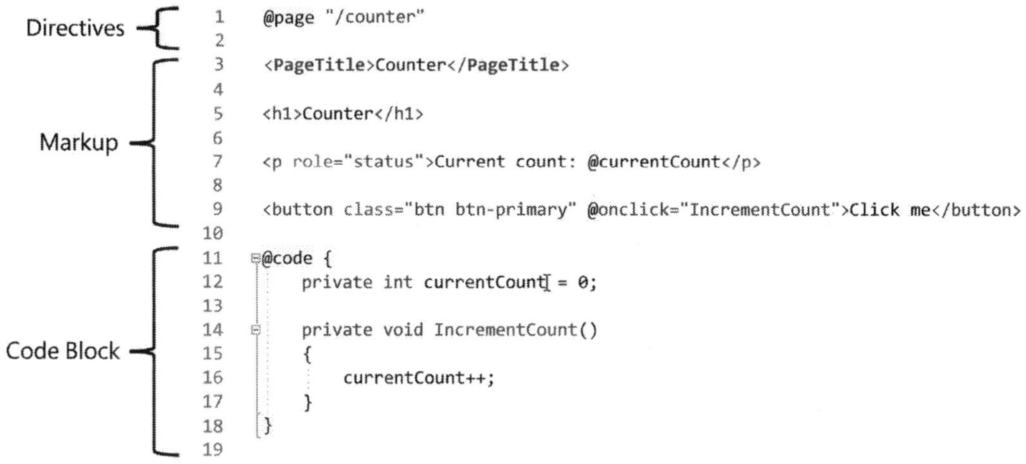

```
Directives   {  1    @page "/counter"
                 2
                 3    <PageTitle>Counter</PageTitle>
                 4
                 5    <h1>Counter</h1>
Markup           6
                 7    <p role="status">Current count: @currentCount</p>
                 8
                 9    <button class="btn btn-primary" @onclick="IncrementCount">Click me</button>
                10
                11    @code {
                12        private int currentCount = 0;
                13
                14        private void IncrementCount()
Code Block      15        {
                16            currentCount++;
                17        }
                18    }
                19
```

Figure 2.3: Component structure

The code in the preceding example is divided into three sections:

- Directives
- Markup
- Code Block

Each of the sections has a different purpose.

Directives

Directives are used to add special functionality, such as routing, layout, and dependency injection. File-level directives are defined within Razor, and you cannot define your own directives. Razor directives start with the @ symbol.

In the preceding example, there is only one directive used – the @page directive. The @page directive is used for routing. In this example, the following URL will route the user to the Counter component:

```
/counter
```

A typical page can include many directives at the top of the page. Also, many pages have more than one @page directive.

Most of the directives in Razor can be used in a Blazor WebAssembly application. These are the Razor directives that are used in Blazor, in alphabetical order:

- @attribute: This directive adds a class-level attribute to the component. The following example adds the [Authorize] attribute:

```
@attribute [Authorize]
```

- @code: This directive adds class members to the component. In the example, it is used to distinguish the code block.

- @implements: This directive implements an interface for the specified class.

- @inherits: This directive provides full control of the class that the view inherits.

- @inject: This directive is used for dependency injection. It enables the component to inject a service from the dependency injection container into the view. The following example injects the **HttpClient** defined in the Program.cs file into the component:

```
@inject HttpClient Http
```

- @layout: This directive is used to specify a layout for the Razor components that include an @page directive.

- @namespace: This directive sets the component's namespace. You only need to use this directive if you do not want to use the default namespace for the component. The default namespace is based on the location of the component.

- @page: This directive is used for routing.

- @preservewhitespace: This directive is used to preserve the whitespace in the rendered markup. If it is set to true, the whitespace is preserved. The default is false.

- @using: This directive controls the components that are in scope.

Markup

Markup is HTML with Razor syntax. The Razor syntax can be used to render text and allows C# to be included as part of the markup. We will cover more about Razor syntax later in this chapter.

Code block

The code block contains the logic for the page. It begins with the @code directive. By convention, the code block is at the bottom of the page. It is the only file-level directive that is not placed at the top of the page.

The code block is where we add C# fields, properties, and methods to the component. Later in this chapter, we will move the code block to a separate code-behind file.

Razor components are the building blocks of a Blazor WebAssembly application. They are easy to use since they are simply a combination of HTML markup and C# code. They are structured with directives, markup, and code blocks. Components have a clearly defined life cycle. They can be nested and leverage different types of parameters to make them dynamic. In the next section, we will explain how routing is used to navigate between components.

Routing

In Blazor WebAssembly, routing is handled on the client, not on the server. As you navigate in the browser, Blazor intercepts that navigation and renders the component with the matching route.

The URLs are resolved relative to the base path that is specified in the `wwwroot/index.html` file. The base path is specified in the head element using the following syntax:

```
<base href="/" />
```

Unlike other frameworks that you may have used, the route is not inferred from the location of its file. For example, in the Demo project, the `Counter` component is in the `/Pages/Counter` folder, yet it uses the following route:

```
/counter
```

This is the @page directive used by the `Counter` component:

```
@page "/counter"
```

Route parameters

Route parameters can be used to populate the parameters of a component. The parameters of both the component and the route must have the same name, but they are not case-sensitive.

You can provide more than one @page directive to a component. The following `RoutingExample` component demonstrates how to include multiple @page parameters:

RoutingExample.razor

```
@page "/routing"
@page "/routing/{text}"

<h1>Blazor WebAssembly is @Text!</h1>
```

```
@code {
    [Parameter] public string? Text { get; set; }
    protected override void OnInitialized()
    {
        Text = Text ?? "fantastic";
    }
}
```

In the preceding code, the first @page directive allows navigation to the component without a parameter, while the second @page directive includes a route parameter. If a value for text is provided, it is assigned to the Text property of the component. If the Text property of the component is null, it is set to fantastic.

The following URL will route the user to the RoutingExample component:

```
/routing
```

The following URL will also route the user to the RoutingExample component, but this time, the Text parameter will be set by the route:

```
/routing/amazing
```

This screenshot shows the results of using the indicated route:

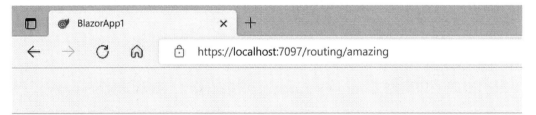

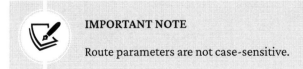

Figure 2.4: The RoutingExample component

IMPORTANT NOTE

Route parameters are not case-sensitive.

Optional route parameters

Optional route parameters are supported by Blazor. In the following version of the `RoutingExample` component, the `Text` property is optional:

RoutingExample.razor

```
@page "/routing/{text?}"


<h1>Blazor WebAssembly is @Text!</h1>


@code {
    [Parameter] public string? Text { get; set; }
    protected override void OnInitialized()
    {
        Text = Text ?? "fantastic";
    }
}
```

The difference between this version of the `RoutingExample` component and the original version is that the two @page directives have been combined and the `text` route parameter has been changed to a nullable type. By using an optional route parameter, we can reduce the number of @page directives that are required by the application.

TIP

If you need a component to navigate to itself with a different optional parameter value, you should set the value in the `OnParametersSet` event instead of the `OnInitialized` event.

Catch-all route parameters

Catch-all route parameters are used to capture paths across multiple folder boundaries. This type of route parameter is a `string` type and can only be placed at the end of the URL. Catch-all route parameters are designated with an asterisk.

This is a sample component that uses a catch-all route parameter:

CatchAll.razor

```
@page "/error/{*path}"
@page "/warning/{*path}"


<h1>Catch All</h1>
Route: @Path


@code {
    [Parameter] public string? Path { get; set; }
}
```

For the /error/type/3 URL, the preceding code will set the value of the Path parameter to type/3, as shown in the following image:

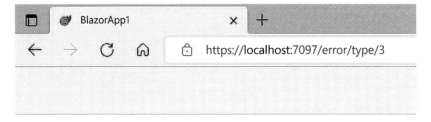

Catch All

Route: type/3

Figure 2.5: Catch-all route parameter example

Route constraints

Route constraints are used to enforce the datatype of a route parameter. To define a constraint, add a colon followed by the constraint type to the parameter. In the following example, the route is expecting a route parameter named Increment with the type of int:

```
@page "/counter/{increment:int}"
```

For route constraints, the following types, and their nullable variants, are supported:

- bool
- datetime
- decimal
- double
- float
- guid
- int
- long

IMPORTANT NOTE

Route constraints use the invariant culture and do not support localization. For example, dates are only valid in the form MM-dd-yyyy or yyyy-MM-dd, and Boolean values must be either true or false.

The following types are not currently supported as constraints:

- Regular expressions
- Enums
- Custom constraints

Route constraints support optional parameters. In the following example, the route parameter named increment with the type of int is optional:

```
@page "/counter/{increment:int?}"
```

Routing is handled on the client. Each routable component can include one or more routes. We can use both route parameters and catch-all route parameters to define routing. Route constraints are used to ensure that a route parameter is of the required datatype. Razor components use Razor syntax to seamlessly merge HTML with C# code, which is what we will see in the next section.

Razor syntax

Razor syntax is made up of HTML, Razor markup, and C#. Rendering HTML from a Razor component is the same as rendering HTML from an HTML file. Razor syntax uses both inline expressions and control structures to render dynamic values.

Inline expressions

Inline expressions start with an @ symbol followed by a variable or function name. This is an example of an inline expression:

```
<h1>Blazor is @Text!</h1>
```

In the preceding example, Blazor will interpret the text after the @ symbol as either a property name or a method name.

Control structures

Control structures also start with an @ symbol. The content within the curly brackets is evaluated and rendered to the output. This is an example of an if statement from the `FetchData` component in the `Demo` project that we will create later in this chapter:

```
@if (forecasts == null)
{
    <p><em>Loading...</em></p>
}
```

Conditionals

The following types of conditionals are included in Razor syntax:

- `if` statements
- `switch` statements

This is an example of an `if` statement:

```
@if (DateTime.Now.DayOfWeek.ToString() != "Friday")
{
    <p>Today is not Friday.</p>
}
else if (DateTime.Now.Day != 13)
{
    <p>Today is not the 13th.</p>
}
else
{
    <p>Today is Friday the 13th.</p>
}
```

The preceding code uses an `if` statement to check if the current day of the week is Friday and/or the current day of the month is the 13th. The result renders the appropriate p element.

This is an example of a `switch` statement:

```
@switch (value)
{
    case 1:
        <p>The value is 1!</p>
        break;
    case 42:
        <p>Your number is 42!</p>
        break;
    default:
        <p>Your number was not 1 or 42.</p>
        break;
}
@code {
    private int value = 2;
}
```

The preceding `switch` statement compares the `value` variable to 1 and 42. The result renders the appropriate p element.

Loops

The following types of loops are provided in Razor syntax:

- **for** loops
- **foreach** loops
- **while** loops
- **do while** loops

Each of the following examples loops through an array of the `WeatherForecast` items to display the `Summary` property of each item in the array.

This is an example of a `for` loop:

```
@for (var i = 0; i < forecasts.Count(); i++)
{
    <div>@forecasts[i].Summary</div>
```

```
    }

@code {
    private WeatherForecast[] forecasts;
    }
```

This is an example of a foreach loop:

```
@foreach (var forecast in forecasts)
{
    <div>@forecast.Summary</div>
}

@code {
    private WeatherForecast[] forecasts;
}
```

This is an example of a while loop:

```
@while (i < forecasts.Count())
{
    <div>@forecasts[i].Summary</div>
    i++;
}

@code {
    private WeatherForecast[] forecasts;
    private int i = 0;
}
```

This is an example of a do while loop:

```
@do
{
    <div>@forecasts[i].Summary</div>
    i++;
} while (i < forecasts.Count());

@code {
    private WeatherForecast[] forecasts;
```

```
        private int i = 0;
}
```

All the preceding examples of loops render the same output. There are many ways to loop through a collection using Razor syntax.

Razor syntax is easy to learn if you already know C#. It includes both inline expressions and control structures such as conditionals and loops. By using Hot Reload, we can edit our code and view the results immediately in the browser.

Hot Reload

Hot Reload allows developers to edit the markup and C# code of a currently running app without requiring the app to be rebuilt or refreshed. Also, it does all of that while maintaining the app's state.

You can use Hot Reload with or without the debugger. To trigger Hot Reload, you can either use the **Hot Reload** drop-down button on the toolbar or press *Alt+F10*.

This is the **Hot Reload** drop-down button that is accessed from the toolbar:

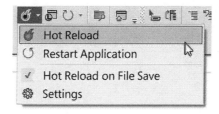

Figure 2.6: Hot Reload drop-down button

As you can see from the **Hot Reload** drop-down button, you can set **Hot Reload** to automatically be triggered whenever you save a file. There are more settings available via the **Settings** option on the menu. **Hot Reload** is supported for most changes to a component, including stylesheets. However, sometimes a change will require that the application be restarted.

This is a list of some of the activities that require a restart:

- Adding new local functions
- Adding new lambdas
- Adding new fields
- Changing a parameter's name
- Adding an await operator

If a restart is required, the following dialog is displayed:

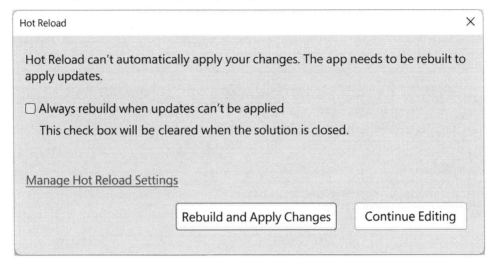

Figure 2.7: Hot Reload warning dialog

If you check the **Always rebuild when updates can't be applied** checkbox, Visual Studio will automatically rebuild and reload the app when Hot Reload is unable to automatically apply the changes. Also, this dialog will no longer be displayed until this setting is changed in **Settings** or the solution is closed.

> **IMPORTANT NOTE**
>
> Hot Reload will not work if native code debugging is enabled. Also, you can disable it at the project level by setting hotReloadEnabled to false in the project's Properties/launchSettings.json file.

Hot Reload makes you more efficient since you don't have to stop and restart your application every time you make an update.

Creating the Demo Blazor WebAssembly project

The Blazor WebAssembly application that we are going to build in this chapter is a simple three-page application. Each page will be used to demonstrate one or more features of Razor components.

This is a screenshot of the completed Demo project:

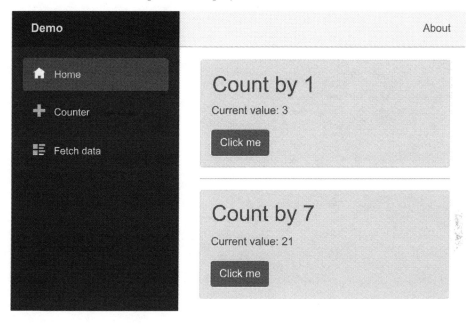

Figure 2.8: Home page of the Demo project

The build time for this project is approximately 60 minutes.

Project overview

The Demo project that we are creating is based on one of the sample projects that are provided by the Blazor WebAssembly App project template. After we have used the template to create the project, we will examine the files in the sample project and update some of the files to demonstrate how to use Razor components. To elevate the development experience, we will enable Hot Reload. Finally, we will separate the code block of one of the components into a separate file to demonstrate how to use the code-behind technique to separate the markup from the code.

Getting started with the project

Visual Studio comes with quite a few project templates. We are going to use the **Blazor WebAssembly App** project template to create our first Blazor WebAssembly project. Since this project template can be used to create many different types of Blazor projects, it is important to follow these instructions precisely:

1.   Open Microsoft Visual Studio 2022.

2.   Click the **Create a new project** button.

3. In the **Search for templates** (*Alt+S*) textbox, enter Blazor and hit the *Enter* key.

The following screenshot shows the **Blazor WebAssembly App** project template that we will be using:

Figure 2.9: Blazor WebAssembly App project template

4. Select the **Blazor WebAssembly App** project template and click the **Next** button.

5. Enter Demo in the **Project name** textbox and click the **Next** button.

This is a screenshot of the dialog used to configure our new project:

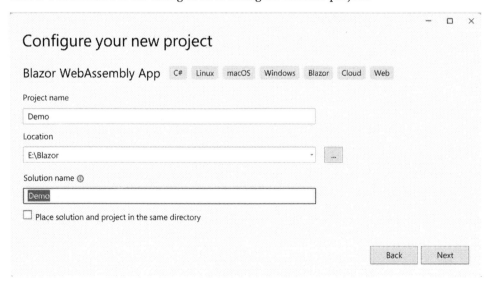

Figure 2.10: The Configure your new project dialog

TIP

In the preceding example, we placed the Demo project into the E:\Blazor folder. However, the location of this project is not important.

6.   Select **.NET 7.0** as the version of the **Framework** to use.

7.   Select **None** as the **Authentication type**.

8.   Check the **Configure for HTTPS** checkbox.

9.   Uncheck the **ASP.NET Core Hosted** checkbox.

10. Uncheck the **Progressive Web Application** checkbox.

11. Check the **Do not use top-level statements** checkbox.

This is a screenshot of the dialog used to create our new Blazor WebAssembly application:

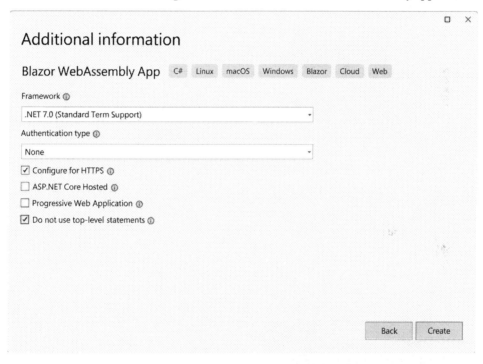

Figure 2.11: Additional information for the Blazor WebAssembly App dialog

12. Click the **Create** button.

You have created the Demo project.

Running the Demo project

Once the project has been created, you need to run it to get an understanding of what it does. The Demo project contains three pages: **Home**, **Counter**, and **Fetch data**:

1.   From the **Debug** menu, select the **Start Without Debugging** (*Ctrl+F5*) option to run the Demo project.

IMPORTANT NOTE

If this is your first web app, Visual Studio will ask to set up a certificate for hosting the web app. You should trust the certificate.

This is a screenshot of the **Home** page from the Demo project:

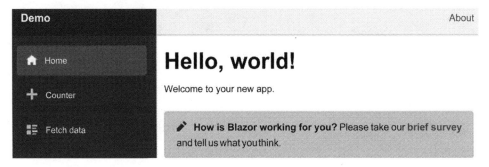

Figure 2.12: The Home page

The **Home** page is split into two sections. The navigation menu is on the left side of the page and the body is on the right side of the page. The body of the **Home** page consists of some static text and a link to a survey.

2.   Click the **Counter** option on the navigation menu to navigate to the **Counter** page.

This is a screenshot of the **Counter** page from the Demo project:

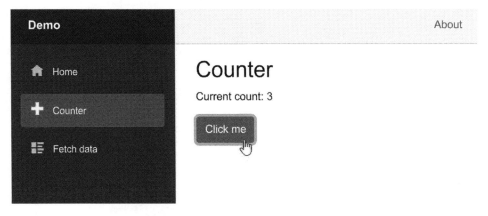

Figure 2.13: The Counter page

The body of the **Counter** page includes the **Current count** and a **Click me** button. Each time the button on the **Counter** page is clicked, the **Current count** is incremented.

IMPORTANT NOTE

Since the Demo project is a **single-page application (SPA)**, only the section of the page that has changed is updated.

3. Click the **Fetch data** option on the navigation menu to navigate to the **Fetch data** page.

This is a screenshot of the **Fetch data** page from the Demo project:

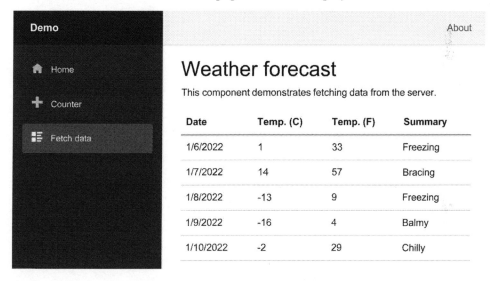

Figure 2.14: The Fetch data page

The body of the **Fetch data** page includes a table that shows a fabricated weather forecast for the second week in January 2022. As you will see, the data displayed in the table is just static data from the `wwwroot\sample-data\weather.json` file.

Examining the Demo project's structure

Now let's return to Visual Studio to examine the files in the Demo project.

The following figure shows the file structure of the project:

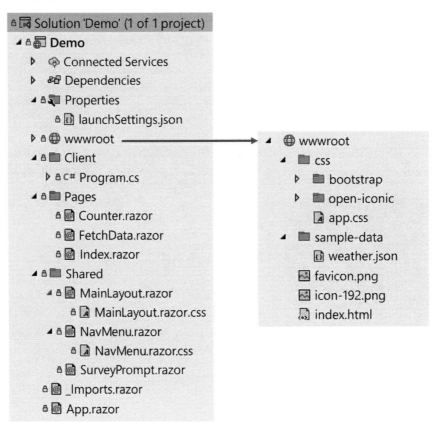

Figure 2.15: File structure of the Demo project

The project includes quite a few files with some of them divided into their own folders. Let's examine them.

The Properties folder

The Properties folder contains the launchSettings.json file. This file contains various settings that can be defined for each profile. As mentioned earlier in this chapter, the applicationUrl is defined in this file. Also, Hot Reload can be disabled by setting hotReloadEnabled to false.

> **TIP**
>
> The settings in the launchSettings.json file are only applied to your local development machine.

The wwwroot folder

The wwwroot folder is the application's web root. Only the files in this folder are web addressable. The wwwroot folder contains a collection of **Cascading Style Sheets (CSS)**, a sample data file, icon files, a font, and index.html. Later in this book, in addition to these types of files, we will use this folder for public static resources such as images and JavaScript files.

The index.html file is the root page of the web application. Whenever a page is initially requested, the contents of the index.html page are rendered and returned in the response. The head element of the index.html file includes links to each of the CSS files in the css folder and specifies the base path to use for the web app. The body element of the index.html file includes two div elements and a reference to the blazor.webassembly.js file.

This is the code in the head element of the index.html file:

```
<head>
    <meta charset="utf-8" />
    <meta name="viewport"
          content="width=device-width,
                   initial-scale=1.0,
                   maximum-scale=1.0,
                   user-scalable=no" />

    <title>Demo</title>

    <base href="/" />

    <link href="css/bootstrap/bootstrap.min.css"
          rel="stylesheet" />
    <link href="css/app.css" rel="stylesheet" />
    <link rel="icon" type="image/png" href="favicon.png" />
    <link href="Demo.styles.css" rel="stylesheet" />
</head>
```

The base element is used to indicate the base path for the URLs that are expressed with the @path directive. In the Demo project, the href attribute points to the root of the application. The base element is required in the index.html file.

The index.html references three different stylesheets. The bootstrap.min.css file is for Bootstrap 5.1 and is in the /css/bootstrap folder. The app.css file is in the /css folder. It includes the styles that are applied globally to the Demo project. Finally, the Demo.styles.css file is used for bundling any of the CSS files that are defined at the component level into one file. This is done to enable CSS isolation. The bundled CSS file is created at build time in the obj folder.

TIP

A copy of Demo.styles.css for the Demo project is in ...\Demo\Demo\obj\Debug\ net7.0\scopedcss\bundle.

This is the code in the body element of the index.html file:

```
<body>
    <div id="app">
        <svg class="loading-progress">
            <circle r="40%" cx="50%" cy="50%" />
            <circle r="40%" cx="50%" cy="50%" />
        </svg>
        <div class="loading-progress-text"></div>
    </div>

    <div id="blazor-error-ui">
        An unhandled error has occurred.
        <a href="" class="reload">Reload</a>
        <a class="dismiss">X</a>
    </div>
    <script src="_framework/blazor.webassembly.js"></script>
</body>
```

The highlighted div element in the preceding code loads the App component. As you can see, the App component includes a loading progress indicator. Since the Demo project is very simple, you may not have noticed it when you ran the application since it loads so quickly. This is an image of the loading progress indicator:

Figure 2.16: Loading Progress Indicator

You can remove the loading progress indicator by updating the highlighted `div` to the following:

```
<div id="app">
</div>
```

Also, you can customize the look and feel of the loading progress indicator by updating the relevant styles in the `\css\app.css` file.

The `blazor-error-ui` `div` element is for displaying unhandled exceptions. The styling for this `div` element is also in the `\css\app.css` file. The `blazor.webassembly.js` file is the script that downloads the .NET runtime, your application's assemblies, and your application's dependencies. It also initializes the runtime to run the web app.

The App component

The App component is defined in the `App.razor` file:

App.razor

```
<Router AppAssembly="@typeof(App).Assembly">
    <Found Context="routeData">
        <RouteView RouteData="@routeData"
                   DefaultLayout="@typeof(MainLayout)" />
        <FocusOnNavigate RouteData="@routeData" Selector="h1" />
    </Found>
    <NotFound>
        <PageTitle>Not found</PageTitle>
        <LayoutView Layout="@typeof(MainLayout)">
            <p role="alert">
                Sorry, there's nothing at this address.
```

```
            </p>
        </LayoutView>
    </NotFound>
</Router>
```

The App component is the root component of a Blazor WebAssembly application. It uses the Router component to set up the routing for the web app. In the preceding code, if the route is found, the RouteView component receives RouteData and renders the specified component using the indicated DefaultLayout. If the route is not found, the NotFound template is used and LayoutView is rendered using the indicated Layout.

As you can see, in the Demo project, both the Found template and the NotFound template use the same layout. They are both using the MainLayout component. However, they do not need to use the same layout component. We will examine the MainLayout component later in this chapter.

The Found template includes a FocusOnNavigate component. It takes two properties:

- RouteData – the route data from the Router component
- Selector – the CSS selector for the element that should have the focus when the navigation completes

In the preceding code, when the Router navigates to a new page, the focus will be on the first h1 element on that page.

The Shared folder

The Shared folder in the Demo project includes the shared Razor components, including the MainLayout component. Each of these components may be used one or more times by other Razor components. None of the components in the Shared folder include an @page directive since they are not routable.

The Pages folder

The Pages folder includes the routable Razor components used by the project. The routable components are Counter, FetchData, and Index. Each of these components includes an @page directive that is used to route the user to the page.

The Client folder

The Client folder contains the Program.cs file. The Program.cs file is the entry point for the application. It contains the method called Main:

```
public static async Task Main(string[] args)
{
    var builder = WebAssemblyHostBuilder.CreateDefault(args);
    builder.RootComponents.Add<App>("#app");
    builder.RootComponents.Add<HeadOutlet>("head::after");

    builder.Services.AddScoped(sp =>
        new HttpClient {
            BaseAddress =
            new Uri(builder.HostEnvironment.BaseAddress)
        });

    await builder.Build().RunAsync();
}
```

In the preceding method, the WebAssemblyHost is built and run. As part of that process, the App component is defined as the RootComponent and is placed into the app object of the wwwroot/ index.html file. Also, the HttpClient base address is configured when the HttpClient is registered in the dependency injection service. Registered services can be injected into components using the @inject directive. For more information on dependency injection, see *Chapter 7, Building a Shopping Cart Using AppState*.

TIP

The HttpClient allows the application to send HTTP requests and receive HTTP responses.

The _Imports.razor file

The _Imports.razor file includes common Razor directives that are shared by multiple Razor components. By including them in this file, they do not need to be included in the individual components. A project can include multiple _Imports.razor files. Each one is applied to its current folder and subfolders.

Any @using directives in the _Imports.razor file are only applied to Razor (RAZOR) files. They are not applied to C# (CS) files. This distinction is important when using the code-behind technique that we will examine later in this chapter.

The Demo project includes many types of files divided into various folders. Next, we will examine the contents of the Shared folder.

Examining the shared Razor components

The shared Razor components are in the Shared folder. There are three shared Razor components in the Demo project:

- The MainLayout component
- The NavMenu component
- The SurveyPrompt component

The MainLayout component

The MainLayout component is used to define the page layout for the Demo project:

Shared/MainLayout.razor

```
@inherits LayoutComponentBase

<div class="page">
    <div class="sidebar">
        <NavMenu />
    </div>

    <main>
        <div class="top-row px-4">
            <a href="https://docs.microsoft.com/aspnet/"
                target="_blank">About</a>
        </div>

        <article class="content px-4">
            @Body
        </article>
    </main>
</div>
```

The highlighted code indicates that the `MainLayout` component inherits from the `LayoutComponentBase` class. The `LayoutComponentBase` class represents a layout and has only one property, which is the `Body` property. The `Body` property gets the content to be rendered inside the layout.

The following diagram illustrates the layout of a page as defined by the `MainLayout` component of the `Demo` project:

App component

MainLayout component

sidebar	main
	top-row
NavMenu component	LayoutComponentBase.Body

Figure 2.17: Page layout of the Demo project

TIP

The `Blazor WebAssembly App` project template uses `Bootstrap 5.1` to style its pages. If you are unfamiliar with Bootstrap 5.1, you can refer to `https://getbootstrap.com/docs/5.1/getting-started/introduction/` to familiarize yourself with its syntax. Regrettably, the project template provided by Microsoft does not use the most current version of Bootstrap. To learn more about the current version of Bootstrap, refer to `https://getbootstrap.com`.

The `MainLayout` component includes its own dedicated CSS styles that are defined in the `MainLayout.razor.css` file. This is an example of **CSS isolation**. By using CSS isolation, we can reduce the number of global styles and avoid style conflicts in nested content. As we mentioned earlier, all the component-level styles will be bundled together into one CSS file during the build process.

The NavMenu component

The `NavMenu` component defines the navigation menu for the `Demo` project. It uses multiple `NavLink` components to define the various menu options. This is the section of the `NavMenu` component that references the `NavLink` components used for the project's navigation:

```
<div class="@NavMenuCssClass nav-scrollable" @onclick="ToggleNavMenu">
    <nav class="flex-column">
        <div class="nav-item px-3">
            <NavLink class="nav-link"
                    href="" Match="NavLinkMatch.All">
                <span class="oi oi-home"
                    aria-hidden="true">
                </span> Home
            </NavLink>
        </div>
        <div class="nav-item px-3">
            <NavLink class="nav-link" href="counter">
                <span class="oi oi-plus"
                    aria-hidden="true">
                </span> Counter
            </NavLink>
        </div>
        <div class="nav-item px-3">
            <NavLink class="nav-link" href="fetchdata">
                <span class="oi oi-list-rich"
                    aria-hidden="true">
                </span> Fetch data
            </NavLink>
        </div>
    </nav>
</div>
```

The NavLink component is defined in the Microsoft.AspNetCore.Components.Routing name-space. It behaves like an a element, except it has added functionality that highlights the current URL. This is the HTML that is rendered by NavLink for the Counter component when the Counter component is selected:

```
<a href="counter" class="nav-link active">
    <span class="oi oi-plus" aria-hidden="true"></span>
    Counter
</a>
```

The style used for the nav-link class is from Bootstrap.

The NavMenu component includes its own dedicated CSS styles that are defined in the NavMenu.razor.css file. This is another example of CSS isolation.

The SurveyPrompt component

The SurveyPrompt component creates a link to a brief survey on Blazor.

In the Demo project, the Shared folder contains the non-routable components. Next, we will examine the routable components in the Pages folder.

Examining the routable Razor components

The routable Razor components are in the Pages folder. A routable Razor component includes one or more @page directives at the top of the file. There are three routable Razor components in the Demo project:

- The Index component
- The Counter component
- The FetchData component

The Index component

The Home page of the Demo project uses the Index component that is defined in the Pages/Index.razor file:

Pages/Index.razor

```
@page "/"

<PageTitle>Index</PageTitle>
```

```
<h1>Hello, world!</h1>

Welcome to your new app.

<SurveyPrompt Title="How is Blazor working for you?" />
```

The preceding code includes an @page directive that references the root of the web app and some markup. The markup includes both a PageTitle component and a SurveyPrompt component.

The PageTitle component is a built-in Razor component that renders an HTML title element. The title element is used to define the page's title in the browser and is the text displayed on the tab in the browser. It also is used when the page is added to favorites.

IMPORTANT NOTE

If your component includes more than one PageTitle component, only the last one to be rendered will be used. The other ones will be ignored.

The SurveyPrompt component is a custom component that is defined in the Shared folder.

The Counter component

The Counter component is more complex than the Index component. Like the Index component, it contains an @page directive that is used for routing and some markup. However, it also contains a C# code block:

Pages/Counter.razor

```
@page "/counter"

<PageTitle>Counter</PageTitle>

<h1>Counter</h1>

<p role="status">Current count: @currentCount</p>

<button class="btn btn-primary" @onclick="IncrementCount">Click me</
button>

@code {
    private int currentCount = 0;
```

```
    private void IncrementCount()
    {
        currentCount++;
    }
}
```

In the preceding code block, a private currentCount variable is used to hold the number of times that the button has been clicked. Each time the Counter button is clicked, the Counter component's registered @onclick handler is called. In this case, it is the IncrementCount method.

The IncrementCount method increments the value of the currentCount variable, and the Counter component regenerates its render tree. Blazor compares the new render tree against the previous one and applies any modifications to the browser's DOM. This results in the displayed count being updated.

The FetchData component

The FetchData component is by far the most complex component in the Demo project.

These are the directives in the Pages/FetchData.razor file:

```
@page "/fetchdata"
@inject HttpClient Http
```

The @page directive is used for routing and the @inject directive is used for dependency injection. In this component, the HttpClient that is defined in the Program.cs file is being injected into the view. For more information on dependency injection, refer to *Chapter 7, Building a Shopping Cart Using Application State*.

The following markup demonstrates the use of a very important pattern that you will often use when developing a Blazor WebAssembly application. Because the application runs on the browser, all data access must be asynchronous. That means that when the page first loads, the data will be null. For that reason, you always need to test for the null case before attempting to process the data.

This is the markup in the Pages/FetchData.razor file:

```
<PageTitle> Weather forecast</PageTitle>
<h1>Weather forecast</h1>

<p>This component demonstrates fetching data from the server.</p>
```

```
@if (forecasts == null)
{
    <p><em>Loading...</em></p>
}
else
{
    <table class="table">
        <thead>
            <tr>
                <th>Date</th>
                <th>Temp. (C)</th>
                <th>Temp. (F)</th>
                <th>Summary</th>
            </tr>
        </thead>
        <tbody>
            @foreach (var forecast in forecasts)
            {
                <tr>
                    <td>@forecast.Date.ToShortDateString()</td>
                    <td>@forecast.TemperatureC</td>
                    <td>@forecast.TemperatureF</td>
                    <td>@forecast.Summary</td>
                </tr>
            }
        </tbody>
    </table>
}
```

The preceding markup includes an if statement and a foreach loop. While the value of forecasts is null, a Loading message is displayed. Once the value of forecasts is no longer null, all the items in the array are presented in a table.

IMPORTANT NOTE

The value of forecasts will be null the first time that the page is rendered. If you do not handle the case when the value of forecasts is null, the framework will throw an exception.

As previously mentioned, Blazor components have a well-defined life cycle. The OnInitializedAsync method is invoked when the component is rendered. After the OnInitializedAsync method completes, the component is rerendered.

This is the code block in the Pages/FetchData.razor file:

```
@code {
    private WeatherForecast[]? forecasts;

    protected override async Task OnInitializedAsync()
    {
        forecasts = await
            Http.GetFromJsonAsync<WeatherForecast[]>
            ("sample-data/weather.json");
    }

    public class WeatherForecast
    {
        public DateOnly Date { get; set; }

        public int TemperatureC { get; set; }

        public string? Summary { get; set; }

        public int TemperatureF =>
            32 + (int)(TemperatureC / 0.5556);
    }
}
```

First, the preceding code block declares a parameter to contain a nullable array of the type WeatherForecast. Next, it uses the OnInitializedAsync asynchronous method to populate the array. To populate the array, the GetFromJsonAsync method of the HttpClient service is used. For more information on HttpClient, refer to *Chapter 11, Building a Task Manager Using the ASP.NET Web API*.

Using a component

Razor components are used by including them in the markup of another component. We will add a Counter component to the Home page. We do this as follows:

1. Return to Visual Studio.

2. Open the Pages/Index.razor file.

3. Delete all the markup after the PageTitle component.

    Be sure you do not remove the @page directive at the top of the file.

4. Add the following markup below the PageTitle component:

    ```
    <Counter />
    ```

5. From the **Build** menu, select the **Build Solution** option.

6. Return to the browser and navigate to the **Home** page. If the Demo project is not running, from the **Debug** menu, select the **Start Without Debugging** (*Ctrl+F5*) option to run it.

7. Press *Ctrl+R* to refresh the browser.

TIP

Whenever you update your C# code, you need to refresh the browser for the browser to load the updated DLL unless you use Hot Reload.

8. Click the **Click me** button 3 times to test the Counter component.

9. The **Current value** is now 3.

    We have nested a Razor component within another Razor component. Next, we will update a component using Hot Reload.

Modifying a component

By using Hot Reload, we can automatically update the app without having to rebuild it or refresh the browser. We will update the Counter component and rebuild the app using Hot Reload. We do this as follows:

1. Return to Visual Studio, without closing the browser.

    If you can, configure your screen to display both the browser and Visual Studio at the same time.

2. Open the Pages/Counter.razor file.

3. Change the text in the h1 element to the following:

    ```
    <h1>Count by 1</h1>
    ```

4. Click the **Hot Reload** drop-down button on the toolbar or press *Alt+F10*.

5. Verify that the text on the browser has changed.

6. Click the **Click me** button 3 times.

7. The **Current value** is now 6.

IMPORTANT NOTE

The value of the current count did not change when Hot Reload was used to update the code.

8. Use the **Hot Reload** drop-down button on the toolbar to select **Hot Reload on File Save**.

9. Update the markup below the PageTitle component to the following:

```
<div class="alert alert-info">
    <h1>Count by 1</h1>
    <p role="status">Current value: @currentCount</p>
    <button class="btn btn-primary"
            @onclick="IncrementCount">
        Click me
    </button>
</div>
```

10. The preceding code will add some formatting to the Counter component and change the label from **Current count** to **Current value**.

11. Add the following code to the top of the code block:

```
private int increment = 1;
```

12. Click *Ctrl+S*.

13. The **Hot Reload** warning dialog is displayed.

14. Check the **Always rebuild when updates can't be applied** checkbox.

15. Click the **Rebuild and Apply Changes** button.

16. Update the IncrementCount method to the following:

```
private void IncrementCount()
{
    currentCount += increment;
}
```

17. Click *Ctrl+S*.

The app rebuilds and refreshes the browser without displaying the **Hot Reload** warning dialog.

By using Hot Reload, we were able to make changes to our code and see those changes immediately reflected in the browser. In this example, we were not in debug mode, but it is important to remember that Hot Reload also works in debug mode. Next, we need to set the value of the increment.

Adding a parameter to a component

Most components require parameters. To add a parameter to a component, use the Parameter attribute. We will add a parameter to specify the increment used by the IncrementCount method. We do this as follows:

1. Return to Visual Studio.

2. Open the Pages/Counter.razor file.

3. Add the following code to the top of the code block to define the new parameter:

```
[Parameter]
[SupplyParameterFromQuery]
public int? Increment { get; set; }
```

4. Add the following OnParametersSet method to set the value of increment to the value of the Increment parameter:

```
protected override void OnParametersSet()
{
    if (Increment.HasValue)
        increment = Increment.Value;
}
```

Adding the OnParametersSet method will require a restart, as indicated by the following image:

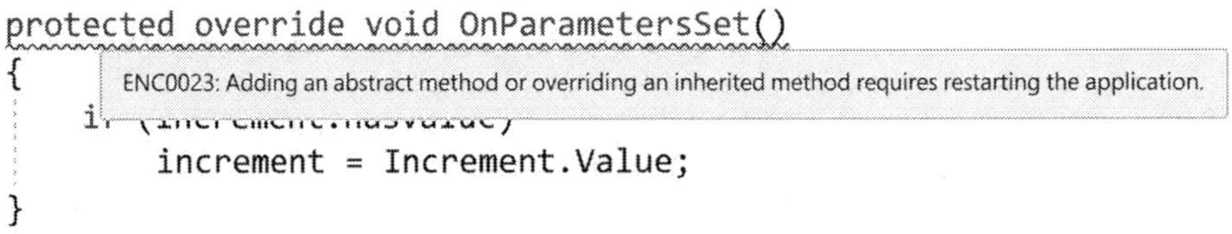

```
protected override void OnParametersSet()
{        ENC0023: Adding an abstract method or overriding an inherited method requires restarting the application.
    if (Increment.HasValue)
        increment = Increment.Value;
}
```

Figure 2.18: Page layout of the Demo project

5. Select **Restart Application** from the **Hot Reload** drop-down button.

6. Change the text in the h1 element to the following:

```
<h1>Count by @increment</h1>
```

7. Update the address bar to the following

```
/counter?increment=5
```

8. Click the **Click me** button 3 times.

9. The **Current value** is now 15.

We have added a parameter that can obtain its value from the query string. It can also obtain its value from an attribute. Next, we will add a Counter component to the Index component that increments its value by 7 each time it is clicked.

Using a parameter with an attribute

We will add another instance of the Counter component to the Home page that uses the new parameter. We do this as follows:

1. Open the Pages/Index.razor file.

2. Add the following markup to the bottom of the Index.razor file:

```
<hr>
<Counter Increment="7"/>
```

As you add the markup, **IntelliSense** is provided for the new Increment parameter:

Figure 2.19: IntelliSense

3. Press *Ctrl+S*.

4. Return to the browser.

5. Navigate to the **Home** page.

    The **Home** page now contains two instances of the Counter component. If you click the first **Click me** button, the first counter will be incremented by 1; if you click the second **Click me** button, the second counter will be incremented by 7.

6. Click each of the **Click me** buttons to verify they both work as intended.

Adding a route parameter

Components can have multiple @page directives. We will add an @page directive to the Counter component that uses a parameter. We do this as follows:

1. Return to Visual Studio.

2. Open the Pages/Counter.razor file.

3. Remove the SupplyParameterFromQuery attribute from the Increment parameter.

4. Add the following @page directive to the top of the file:

```
@page "/counter/{increment:int}"
```

5. The Counter component now includes two @page directives.

6. Press *Ctrl+S*.

7. Navigate to the Counter page.

8. Update the URL to the following:

```
/counter/4
```

IMPORTANT NOTE

Since the page is automatically reloaded when you change the URL, you do not need to refresh the browser to reload the page.

9. Click the **Click me** button.

    The counter should now increment by 4.

10. Update the URL to an invalid route:

```
/counter/a
```

Since this is not a valid route, you will be directed to the NotFound content defined in the App component:

Figure 2.20: Page not found

TIP

If you need to navigate to a URL in code, you should use `NavigationManager`. `NavigationManager` provides a `NavigateTo` method that is used to navigate the user to the specified URI without forcing a page load.

Using partial classes to separate markup from code

Many developers prefer to separate their markup from their C# fields, properties, and methods. Since Razor components are regular C# classes, they support partial classes. The `partial` keyword is used to create a partial class. We will use a partial class to move the code block from the RAZOR file to a CS file. We do this as follows:

1. Return to Visual Studio.
2. Right-click the Pages folder and select **Add, Class** from the menu.
3. Name the new class `Counter.razor.cs`.
4. Update the `Counter` class to be a partial class by using the `partial` keyword:

   ```
   public partial class Counter{}
   ```

5. Open the `Pages/Counter.razor` file.
6. Copy all the code in the code block to the partial `Counter` class in the `Counter.razor.cs` file.
7. Delete the code block from the `Counter.razor` file.
8. Press *Ctrl+S*.

9. Navigate to the **Counter** page.

10. Click the **Click me** button to verify that it still works.

11. Close the browser.

Using partial classes gives you the flexibility to move the code in the code block to a separate file, allowing you to use the code-behind technique.

TIP

A quick way to create the code-behind page is to right-click on the code block and use the **Quick Actions and Refactorings** option to extract the block to code behind.

We have created a Demo project by using the **Blazor WebAssembly App** project template provided by Microsoft. We added a parameter to the Counter component and moved the code in the code block of the Counter component to a separate file.

Summary

You should now be able to create a Blazor WebAssembly application.

In this chapter, we introduced Razor components. We learned about their parameters, naming conventions, life cycle, and structure. We also learned about routing and Razor syntax. Finally, we learned how to use Hot Reload.

After that, we used the **Blazor WebAssembly App** project template provided by Microsoft to create the Demo project. We examined each of the files in the Demo project. We added a parameter to the Counter component and examined how routing works. Finally, we practiced using Hot Reload.

Questions

The following questions are provided for your consideration:

1. Can Razor components include JavaScript?

2. What types of loops are supported by Razor syntax?

3. Can the parameter of a component be defined using a POCO?

4. Will Hot Reload render changes to CSS files?

5. How can a child component trigger an infinite loop?

Further reading

The following resources provide more information concerning the topics in this chapter:

- For more information on Bootstrap, refer to `https://getbootstrap.com`.
- For more information on Razor syntax, refer to `https://learn.microsoft.com/en-us/aspnet/core/mvc/views/razor`.
- For more information on Hot Reload, refer to `https://learn.microsoft.com/en-us/visualstudio/debugger/hot-reload`.

3

Debugging and Deploying a Blazor WebAssembly App

Debugging is not always fun, but it is an important aspect of software development. When debugging a Blazor WebAssembly app, Microsoft Visual Studio provides most of the functionality we need. However, since apps built with Blazor WebAssembly run on the client, we also need to learn how to use the browser's **developer tools (DevTools)** to debug the app. After we finish debugging a Blazor WebAssembly app, we can use Microsoft Visual Studio to deploy it.

In this chapter, we will create a simple game that we will use to practice both debugging and deploying a Blazor WebAssembly app. We will debug the app using both Visual Studio and DevTools. We will learn how to log errors using the ILogger interface and we will examine different ways to handle exceptions. After we have completed the debugging, we will apply **ahead-of-time (AOT)** compilation to the app before deploying it to Microsoft Azure.

Shift+Alt+D

debugging in the browser.

Knowledge is power!

In this chapter, we will cover the following topics:

- Debugging a Blazor WebAssembly app
- Understanding logging

- Handling exceptions
- Using **ahead-of-time** (**AOT**) compilation
- Deploying a Blazor WebAssembly app to Microsoft Azure
- Creating the "guess the number" project

Technical requirements

To complete this project, you need to have Microsoft Visual Studio 2022 installed on your PC. For instructions on how to install the free community edition of Microsoft Visual Studio 2022, refer to *Chapter 1, Introduction to Blazor WebAssembly*. Since we will be deploying this project to Microsoft Azure, you will need an account on Microsoft Azure. If you do not have an account on Microsoft Azure, refer to *Chapter 1, Introduction to Blazor WebAssembly*, to create a free account.

The source code for this chapter is available in the following GitHub repository: `https://github.com/PacktPublishing/Blazor-WebAssembly-by-Example-Second-Edition/tree/main/Chapter03`.

The Code in Action video is available here: `https://packt.link/Ch3`.

Debugging a Blazor WebAssembly.app

Debugging is an important and useful skill. You can debug a Blazor WebAssembly app by using the debugging tools within Visual Studio or by using `DevTools`. To debug on the browser, you must use one of the following browsers:

- Microsoft Edge (version 80 or later)
- Google Chrome (version 70 or later)

All the usual debugging scenarios are supported by both Visual Studio and `DevTools`:

- Setting and removing breakpoints.
- Pressing *F10* to single-step through the code.
- Pressing *F11* to step into the next function.
- Pressing *F5* in Visual Studio and *F8* in the browser to resume code execution.
- Viewing the value of local variables in the `Locals` display.
- Viewing the `Call Stack`.
- Setting `Watch` values.

The following scenarios are not currently supported. But, since Microsoft is continuing to make large improvements to the debugging process, they will be supported in the future:

- Breaking on unhandled exceptions.
- Hitting the breakpoints during startup.

First, we will look at debugging in Visual Studio.

Debugging in Visual Studio

If you have any experience with using Visual Studio, you probably have used the debugging tools. To start debugging, select **Debug**, **Start Debugging** from the Visual Studio menu, or press *F5*.

Once you have started debugging, you can use any of the scenarios listed above to debug the code. For example, to set a breakpoint on a line of code, simply click in the margin to the left of the line code.

The following screenshot shows a breakpoint that has been set on line 36:

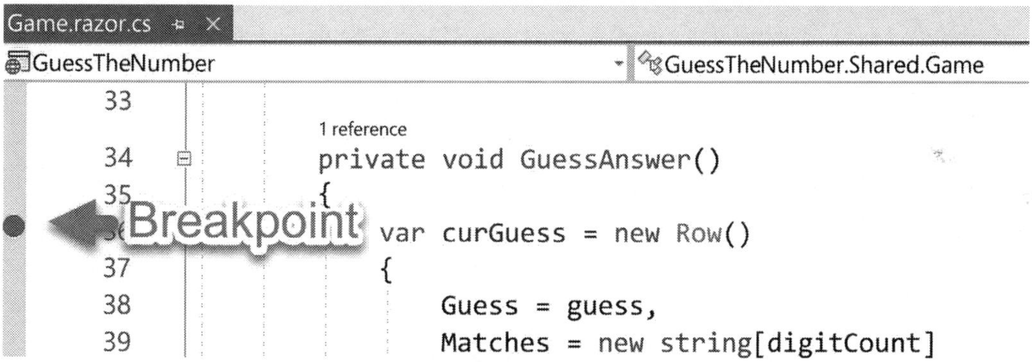

Figure 3.1: Breakpoint in Visual Studio

Debugging in Visual Studio is as easy as pressing *F5*. Debugging in the browser requires a bit more effort.

Debugging in the browser

Debugging a Blazor WebAssembly app on the browser takes a few steps. The following image shows the steps required to start debugging an app in the browser:

Figure 3.2: Enabling debugging in the browser

These are the steps to enable debugging in the browser:

1. Press *Ctrl+F5* to start the application without debugging.

2. Press *Shift+Alt+D* to start debugging.

> **TIP**
>
> To successfully start debugging, make sure that your application has focus
> before pressing *Shift+Alt+D*.

Since your browser is not yet running with remote debugging enabled, after you press
Shift+Alt+D, you will receive the following warning:

Unable to find debuggable browser tab

Could not get a list of browser tabs from `http://localhost:9222/json`. Ensure your browser is running with debugging enabled.

Resolution

If you are using Google Chrome for your development, follow these instructions:

Press Win+R and enter the following:

`chrome --remote-debugging-port=9222 --user-data-dir="C:\Users\toi\AppData\Local\Temp\blazor-chrome-debug" https://localhost:7092/`

If you are using Microsoft Edge (80+) for your development, follow these instructions:

Press Win+R and enter the following:

`msedge --remote-debugging-port=9222 --user-data-dir="C:\Users\toi\AppData\Local\Temp\blazor-edge-debug" --no-first-run https://localhost:7092/`

This should launch a new browser window with debugging enabled..

Figure 3.3: Unable to find debuggable browser tab warning

The **Unable to find debuggable browser tab** warning gives instructions on how to proceed for both Google Chrome and Microsoft Edge. Since we are using Microsoft Edge for these screenshots, we have highlighted the instructions for Microsoft Edge in the preceding image.

3. To enable debugging in the browser, we need to copy the provided text from the **Unable to find debuggable browser tab** warning to the Windows run command dialog box. Press *Win+R* to open the run command dialog box, paste the text, and press *Enter*.

    This process will launch another browser window that has debugging enabled. If you are asked to sync your devices, you can select **No**.

4. Close the previous browser window.

    This step is not required. We have included it because it can be confusing to have multiple browsers open.

5. Press *Shift+Alt+D*.

    We have enabled debugging on the browser.

    There are now two tabs open in the browser. The first tab is running the app and the second tab is running DevTools:

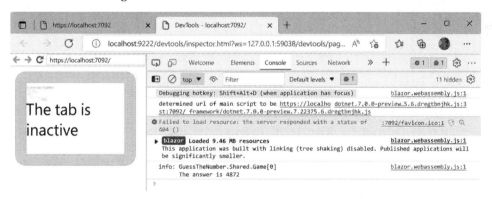

Figure 3.4: Browser with debugging enabled

The preceding image shows the DevTools tab. The area on the left is inactive. It is used to display the screen contents from the other tab. The **Console** tab in DevTools is selected. However, the **Sources** tab is the one that we will use for debugging.

Once we have started debugging, we can use any of the scenarios listed above to debug the code. For example, to set a breakpoint on a line of code, we simply click in the margin to the left of the line code.

The following screenshot shows a breakpoint that has been set on line 36:

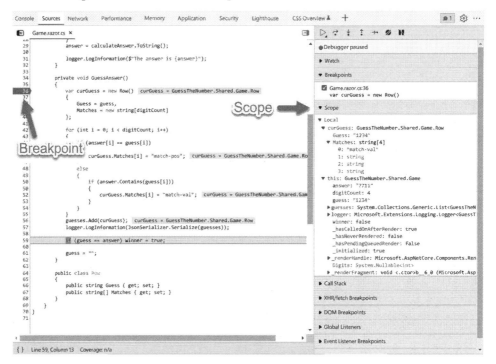

Figure 3.5: Source tab of DevTools

It is possible to debug a Blazor WebAssembly app using Visual Studio or directly in the browser. Enabling debugging in the browser takes a little more effort, but offers the same robust features as found in Visual Studio.

By efficiently using logging, debugging can be more efficient. Next, we will learn how to use logging in a Blazor WebAssembly app.

Understanding logging

Logging is an essential tool for troubleshooting any application. It helps to identify and solve problems. Logging is enabled by default in the Blazor WebAssembly project templates provided by Microsoft. However, the only logging provider that is enabled is the **Console** provider.

IMPORTANT NOTE

The **Console** provider does not store the logs, it only displays them. If you need to retain your logs, you will need to use a different provider.

The following code sample does the following:

- Injects an ILogger<Counter> object into the page. It uses the fully qualified name of the class type as the log category. The log category is included with each log message that is created by that instance of ILogger.

- Calls LogInformation to log the indicated string at the Information log level.

The following code writes to the log each time the button is clicked:

Counter.razor

```
@page "/counter"
@inject ILogger<Counter> logger;


<PageTitle>Counter</PageTitle>


<h1>Counter</h1>


<p role="status">Current count: @currentCount</p>


<button class="btn btn-primary" @onclick="IncrementCount">
    Click me
</button>


@code {
    private int currentCount = 0;

    private void IncrementCount()
    {
        logger.LogInformation("Button Clicked!");
        currentCount++;
    }
}
```

The following screenshot of the **Console** tab within `DevTools` shows the results of clicking the **Click me** button:

Figure 3.6: Logging example

Understanding log levels

Whenever we log an item to the logger, we must provide the log level. The log level indicates the severity of the message.

The following table lists the log level values from the lowest to the highest level of severity:

Log Level	Method	Description
Trace	`LogTrace`	These messages are extremely detailed and may contain sensitive data. They are disabled by default and should never be enabled in production.
Debug	`LogDebug`	These messages are used only during debugging and development.
Information	`LogInformation`	These messages track the general flow of the application.
Warning	`LogWarning`	These messages are for unexpected or abnormal events.
Error	`LogError`	These messages are for errors in the current operation, such as a failed save.
Critical	`LogCritical`	These messages are for critical errors that cause the entire application to fail.

Table 3.1: Log levels

TIP

You should use ILogger rather than System.Console.WriteLine or System.Diagnostics.Debug.WriteLine since those methods only allow you to send text to the console and they do not include the name of the class that originated the message. Also, they must be either removed or hidden before the app is deployed.

When using logging, try to log using the appropriate log level and try to make your messages as short as possible without rendering them meaningless. Use a consistent format for your messages so that they can be easily filtered. Finally, avoid logging redundant or irrelevant information because logging is not free; it consumes some resources.

You can adjust the minimum log level as necessary.

The following Logging component demonstrates how to use each of the various log levels:

Logging.razor

```
@page "/logging"
@inject ILogger<Logging> logger;

<PageTitle>Logging</PageTitle>

<h1>Logging</h1>

<button class="btn btn-primary" @onclick="DemoLogging">
    Click me
</button>

@code {
    private void DemoLogging()
    {
        logger.LogTrace("Logger: Trace");
        logger.LogDebug("Logger: Debug");
        logger.LogInformation("Logger: Information");
        logger.LogWarning("Logger: Warning");
        logger.LogError("Logger: Error");
        logger.LogCritical("Logger: Critical");
```

```
        logger.Log(LogLevel.None, "Logger: None");
    }
}
```

The following screenshot shows how each of the different log levels is rendered in DevTools.

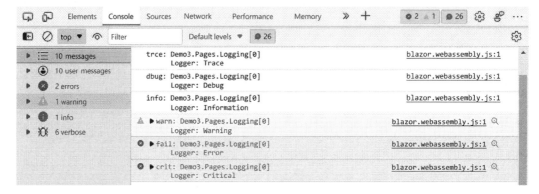

Figure 3.7: Log levels

Setting the minimum log level

By default, the project is configured to display all the logged items with a minimum log level of Information. You can adjust this setting by completing the following steps:

1. From the **Tools** menu, select **NuGet Package Manager**, **Package Manager Console** to open the **Package Manager Console**.

2. Enter the following text into the **Package Manager Console** and press the *Enter* key:

    ```
    Install-Package Microsoft.Extensions.Logging.Configuration
    ```

    The preceding code will add the **Microsoft.Extenstions.Logging.Configuration** NuGet package to the project.

3. Right-click the wwwroot folder and select the **Add**, **New Item** option from the menu.

4. Press *Ctrl+E* to enter the **Search** textbox.

5. Enter app settings file in the **Search** textbox.

6. Enter appsettings.json in the **Name** textbox and click the **Add** button.

7. Replace the default JSON with the following JSON:

```json
{
  "Logging": {
    "LogLevel": {
      "Default": "Information",
      "Microsoft.AspNetCore": "Debug"
    }
  }
}
```

8. Add the following line to the `Main` method of the `Client/Program.cs` file:

```
builder.Logging.AddConfiguration(
    builder.Configuration.GetSection("Logging"));
```

The proceeding code will configure the browser to only log items that have a log level of at least Debug.

Logging is an essential tool for understanding the flow of a Blazor WebAssembly app. There are different log levels depending on the type of message. The minimum log level displayed can be adjusted with an `appsetting.json` file.

Now let's look at some different ways to handle exceptions.

Handling exceptions

As part of the template, when an unhandled exception occurs in a Blazor WebAssembly app, a yellow bar is displayed at the bottom of the screen:

Figure 3.8: Sample unhandled exception

You can modify the text and style of the error message that is displayed by modifying the `index.html` file. The UI for the yellow bar is defined in the `wwwroot/index.html` file:

```
<div id="blazor-error-ui">
    An unhandled error has occurred.
    <a href="" class="reload">Reload</a>
    <a class="dismiss">X</a>
</div>
```

TIP

You can modify the style of the error message that is displayed in the `wwwroot/css/app.css` file.

In the preceding screenshot, clicking the **Throw Exception** button throws an unhandled exception. This is the code for the `ThrowException` component that we used to create the **Throw Exception** button in the preceding screenshot:

```
<button class="btn btn-primary" @onclick="NewException">
    Throw Exception
</button>

@code {
    private void NewException()
    {
        throw new Exception("This is a sample error!");
    }
}
```

To view the exception, we need to open `DevTools` by pressing *F12* and selecting the **Console** tab. By default, unhandled exceptions are logged to the **Console**. The following screenshot shows the **Console** tab:

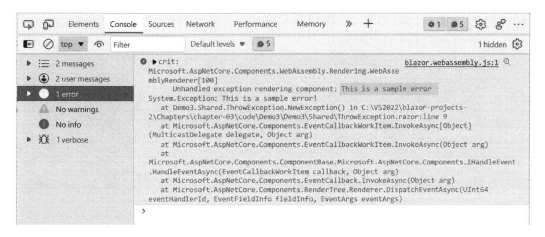

Figure 3.9: Sample critical log

In a perfect world, there are not any unhandled exceptions. In our world, there are error boundaries and custom error components.

Setting error boundaries

Error boundaries can be used to handle exceptions. The **ErrorBoundary** component is a built-in component used to handle unhandled errors at the UI level. It includes a **ChildContent** property that renders when an error has not occurred and an **ErrorContent** property that renders when an error has occurred. The ErrorBoundary component can be wrapped around any other component.

The following code wraps an ErrorBoundary component around the ThrowException component:

```
<ErrorBoundary>
    <ChildContent>
        <ThrowException />
    </ChildContent>
</ErrorBoundary>
```

When the **Throw Exception** button is pressed, the following information will be displayed:

Figure 3.10: Default ErrorBoundary UI

The default UI for the ErrorBoundary component is defined in the wwwroot/css/app.css file. The default message is very generic. We can add our own custom error message by using the ErrorContent property of the ErrorBoundary component. This is the updated ErrorBoundary component that includes the ErrorContent property:

```
<ErrorBoundary>
    <ChildContent>
        <ThrowException />
    </ChildContent>
    <ErrorContent>
        <h3>The Throw Exception button caused this error!</h3>
    </ErrorContent>
</ErrorBoundary>
```

The following screenshot shows the result of the custom ErrorContent:

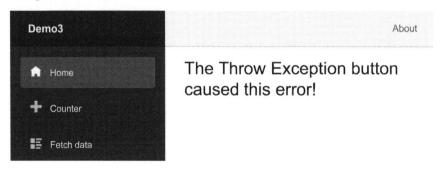

Figure 3.11: Custom ErrorContent

The ErrorBoundary component only handles errors on the UI level. It allows the developer to catch the error at a single point in the UI. To handle the errors programmatically, we need to create a custom error component.

Creating a custom error component

A custom error component can be passed to each child component. The following ErrorHandler component writes to the log when an error is encountered:

ErrorHandler.razor

```
@inject ILogger<ErrorHandler> Logger

<CascadingValue Value="this">
    @ChildContent
</CascadingValue>

@code {
    [Parameter]
    public RenderFragment? ChildContent { get; set; }

    public void ProcessError(Exception ex)
    {
        Logger.LogError("Message: {Message}", ex.Message);
    }
}
```

The ErrorHandler needs to be added as a CascadingParameter into the component that will use it. This is the ThrownExceptionHandled component:

ThrownExceptionHandled.razor

```
<button class="btn btn-primary" @onclick="NewException">
    Throw Exception
</button>

@code {
    [CascadingParameter]
    public ErrorHandler? Error { get; set; }
```

```
    private void NewException()
    {
        try
        {
            throw new Exception("This is a sample error!");
        }
        catch (Exception ex)
        {
            Error?.ProcessError(ex);
        }
    }
}
```

When the ThrownExceptionHandled component is wrapped in the ErrorHandler component, all the unhandled errors are logged to the **Console**:

```
<ErrorHandler>
    <ThrowExceptionHandled />
</ErrorHandler>
```

The following screenshot shows how the error is rendered to the **Console**:

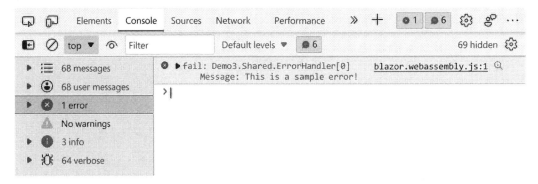

Figure 3.12: Handled error

The Blazor WebAssembly project templates provided by Microsoft render a generic yellow bar at the bottom of the page when an unhandled exception is encountered. We can use an ErrorBoundary component to customize the UI. Even better, we can create a custom error component for more control over how errors are handled.

Now that we know how to handle errors, let's learn how to prepare our application for deployment.

Using ahead-of-time (AOT) compilation

By default, Blazor WebAssembly apps use a .NET **Intermediate Language** (**IL**) interpreter when running on the browser. **Ahead-of-time** (**AOT**) compilation allows you to compile your .NET code into WebAssembly before deployment. Since compiled code is more performant than interpreted code, your app will run faster. The only downside to using AOT is that the app may be larger and, therefore, will take more time to load during application startup.

These are the steps to enable AOT:

1. Right-click the project in the **Solution Explorer** and select **Properties** from the menu.
2. Enter AOT in the **Search properties** textbox.
3. Check the **Use ahead-of-time (AOT) compilation on publish** checkbox.

Once AOT is enabled, AOT compilation will occur every time the project is published. It takes much longer to publish an app using AOT compilation, but it can make the Blazor WebAssembly app run much faster. This is especially true for CPU-intensive apps.

> **IMPORTANT NOTE**
>
> You must have `wasm-tools` installed to use AOT. To install `wasm-tools`, run the following command and restart Visual Studio:
>
> ```
> dotnet workload install wasm-tools
> ```

Now we are ready to deploy the Blazor WebAssembly app.

Deploying a Blazor WebAssembly app to Microsoft Azure

Deploying a Blazor WebAssembly app using Visual Studio is quite simple. There is an easy-to-follow wizard that is included in Visual Studio. These are the steps for deploying a Blazor WebAssembly app to Microsoft Azure using Visual Studio 2022:

1. Right-click the project and select **Publish** from the menu.

This is the first page of the **Publish** wizard:

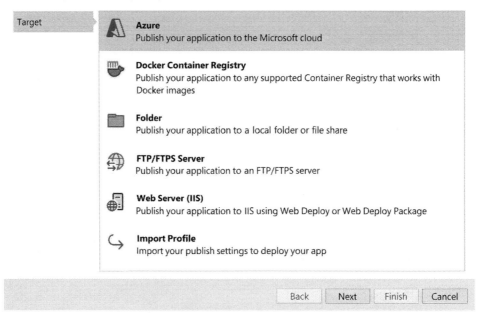

Figure 3.13: First page of Publish wizard

As you can see, there are many options provided. For this project, we will be publishing the application to the Microsoft cloud.

2.   Select **Azure** and click the **Next** button.

This is the second page of the **Publish** wizard:

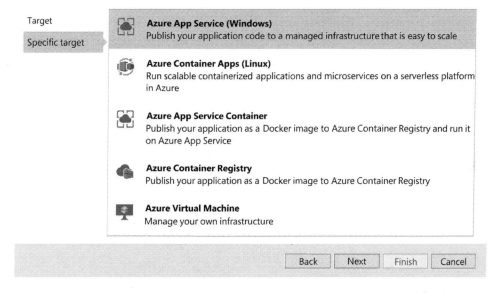

Figure 3.14: Second page of Publish wizard

3. Select **Azure App Service (Windows)** and click the **Next** button.

    This is the last page of the **Publish** wizard. This page is used to select the **Azure App Service** to use for the application. You can also use this page to create an **Azure App Service**.

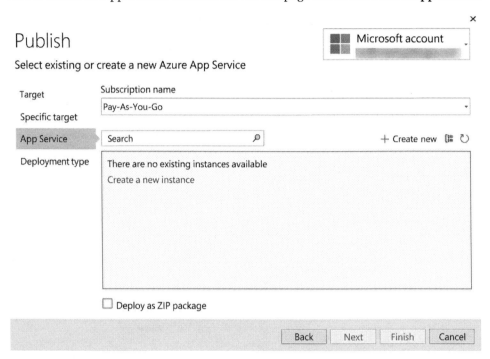

Figure 3.15: Last page of Publish wizard

4. Create an **Azure App Service** if you do not have one.

This is a screenshot of the **Create New App Service** dialog:

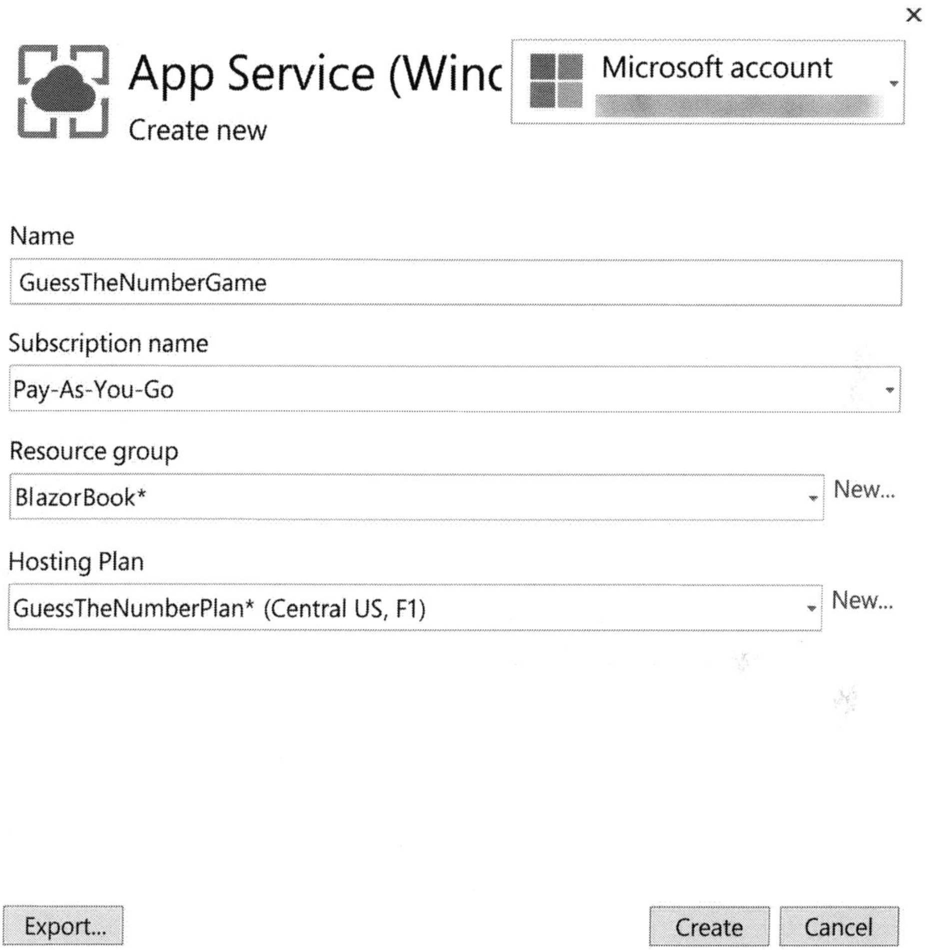

Figure 3.16: Create New App Service dialog

If you do not already have a Hosting Plan, we recommend that you create a **Free** hosting plan for this project. The following screenshot shows the **Create New Hosting Plan** dialog with the **Free** option selected:

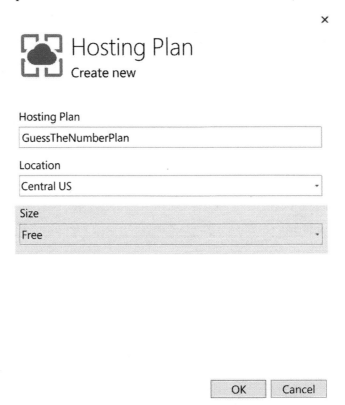

Figure 3.17: Create New Hosting Plan dialog

5.   Click the **Finish** button.

6. Click the **Close** button.

The application is now ready to be published.

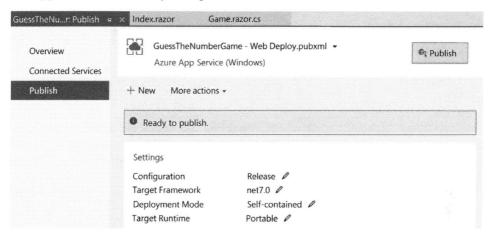

Figure 3.18: Publish dialog

7. Click the **Publish** button and wait.

The browser will automatically open once the app is published.

Deploying a Blazor WebAssembly app to Microsoft Azure is as simple as following the steps in a wizard.

Creating the "guess the number" project

In this section, we will build a simple number-guessing game. The game will allow for multiple guesses and will alert us when we win.

This is a screenshot of the completed application:

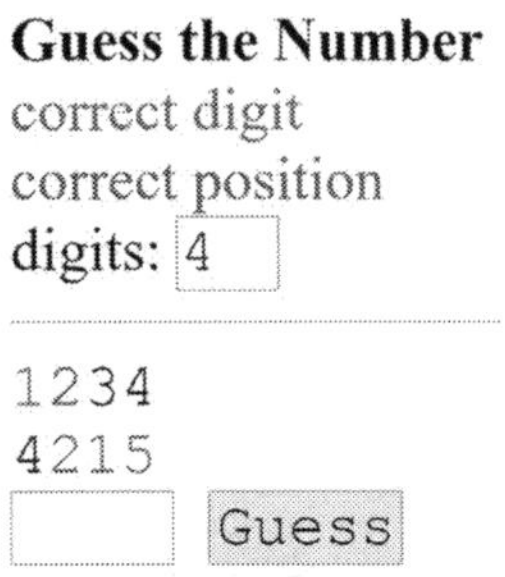

Guess the Number
correct digit
correct position
digits: 4

1234
4215
[   ] Guess

Figure 3.19: Guess the Number game

The build time for this project is approximately 60 minutes.

Project overview

The GuessTheNumber project will be created by using Microsoft's **Blazor WebAssembly App Empty** project template to create an empty Blazor WebAssembly project. First, we will add the components needed for the project. Then, we will add logging. We will debug the app in both Visual Studio and the browser. We will add an ErrorBoundary component. Finally, we will deploy the project to Microsoft Azure.

Getting started with the project

We need to create a new Blazor WebAssembly app. We do this as follows:

1.   Open Visual Studio 2022.

2.   Click the **Create a new project** button.

3.   Press *Alt+S* to enter the **Search for templates** textbox.

4. Enter Blazor and press the *Enter* key.

The following screenshot shows the **Blazor WebAssembly App Empty** project template.

Figure 3.20: Blazor WebAssembly App Empty project template

5. Select the **Blazor WebAssembly App Empty** project template and click the **Next** button.

6. Enter GuessTheNumber in the **Project name** textbox and click the **Next** button.

This is a screenshot of the dialog used to configure our new project:

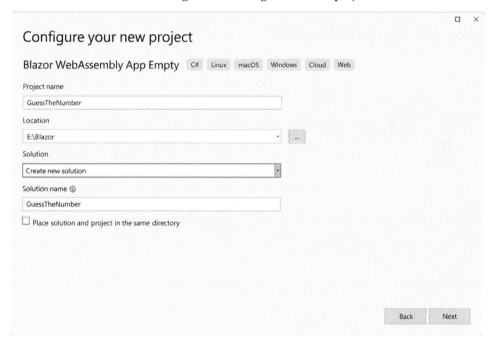

Figure 3.21: Configure your new project dialog

TIP

In the preceding example, we placed the GuessTheNumber project into the
E:\Blazor folder. However, the location of this project is not important.

7. Select **.NET 7.0** as the version of the **Framework** to use.

8. Check the **Configure for HTTPS** checkbox.

9. Uncheck the **ASP.NET Core Hosted** checkbox.

10. Uncheck the **Progressive Web Application** checkbox.

    This is a screenshot of the **Additional information** dialog:

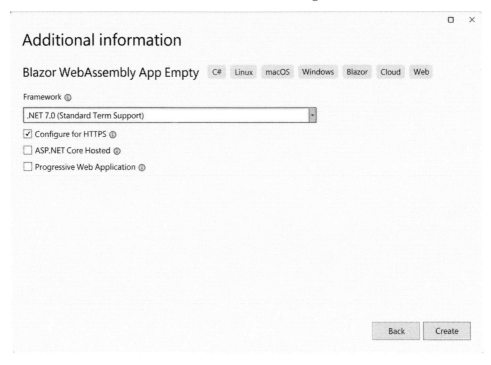

Figure 3.22: Additional information dialog

11. Click the **Create** button.

We have created the GuessTheNumber Blazor WebAssembly project. Now we need to add a component.

Adding a Game component

We need to add a Game component that includes a Razor page, a code-behind page, and a cascading style sheet. We do this as follows:

1. Right-click the GuessTheNumber project and select the **Add, New Folder** option from the menu.

2. Name the new folder Shared.

3. Right-click the Shared folder and select the **Add, Razor Component** option from the menu.

4. Name the new component Game.

5. Replace the default code in the Game component with the following markup:

    ```
    <div class="game">
        <strong>Guess the Number</strong>
        <div class="match-val">correct digit</div>
        <div class="match-pos">correct position</div>
        <div>digits: @digitCount</div>
        <hr />
        @if (guesses == null)
        {
            <h1>Loading...</h1>
        }
        else
        {
            <div class="guesses">
            </div>
        }
    </div>
    ```

    The preceding code creates the framework for the game.

6. Enter the following code in the guesses div:

    ```
    @foreach (var row in guesses)
    {
        @for (int i = 0; i < digitCount; i++)
        {
            <span class="@row.Matches[i]">
                @row.Guess[i]
    ```

```
        </span>
    }
    <br />
}
```

The preceding code loops through each of the guesses to render them on the screen.

7. Enter the following code beneath the @foreach statement:

```
@if (winner)
{
    <span>Winner!</span>
    <div>
        <button @onclick="PlayAgain">Play Again</button>
    </div>
}
else
{
    <input type="text"
        @bind=guess
        class="guess"
        inputmode="numeric"
        size="@digitCount"
        maxlength="@digitCount" />
    <button @onclick="GuessAnswer">Guess</button>
}
```

The preceding code checks to see if the player is a winner. If they are a winner, it displays the **Play Again** button. If they are not a winner, it provides them with an input element for them to enter another guess.

Now that we have added the markup, we need to add the code.

Adding the code

We will add the code for the project in a separate file. We do this as follows:

1. Right-click the Shared folder and select the **Add**, **Class** option from the menu.
2. Enter Game.razor.cs and click the **Add** button.

3. Add the following using statement to the top of the file:

```
using System.Text;
```

4. Add the partial keyword to the Game class:

```
public partial class Game
{
}
```

5. Add the following code to the Game class:

```
[Parameter] public int? Digits { get; set; }

private int digitCount = 4;
private string answer = "";
private string guess = "";
private List<Row> guesses = new();
private bool winner = false;

protected override void OnParametersSet(){ }

private void CalculateAnswer(){ }

private void GuessAnswer(){ }

private void PlayAgain(){ }

public class Row
{
    public string Guess { get; set; }
    public string[] Matches { get; set; }
}
```

The preceding code defines the properties and methods we will use in the Game component. It also defines the Row class.

6. Add the following code to the OnParametersSet method:

```
if (Digits.HasValue) { digitCount = (int)Digits; };
CalculateAnswer();
```

The preceding code sets the value of digitCount. After it has determined the value of digitCount, it calls the CalculateAnswer method.

7. Add the following code to the CalculateAnswer method:

```
StringBuilder calculateAnswer = new StringBuilder();
for (int i = 0; i < digitCount; i++)
{
    int nextDigit = new Random().Next(0, 10);
    calculateAnswer.Append(nextDigit);
}
answer = calculateAnswer.ToString();
```

The preceding code calculates the answer based on the number of digits specified by digitCount.

8. Add the following code to the GuessAnswer method:

```
var curGuess = new Row()
{
    Guess = guess,
    Matches = new string[digitCount]
};

for (int i = 0; i < digitCount; i++)
{
    if (answer[i] == guess[i])
    {
        curGuess.Matches[i] = "match-pos";
    }
    else
    {
        if (answer.Contains(guess[i]))
        {
            curGuess.Matches[i] = "match-val";
        }
```

```
        }
    }
    guesses.Add(curGuess);
    guess = "";

    if (guess == answer) winner = true;
```

The preceding code compares each digit in the answer with each digit in the guess. If the guess is equal to the answer, they are a winner.

9. Add the following code to the PlayAgain method:

```
winner = false;
guesses = new();
CalculateAnswer();
```

The preceding code resets the game.

We are almost done creating the Game component. We just need to add some styling.

Adding a style sheet

We will add a style sheet using CSS isolation. We do this as follows:

1. Right-click the Shared folder and select the **Add, New Item** option from the menu.

2. Press *Ctrl+E* to enter the **Search** textbox.

3. Enter css in the **Search** textbox.

4. Enter Game.razor.css in the **Name** textbox and click the **Add** button.

5. Enter the following styles:

```
.game {
    padding: 15px;
    font-size: 4rem;
}

input, button, .guesses {
    font-size: 4rem;
    font-family: Courier New, Courier, monospace
}

.match-pos {
```

```
        color: green;
    }


    .match-val {
        color: red
    }
```

The style sheet sets the font to a monospaced font for both the list of past guesses and the current guess. Also, the classes used to designate the color are defined.

6.   Open the wwwroot/index.html file.

7.   Uncomment the link to the GuessTheNumber.styles.css style sheet in the head element:

```
<head>
    <meta charset="utf-8" />
    <base href="/" />
    <link href="css/app.css" rel="stylesheet" />
    <link href="GuessTheNumber.styles.css"
        rel="stylesheet" />
</head>
```

Let's test the app by playing the game.

Setting up and playing the game

We need to add the Game component to the Index component to play the game. We do this as follows:

1.   Open the _Imports.razor file.

2.   Add the following using statement to the file:

```
@using GuessTheNumber.Shared
```

By adding the preceding using statement to the _Imports.razor file, it is automatically imported into the other .razor files within the same folder and its subfolders.

3.   Open the Pages/Index.razor file.

4.   Replace the h1 element with the following:

```
<PageTitle>Guess the Number</PageTitle>
<Game />
```

5. Press *Ctrl+F5* to start the application without debugging.

6. Enter a 4-digit number and click the **Guess** button.

   If a digit is in the answer, it will appear in red. If the digit is in the answer and it is in the correct position, it will appear in green. The goal is to guess the answer.

7. Enter another 4-digit number and click the **Guess** button.

8. Try to win the game.

It is impossible to win the game because there is a bug in our code. Let's add some logging to try and find the issue.

Adding logging

We will add logging to the application. We do this as follows:

1. Open the Game.razor.cs file.

2. Add the following using statement to the top of the file:

   ```
   using System.Text.Json;
   ```

3. Add the following code to the top of the Game class:

   ```
   [Inject] ILogger<Game>? logger { get; set; }
   ```

   The preceding code injects an ILogger object into the Game component to create a logger.

4. Add the following code to the end of the CalculateAnswer method:

   ```
   logger.LogInformation($"The answer is {answer}");
   ```

5. Add the following code to the end of the GuessAnswer method:

   ```
   logger.LogInformation(JsonSerializer.Serialize(guesses));
   ```

6. Press *Ctrl+F5* to start the application without debugging.

7. Press *F12* to open DevTools.

8. Select the **Console** tab.

9. Enter a 4-digit number and click the **Guess** button.

10. Enter another 4-digit number and click the **Guess** button.

The following screenshot shows the messages that have been logged to the **Console** tab:

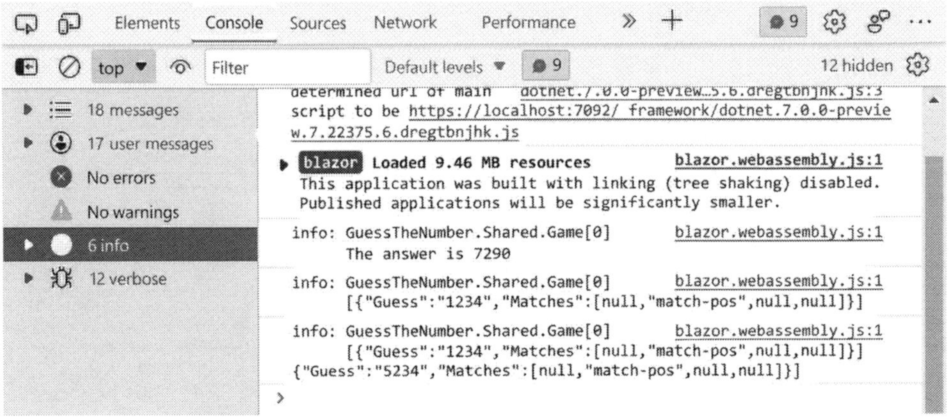

Figure 3.23: Logged information

By using logging, we can determine that our guesses are being correctly evaluated. Let's try debugging our code to find the issue.

Debugging in Visual Studio

First, we will debug the Blazor WebAssembly app using Visual Studio. We do this as follows:

1. Open the Game.razor.cs file.

2. Add a breakpoint to the first line of the GuessAnswer method.

3. Press *F5* to run the application with debugging.

4. Enter a 4-digit number and click the **Guess** button.

5. Hover over curGuess to view its contents.

6. View the **Locals** window.

7. Set a **Watch** on guess.

8. Press *F10* to step through the code.

9. Verify that the code is working correctly.

10. View the **Output** window in Visual Studio to help understand the flow:

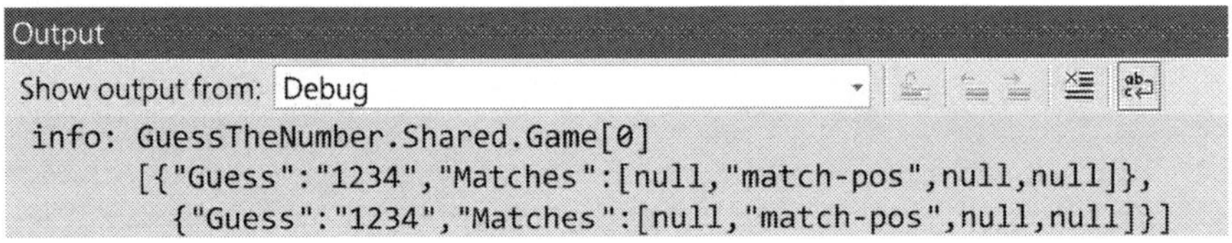

Figure 3.24: Output window in Visual Studio

11. The problem is that guess is being set to an empty string before its value is compared to the answer.

12. Move the following code to the end of the GuessAnswer method:

```
guess = "";
```

13. Press *F5* to run the application without debugging.

14. Play the game until you win.

    The following screenshot shows a winning game:

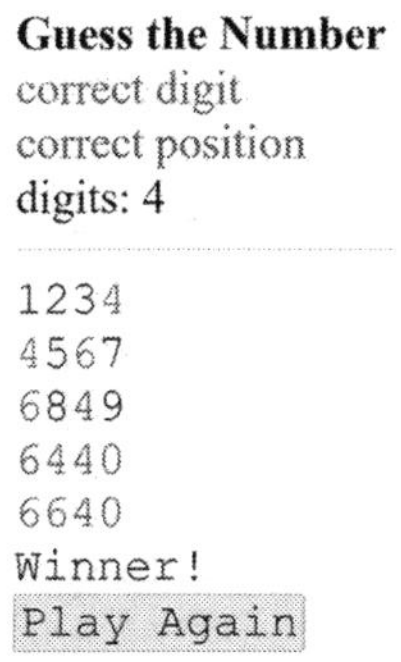

Guess the Number
correct digit
correct position
digits: 4

```
1234
4567
6849
6440
6640
Winner!
Play Again
```

Figure 3.25: Guess the Number – Winner

When your guess matches the answer, you win the game. Let's make the game harder by varying the number of digits.

Updating the code

To make the game harder, we will allow the player to decide how many digits they need to guess. We do this as follows:

1. Return to Visual Studio 2022.

2. Open the Game.razor file.

3. Replace @digitCount with the following:

```
<input type="number"
    value=@digitCount
    inputmode="numeric"
    min="1" max="10"
    @onchange="RestartGame" />
```

4. Open the `Game.razor.cs` file.

5. Add the following `RestartGame` method:

```
private void RestartGame(ChangeEventArgs e) {
    digitCount = Convert.ToInt16(e.Value);
    PlayAgain();
}
```

The preceding code resets the game every time the number of digits is changed.

6. Press *Ctrl+F5* to start the application without debugging.

7. Play the updated game.

Now we will use the browser to debug our updates.

Debugging in the browser

We will debug the new code in the browser. We do this as follows:

1. Press *Shift+Alt+D*.

2. Copy the indicated text into your clipboard that corresponds with the browser that you are using.

3. Press *Win+R*, paste the text that you copied, and click the **OK** button.

4. Press *Shift+Alt+D*.

    A second tab opens in the browser.

5. Click the **Sources** tab and view the files in the `file://` node.

6. Open the Shared folder:

Figure 3.26: Folders in the browser

7. Add a breakpoint in the GuessAnswer method.

8. Return to the first tab.

9. Change the number of digits to 5.

10. Enter a 5-digit number and click the **Guess** button.

11. Return to the second tab.

12. View the Scope, Local value of curGuess.

13. Press *F10* multiple times to step through the function call.

14. Press *F8* to resume script execution.

15. Return to the first tab.

16. Enter a 3-digit number and press the **Guess** button.

17. Press *F8* to resume script execution.

18. Click the **reload** link at the bottom of the page.

We encountered an unhandled error when we entered a guess with fewer digits than the answer. Let's address that issue by adding an ErrorBoundary component.

Adding an ErrorBoundary component

We need to wrap the Game component in an ErrorBoundary component. We do this as follows:

1. Return to Visual Studio.

2. Open the Index.razor file.

3. Replace the Game element with the following:

```
<ErrorBoundary>
    <ChildContent>
        <Game />
    </ChildContent>
    <ErrorContent>
        <h1>You have entered an invalid guess!</h1>
    </ErrorContent>
</ErrorBoundary>
```

4. Press *Ctrl+F5* to start the application without debugging.

5. Enter a 3-digit number and press the **Guess** button.

6. Verify that the message defined by the ErrorContent property is displayed.

We have added an ErrorBoundary component to update the UI when an unhandled exception is encountered. The ErrorContent property is used to define the UI. Now that the application is tested, it's time to deploy it.

Deploying the application to Microsoft Azure

We will enable AOT compilation and deploy the app to Microsoft Azure. We do this as follows:

1. Right-click the GuessTheNumber project and select **Properties** from the menu.

2. Enter AOT in the **Search properties** textbox.

3. Check the **Use ahead-of-time (AOT) compilation on publish** checkbox.

4. Right-click the GuessTheNumber project and select the **Publish** option from the menu.

5. Select **Azure** and click the **Next** button.

6. Select **Azure App Service (Windows)** and click the **Next** button.

7. Select an existing Azure App Service or create a new one.

8. Click the **Finish** button.

> **IMPORTANT NOTE**
>
> Be patient, it will take some time to deploy the app to Microsoft Azure.

9. Play the game.

We have deployed the Guess the Number web app to Microsoft Azure.

> **IMPORTANT NOTE**
>
> After you have finished testing your application, don't forget to remove the resources that you added to your Azure account.

Summary

You should now be able to debug and deploy a Blazor WebAssembly app.

In this chapter, we learned about debugging in both Visual Studio and DevTools. We learned about the different levels of logging and how to write to the log. We learned how to handle exceptions. Finally, we learned how to use AOT compilation before deploying a Blazor WebAssembly app to Microsoft Azure.

After that, we created a new project using the **Blazor WebAssembly App Empty** project template in Visual Studio. We added a simple Game component. We added some logging to the app. We added a breakpoint to the app using both Visual Studio and DevTools. We added an ErrorBoundary component to capture the unhandled errors. Finally, we enabled AOT compilation and deployed the application to Microsoft Azure.

In the next chapter, we will build a modal dialog using templated components.

Questions

The following questions are provided for your consideration:

1. How would you rewrite the Guess the Number game to use a custom error component?
2. What types of applications benefit the most from AOT?
3. What are the different log levels and when should you use each one?

4. How do you debug a Blazor WebAssembly app in the browser?

5. Can you deploy a Blazor WebAssembly app to Microsoft Azure for free?

Further reading

The following resources provide more information concerning the topics in this chapter:

- For more information on debugging C# code in Visual Studio, refer to `https://learn.microsoft.com/en-us/visualstudio/get-started/csharp/tutorial-debugger`.

- For more information on DevTools, refer to `https://learn.microsoft.com/en-us/microsoft-edge/devtools-guide-chromium/overview`.

- For more information on logging, refer to `https://learn.microsoft.com/en-us/dotnet/core/extensions/logging`.

- For more information on Microsoft Azure, refer to `https://azure.microsoft.com`.

4

Building a Modal Dialog Using Templated Components

A modal dialog is a dialog box that appears on top of all other content in a window and requires user interaction to close it. A templated component is a component that accepts one or more UI templates as parameters. The UI templates of a templated component can contain any Razor markup.

In this chapter, we will learn about **RenderFragment** parameters, **EventCallback** parameters, and CSS isolation. RenderFragment parameters are used when a parent component needs to share information with a child component, and conversely, EventCallback parameters are used when a child component needs to share information with its parent component. CSS isolation is used to scope CSS styles to a specific component.

In this chapter, we will create a modal dialog component. The component will be a templated component that can render different HTML based on its parameters. It will use event callbacks to return events to the calling component. It will use CSS isolation to add the formatting that will make it behave like a modal dialog. We will test the modal dialog component by adding it to another component. Finally, we will move the component to a **Razor class library** so that it can be easily shared with other projects.

Custom components

can be used over again.

Make a library!

In this chapter, we will cover the following topics:

- Using `RenderFragment` parameters
- Using `EventCallback` parameters
- Understanding CSS isolation
- Creating a Razor class library
- Creating the modal dialog project

Technical requirements

To complete this project, you need to have Visual Studio 2022 installed on your PC. For instructions on how to install the free Community Edition of Visual Studio 2022, refer to *Chapter 1, Introduction to Blazor WebAssembly*.

The source code for this chapter is available in the following GitHub repository: `https://github.com/PacktPublishing/Blazor-WebAssembly-by-Example-Second-Edition/tree/main/Chapter04`.

The Code in Action video is available here: `https://packt.link/Ch4`.

Using RenderFragment parameters

A `RenderFragment` parameter is a segment of UI content. It is used to communicate UI content from the parent to the child. The UI content can include plain text, HTML markup, Razor markup, or another component.

The following code is for the `Alert` component. The UI content of the `Alert` component is displayed when the value of its `Show` property is `true`:

Alert.razor

```
@if (Show)
{
    <div>
        <div>
            <div>
                @ChildContent
            </div>
            <div>
                <button @onclick="OnOk">
                    OK
```

```
                    </button>
                </div>
            </div>
        </div>
}
@code {
    [Parameter] public bool Show { get; set; }
    [Parameter] public EventCallback OnOk { get; set; }
    [Parameter] public RenderFragment ChildContent { get; set;}
}
```

The preceding code, for the Alert component, includes three different types of parameters: simple type, EventCallback, and RenderFragment:

- The first parameter is the Show property. It is of type Boolean, which is a simple type. For more information on using simple types as parameters, see *Chapter 2, Building Your First Blazor WebAssembly Application*.

- The second parameter is the OnOk property. It is of type EventCallback. We will learn more about EventCallback parameters in the next section.

- The last parameter is the ChildContent property. It is of type RenderFragment and is the subject of this section.

The following markup uses the Alert component to display the current day of the week in a dialog when the **Show Alert** button is clicked. The Razor markup between the opening tag and the closing tag of the Alert element is bound to the ChildContent property of the Alert component:

```
@page "/"

<PageTitle>Home</PageTitle>

<Alert Show="showAlert" OnOk="@(() => showAlert = false)">
    <h1>Alert</h1>
    <p>Today is @DateTime.Now.DayOfWeek.</p>
</Alert>

@if (!showAlert)
{
    <button @onclick="@(() => showAlert = true)">
        Show Alert
```

```
        </button>
    }


@code {
    private bool showAlert = false;
}
```

The following screenshot shows the dialog that is displayed when the **Show Alert** button is clicked:

Alert

Today is Tuesday.

 OK

Figure 4.1: Sample alert

The name of the RenderFragment parameter must be ChildContent to use the content of the element without explicitly specifying the parameter's name. For example, the following markup results in the same output as the preceding markup that did not explicitly specify the ChildContent element:

```
<Alert Show="showAlert" OnOk="@(() => showAlert = false)">
    <ChildContent>
        <h1>Alert</h1>
        <p>Today is @DateTime.Now.DayOfWeek.</p>
    </ChildContent>
</Alert>
```

The ChildContent element is highlighted in the preceding markup.

 IMPORTANT NOTE

By convention, the name of the RenderFragment parameter used to capture the content of a parent element must be ChildContent.

It is possible to include multiple RenderFragment parameters in a component by explicitly specifying each parameter's name in the markup. We will use multiple RenderFragment parameters to complete the project in this chapter.

A RenderFragment parameter enables a parent component to communicate the UI content to be used by its child component, while an EventCallback parameter is used to communicate from the child component back to the parent component. In the next section, we will explain how to use EventCallback parameters.

Using EventCallback parameters

An event callback is a method that is passed to another method when a particular event occurs. For example, when the button on the Alert component is clicked, the @onclick event uses the OnOk parameter to determine the method that should be called. The method that the OnOK parameter references is defined in the parent component.

As previously stated, EventCallback parameters are used to share information from the child component to the parent component. They share information with their parent and notify their parent when something, such as a button click, has occurred. The parent component simply specifies the method to call when the event is triggered.

This is an example of an EventCallback parameter:

```
[Parameter] public EventCallback OnOk { get; set; }
```

The following example uses a **lambda expression** for the OnOk method. When the OnOk method is called, the value of the showAlert property is set to false:

```
<Alert Show="showAlert" OnOk="@(() => showAlert = false)">
        <h1>Alert</h1>
        <p>Today is @DateTime.Now.DayOfWeek.</p>
</Alert>

@code {
    private bool showAlert = false;
}
```

A lambda expression is used to create an anonymous function. However, we do not need to use anonymous functions when using EventCallback parameters. The following example shows how to use a method for the OnOk method instead of an anonymous function:

```
<Alert Show="showAlert" OnOk="OkClickHandler">
    <h1>Alert</h1>
    <p>Today is @DateTime.Now.DayOfWeek.</p>
</Alert>
```

```
@code {
    private bool showAlert = false;

    private void OkClickHandler()
    {
        showAlert = false;
    }
}
```

The preceding code defines a new OkClickHandler method that is called when the button is clicked.

When writing the Alert component, you might be tempted to update the Show parameter directly from the OnOk event on the component. You must not do so because if you update the values directly in the component and the component needs to be re-rendered, any state changes will be lost. If you need to maintain state in the component, you should add a private field to the component.

IMPORTANT NOTE

Components should never write to their own parameters.

For more information on using events, refer to *Chapter 8, Building a Kanban Board Using Events*.

The Alert component displays text on the page, but it does not yet work like a modal dialog. To make it work like a modal dialog, we need to update the style sheets that are used by the component. We can do that by using CSS isolation. In the next section, we will explain how to use CSS isolation.

Understanding CSS isolation

The location of the **cascading style sheets (CSS)** used to style our Blazor WebAssembly apps is usually the wwwroot folder. Usually, the styles defined in those CSS files are applied to all the components in the web app. However, there are times when we want more control over the styles that are applied to a particular component. To achieve that, we use CSS isolation. With CSS isolation, the styles in the designated CSS file will override the global styles and will target only a specific component and its child components.

Enabling CSS isolation

To add a CSS file that is scoped to a specific component, create a CSS file in the same folder as the component with the same name as the component, but with a CSS file extension. For example, the CSS file for the Alert.razor component would be called Alert.razor.css.

The following markup is for an updated version of the Alert component. In this version, we have added the two highlighted classes:

Alert.razor

```razor
@if (Show)
{
    <div class="dialog-container">
        <div class="dialog">
            <div>
                @ChildContent
            </div>
            <div>
                <button @onclick="OnOk">
                    OK
                </button>
            </div>
        </div>
    </div>
}
```

The following Alert.razor.css file defines the styles used by the new classes:

Alert.razor.css

```css
.dialog-container {
    position: absolute;
    top: 0;
    bottom: 0;
    left: 0;
    right: 0;
    background-color: rgba(0,0,0,0.6);
    z-index: 2000;
}
```

```
.dialog {
    background-color: white;
    margin: auto;
    width: 15rem;
    padding: .5rem
}
```

The preceding CSS includes styles for both the dialog-container class and the dialog class:

- dialog-container: This class sets the background color of the element to black with 60% opacity and places it on top of the other elements, by setting its z-index to 2,000.
- dialog: This class sets the background color of the element white, centers it horizontally within its parent, and sets its width to 15 REM.

To enable the project to use the CSS, we need to add a link to the wwwroot/index.html file. By convention, the name of the CSS file that needs to be linked is the assembly's name followed by .styles.css. For example, if the name of the project is Demo4, a link to Demo4.styles.css needs to be added to the wwwroot/index.html file. The following highlighted markup shows the link to apply the styles defined in the Alert.razor.css file:

```
<head>
    <meta charset="utf-8" />
    <base href="/" />
    <link href="css/app.css" rel="stylesheet" />
    <link href="Demo4.styles.css" rel="stylesheet" />
</head>
```

The following screenshot shows the Alert component using the preceding Alert.razor.css file:

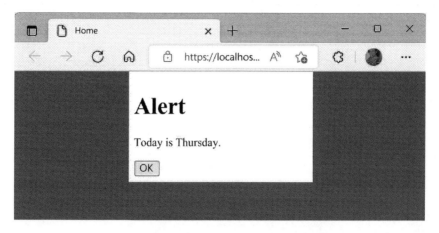

Figure 4.2: Alert component

In the preceding example, the linked `Demo4.style.css` file is created at build time. When it is created, the Blazor engine rewrites the CSS and HTML for each component by appending a string generated by the framework that is unique for each component. The rewritten CSS styles are bundled into one file and saved as a static resource.

This is a portion of the `Demo4.styles.css` file:

```
.dialog-container[b-j4grw2wm7a] {
    position: absolute;
    top: 0;
    bottom: 0;
    left: 0;
    right: 0;
    background-color: rgba(0,0,0,0.6);
    z-index: 2000;
}

.dialog[b-j4grw2wm7a] {
    background-color: white;
    margin: auto;
    width: 15rem;
    padding: .5rem
}
```

This is the rewritten HTML that references the rewritten styles:

```
▼ <div class="dialog-container" b-j4grw2wm7a>
  ▶ <div class="dialog" b-j4grw2wm7a>...</div>
  </div>
```

Figure 4.3: Rewritten HTML

By convention, the contents of the `Demo4.styles.css` file are in the `obj/{CONFIGURATION}/`
`{TARGET FRAMEWORK}/scopedcss/projectbundle/{ASSEMBLY NAME}.bundle.scp.css` file. In
the preceding example, the file was in the `\Demo4\obj\Debug\net7.0\scopedcss\bundle` folder.

Supporting child components

By default, when using CSS isolation, the CSS styles only apply to the current component. If we
want the CSS styles to apply to a child component of the current component, we need to use
the `::deep` pseudo-element within our style. This pseudo-element selects the elements that are
descendants of the element's identifier.

For example, the following style will be applied to any `H1` headings within the current component,
as well as any `H1` headings within the child components of the current component:

```
::deep h1 {
    color: red;
}
```

CSS isolation is useful if you don't want your component to use the global styles or want to share
your component via a Razor class library.

> **IMPORTANT NOTE**
>
> Scoped CSS does not apply to Razor components. It only applies to the HTML ele-
> ments that are rendered by the Razor component.

Now let's take a look at the project that we will be building in this chapter.

Creating the modal dialog project

In this chapter, we will build a modal dialog component. We will enable both the `Title` and the
`Body` of the modal dialog component to be customized using Razor markup. We will add the
modal dialog component to another component.

This is a screenshot of the modal dialog:

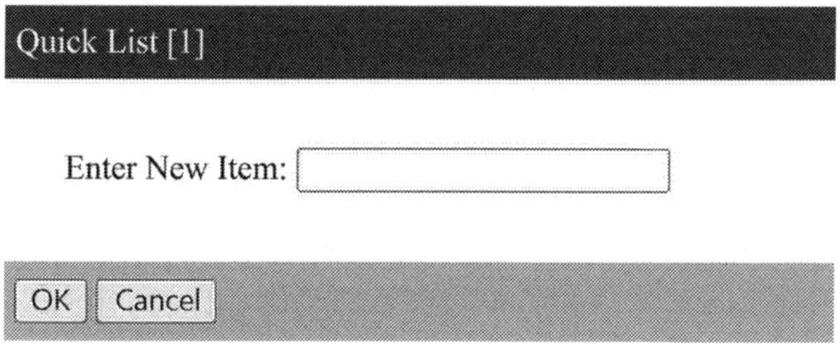

Figure 4.4: Modal dialog

After we have completed the modal dialog component, we will move it into a Razor class library so that it can be shared with other projects.

The build time for this project is approximately 90 minutes.

Project overview

The ModalDialog project will be created by using Microsoft's **Blazor WebAssembly App Empty** project template to create an empty Blazor WebAssembly project. We will add a Dialog component that includes multiple sections and use CSS isolation to apply styles that make it behave like a modal dialog. We will use EventCallback parameters to communicate from the component back to the parent when a button is clicked. We will use RenderFragment parameters to allow Razor markup to be communicated from the parent to the component. Finally, we will create a Razor class library and move the Dialog component into it so that the modal dialog can be shared with other projects.

Getting started with the project

We need to create a new Blazor WebAssembly app. We do this as follows:

1. Open Visual Studio 2022.
2. Click the **Create a new project** button.
3. Press *Alt+S* to enter the search for the templates textbox.
4. Enter Blazor and press the *Enter* key.

The following screenshot shows the **Blazor WebAssembly App Empty** project template.

Figure 4.5: Blazor WebAssembly App Empty project template

5.   Select the **Blazor WebAssembly App Empty** project template and click the **Next** button.

6.   Enter ModalDialog in the **Project name** textbox and click the **Next** button.

This is a screenshot of the dialog used to configure our new project:

□   ×

Configure your new project

Blazor WebAssembly App Empty   C#   Linux   macOS   Windows   Cloud   Web

Project name

ModalDialog

Location

E:\Blazor

Solution

Create new solution

Solution name ⓘ

ModalDialog

☐ Place solution and project in the same directory

Back   Next

Figure 4.6: Configure your new project dialog

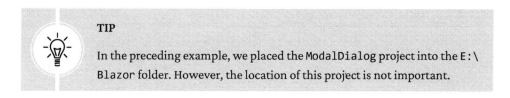

TIP

In the preceding example, we placed the `ModalDialog` project into the `E:\` `Blazor` folder. However, the location of this project is not important.

7. Select **.NET 7.0** as the version of the **Framework** to use.

8. Check the **Configure for HTTPS** checkbox.

9. Uncheck the **ASP.NET Core Hosted** checkbox.

10. Uncheck the **Progressive Web Application** checkbox.

This is a screenshot of the dialog used to collect additional information about our new project.

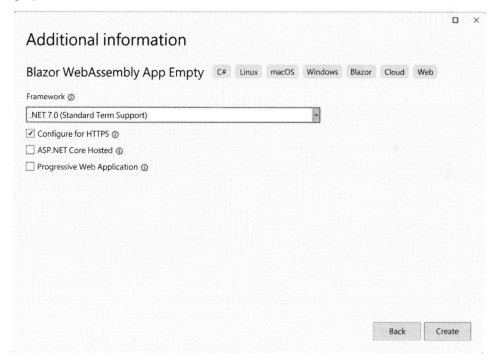

Figure 4.7: Additional information dialog

11. Click the **Create** button.

We have created the `ModalDialog` Blazor WebAssembly project. However, it is practically empty. Let's add the `Dialog` component.

Adding the Dialog component

The Dialog component will be shared. Therefore, we will add it to the Shared folder. We do this as follows:

1. Right-click the ModalDialog project and select the **Add, New Folder** option from the menu.

2. Name the new folder Shared.

3. Right-click the Shared folder and select the **Add, Razor Component** option from the menu.

4. Name the new component Dialog.

5. Click the **Add** button.

6. Replace the markup in the Dialog.razor file with the following markup:

```
@if (Show)
{
    <div class="dialog-container">
        <div class="dialog">
            <div class="dialog-title">Title</div>
            <div class="dialog-body">Body</div>
            <div class="dialog-buttons">
                <button>
                    Ok
                </button>
                <button>
                    Cancel
                </button>
            </div>
        </div>
    </div>
}
@code {
    [Parameter] public bool Show { get; set; }
}
```

In the preceding code, the Show property is used to show and hide the contents of the component.

We have added a Dialog component, but it will not behave like a modal dialog box until the appropriate styles have been added to the project.

Add a CSS file

The preceding markup includes five classes that we will use to style the `Dialog` component to make it behave like a modal dialog:

- `dialog-container`: This class is used to set the background color of the element to black with 60% opacity and place it on top of the other elements, by setting its z-index to 2,000.
- `dialog`: This class is used to set the background color of the element to white, center it horizontally within its parent, and set its width to 25 REM.
- `dialog-title`: This class is used to set the background color to dark gray, set the text to white, and add some padding.
- `dialog-body`: This class is used to add some padding to the body.
- `dialog-buttons`: This class is used to set the background color to silver and add some padding.

We need to create a CSS file to define how to style each of these classes. We do this as follows:

1. Right-click the `Shared` folder and select the **Add**, **New Item** option from the menu.
2. Enter `css` in the **Search** box.
3. Select **Style Sheet**.
4. Name the style sheet `Dialog.razor.css`.
5. Click the **Add** button.
6. Enter the following styles into the `Dialog.razor.css` file:

```
.dialog-container {
    position: absolute;
    top: 0;
    bottom: 0;
    left: 0;
    right: 0;
    background-color: rgba(0,0,0,0.6);
    z-index: 2000;
}
.dialog {
    background-color: white;
    margin: auto;
```

```
        width: 25rem;
    }
    .dialog-title {
        background-color: #343a40;
        color: white;
        padding: .5rem;
    }
    .dialog-body {
        padding: 2rem;
    }
    .dialog-buttons {
        background-color: silver;
        padding: .5rem;
    }
```

7.   Open the wwwroot/index.html file.

8.   Uncomment the following link element to the bottom of the head element:

```
<link href="ModalDialog.styles.css" rel="stylesheet" />
```

The styles in the Dialog.razor.cs file will only be used by the Dialog component due to CSS isolation. Next, let's test the Dialog component.

Test the Dialog component

To test the Dialog component, we need to add it to another component. We will add it to the Index component that is used as the Home page of the application. We do this as follows:

1.   Open the _Imports.razor file.

2.   Add the following using statement:

```
@using ModalDialog.Shared
```

3.   Open the Pages/Index.razor file.

4.   Remove the h1 element from the Index.razor file.

5.   Add the following markup to the Index.razor file:

```
<PageTitle>Home</PageTitle>

<Dialog Show="showDialog"></Dialog>
```

```
<button @onclick="OpenDialog">Show Dialog</button>

@code {
    private bool showDialog = false;
    private void OpenDialog()
    {
        showDialog = true;
    }
}
```

 IMPORTANT NOTE

Do not remove the @page directive from the top of the file while editing the Index component.

6. Press *Ctrl+F5* to start the application without debugging.

7. Click the **Show Dialog** button.

    This is the modal dialog that is displayed:

Figure 4.8: Sample modal dialog

8. Click the **Ok** button.

    Nothing happens when you click the **Ok** button because we have not yet added an @onclick event.

9. Close the browser.

We will add a couple of EventCallback parameters to communicate from the Dialog component back to the Index component.

Add EventCallback parameters

We need to add @onclick events for both the **Ok** button and the **Cancel** button. We do this as follows:

1. Return to Visual Studio.

2. Open the Shared/Dialog.razor file.

3. Add @onclick events to each of the buttons as indicated by the following highlighted code:

    ```
    <button @onclick="OnOk">
        OK
    </button>
    <button @onclick="OnCancel">
        Cancel
    </button>
    ```

4. Add the following parameters to the code block:

    ```
    [Parameter]
    public EventCallback<MouseEventArgs> OnOk { get; set; }
    [Parameter]
    public EventCallback<MouseEventArgs> OnCancel { get; set; }
    ```

    TIP

    The Parameter attribute does not need to be on the same line as the property that it applies to.

5. Open the Pages/Index.razor file.

6. Update the markup for the Dialog element by adding the highlighted markup:

    ```
    <Dialog Show="showDialog"
            OnCancel="DialogCancelHandler"
            OnOk="DialogOkHandler">
    </Dialog>
    ```

7. Add the following methods to the code block:

    ```
    private void DialogCancelHandler(MouseEventArgs e)
    {
    ```

```
        showDialog = false;
    }
    private void DialogOkHandler(MouseEventArgs e)
    {
        showDialog = false;
    }
```

TIP

Since e is not being used in the preceding methods, we do not need to specify MouseEventArgs in the method's definition. We have included it for
demonstration purposes.

8. Press *Ctrl+F5* to start the application without debugging.

9. Click the **Show Dialog** button.

10. Click the **Ok** button.

The dialog box closes when you click the **Ok** button.

Now let's update the Dialog component to allow us to customize both the Title and Body properties of the modal dialog that it creates.

Add RenderFragment parameters

We will use RenderFragment parameters for both the Title and Body properties of the Dialog
component. We do this as follows:

1. Return to Visual Studio.

2. Open the Shared/Dialog.razor file.

3. Update the markup for dialog-title to the following:

```
<div class="dialog-title">@Title</div>
```

4. Update the markup for dialog-body to the following:

```
<div class="dialog-body">@Body</div>
```

5. Add the following parameters to the code block:

```
[Parameter]
public RenderFragment Title { get; set; }
[Parameter]
public RenderFragment Body { get; set; }
```

6. Open the Pages/Index.razor file.

7. Update the markup for the Dialog element to the following:

```
<Dialog Show="showDialog"
        OnCancel="DialogCancelHandler"
        OnOk="DialogOkHandler">
    <Title>Quick List [@(Items.Count + 1)]</Title>
    <Body>
        Enter New Item: <input @bind="NewItem" />
    </Body>
</Dialog>
```

The preceding markup will change the title of the dialog to Quick List and provide a textbox for the user to enter items for a list.

8. Add the following markup under the Dialog element:

```
<ol>
    @foreach (var item in Items)
    {
        <li>@item</li>
    }
</ol>
```

The preceding code will display each of the items in the Items list in an ordered list.

9. Add the following variables to the top of the code block:

```
private string? NewItem;
private List<string> Items = new List<string>();
```

10. Update `DialogCancelHandler` to the following:

```
private void DialogCancelHandler(MouseEventArgs e)
{
    NewItem = "";
    showDialog = false;
}
```

The preceding code will clear the textbox and hide the contents of the `Dialog` component.

11. Update `DialogOkHandler` to the following:

```
private void DialogOkHandler(MouseEventArgs e)
{
    if (!string.IsNullOrEmpty(NewItem))
    {
        Items.Add(NewItem);
        NewItem = "";
    };
    showDialog = false;
}
```

The preceding code will add `NewItem` to the `Items` list, clear the textbox, and hide the contents of the `Dialog` component.

12. Press *Ctrl+F5* to start the application without debugging.

13. Click the **Show Dialog** button.

14. Enter some text in the **Enter New Item** field.

15. Click the **Ok** button.

16. Repeat.

Each time the **Ok** button is clicked, the text in the **Enter New Item** field will be added to the list. The following screenshot shows a list where three items have already been added and a fourth item is about to be added using the modal dialog:

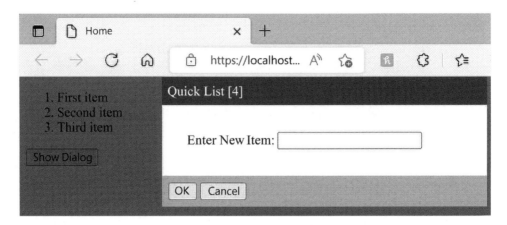

Figure 4.9: Sample Quick List

17. Close the browser.

To share this new component with other projects, we need to add it to a Razor class library.

Create a Razor class library

We can share components across projects by using a Razor class library. To create a Razor class library, we will use the **Razor Class Library** project template. We do this as follows:

1. Right-click the solution and select the **Add**, **New Project** option from the menu.

2. Enter Razor Class Library in the **Search for templates** textbox to locate the **Razor Class Library** project template.

    The following screenshot shows the **Razor Class Library** project template:

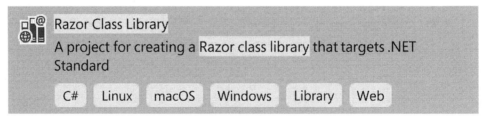

Figure 4.10: Razor Class Library project template

3. Select the **Razor Class Library** project template.

4. Click the **Next** button.

5. Name the project MyComponents and click the **Next** button.

6. Select **.NET 7.0** as the version of the **Framework** to use.

7. Uncheck the **Support pages and views** checkbox.

8. Click the **Create** button.

9. Right-click the ModalDialog project and select the **Add**, **Project Reference** option from the menu.

10. Check the MyComponents checkbox and click the **OK** button.

We have created the MyComponents Razor class library, and we have added a reference to it from the ModalDialog project. Let's test it.

Test the Razor class library

The MyComponents Razor class library that we have just created using the project template includes one component, called Component1. Before we continue, we need to test that the new Razor class library is working properly. We do this as follows:

1. Open the ModalDialog.Pages/Index.razor file.

2. Add the following using statement right below the @page directive:

```
@using MyComponents;
```

TIP

If you will be using this project on multiple pages, you should consider adding the using statement to the ModalDialog._Imports.razor file so that you do not need to include it in every component that uses it.

3. Add the following markup below the PageTitle element:

```
<Component1 />
```

4. Press *Ctrl+F5* to start the application without debugging.

The following screenshot shows how the Component1 component should render:

This component is defined in the **MyComponents** library

Figure 4.11: Component1

IMPORTANT NOTE

If the Component1 component is missing its styling, it is because the CSS file is cached. Use the following key combination, *Ctrl+Shift+R*, to empty the cache and reload the page.

5.   Close the browser.

6.   Return to Visual Studio.

7.   Delete the Component1 element from the Index component.

We have finished testing the MyComponents Razor class library. Now it's time to add our custom Dialog component to the MyComponents Razor class library.

Add a component to the Razor class library

To share the Dialog component, we need to move it into the Razor class library that we just created and tested. We do this as follows:

1.   Right-click the ModalDialog.Shared/Dialog.razor file and select the **Copy** option from the menu.

2.   Right-click the MyComponents project and select the **Paste** option from the menu.

3.   Right-click the MyComponents.Dialog.razor file and select the **Rename** option from the menu.

4.   Rename the file BweDialog.razor.

     In this case, Bwe stands for *Blazor WebAssembly by Example*.

TIP

When naming components in a Razor class library, you should give them unique names to avoid ambiguous reference errors. Most organizations prefix all their shared components with the same text. For example, a company named **One Stop Designs (OSD)** might prefix all their shared components with Osd.

5.   Open the ModalDialog.Pages/Index.razor file.

6.   Rename the Dialog element BweDialog.

7.   Press *Ctrl+F5* to start the application without debugging.

8.   Click the **Show Dialog** button.

9.   Enter some text in the **Enter New Item** field.

10. Click the **Ok** button.

11. Repeat.

The BweDialog component is now being used from the MyComponents Razor class library. Since the BweDialog component is included in a Razor class library, it can easily be shared with other projects.

Summary

You should now be able to create a modal dialog and share it with multiple projects by using a Razor class library.

In this chapter, we introduced RenderFragment parameters, EventCallback parameters, and CSS isolation.

After that, we used the **Blazor WebAssembly App Empty** project template to create a new project. We created a Dialog component that acts like a modal dialog. The Dialog component uses both RenderFragment parameters and EventCallback parameters to share information between it and its parent. Also, it uses CSS isolation for its styles.

In the last part of the chapter, we created a Razor custom library and moved the Dialog component to the new library.

So far, in this book, we have avoided using JavaScript. Unfortunately, there are still some functions that we can only accomplish with JavaScript. In the next chapter of this book, we will learn how to use JavaScript interop to use JavaScript in a Blazor WebAssembly app.

Questions

The following questions are provided for your consideration:

1.   How can you replace a table with a templated component?

2.   How would you add default values for the Title property and the Body property of the Dialog component?

3.   How can you determine which button was clicked when handling the @onclick event?

4.   Can you distribute your Dialog component using a NuGet package?

Further reading

The following resources provide more information concerning the topics in this chapter:

- For more information on CSS, refer to `https://www.w3schools.com/css/default.asp`.
- For more information on lambda expressions, refer to `https://learn.microsoft.com/en-us/dotnet/csharp/language-reference/operators/lambda-expressions`.
- For more information on ASP.NET Core Razor components class libraries, refer to `https://learn.microsoft.com/en-us/aspnet/core/blazor/components/class-libraries`.
- For more information on NuGet, refer to `https://www.nuget.org`.

Join our community on Discord

Join our community's Discord space for discussions with the author and other readers:

`https://packt.link/BlazorWASM2e`

5

Building a Local Storage Service Using JavaScript Interoperability (JS Interop)

The Blazor WebAssembly framework makes it possible for us to run C# code on the browser. However, there are some scenarios that C# simply cannot handle, and for those scenarios, we need to use JavaScript functions.

In this chapter, we will learn how to use JavaScript with Blazor WebAssembly. We will learn how to invoke a JavaScript function from a .NET method with and without a return value. Conversely, we will learn how to invoke a .NET method from a JavaScript function. We will accomplish both scenarios by using **JavaScript interop (JS interop)**. Finally, we will learn how to store data on the browser by using the Web Storage API for JavaScript.

The project that we will create in this chapter will be a local storage service that will read and write to the application's local storage. To access the application's local storage, we will use JavaScript. We will also create a test component to test the local storage service. The test component will use JavaScript to display text in a JavaScript alert box.

It is sad, but true.

We may not like JavaScript,

but we still need it!

In this chapter, we will cover the following topics:

- Why use JavaScript?
- Exploring JS interop
- Using local storage
- Creating the local storage service

Technical requirements

To complete this project, you need to have Visual Studio 2022 installed on your PC. For instructions on how to install the free Community Edition of Visual Studio 2022, refer to *Chapter 1, Introduction to Blazor WebAssembly*.

The source code for this chapter is available in the following GitHub repository: `https://github.com/PacktPublishing/Blazor-WebAssembly-by-Example-Second-Edition/tree/main/Chapter05`.

The Code in Action video is available here: `https://packt.link/Ch5`.

Why use JavaScript?

With Blazor WebAssembly, we can create robust applications without writing any JavaScript. However, there are some scenarios that require the use of JavaScript. For example, we may have a favorite JavaScript library that we want to continue to use. Also, without JavaScript, we can't manipulate the DOM or call any of the JavaScript APIs.

This is a partial list of things that we do not have access to directly from the Blazor WebAssembly framework:

- **DOM manipulation**
- The **Media Capture and Streams API**
- The **WebGL API** (2D and 3D graphics for the web)
- The **Web Storage API** (`localStorage` and `sessionStorage`)
- The **Geolocation API**
- JavaScript pop-up boxes (an alert box, a confirm box, and a prompt box)
- The online status of the browser
- The browser's history
- **Chart.js**
- Other third-party JavaScript libraries

The preceding list is not at all comprehensive since there are hundreds of JavaScript libraries that are currently available. However, the key point to remember is that we cannot manipulate the DOM without using JavaScript. Therefore, we will probably always need to use some JavaScript in our web apps. Luckily, by using JS interop, this is easy to do.

Exploring JS interop

To invoke a JavaScript function from .NET, we use the `IJSRuntime` abstraction. This abstraction represents an instance of a JavaScript runtime that the framework can call into. To use `IJSRuntime`, we must first inject it into our component using dependency injection. For more information on dependency injection, refer to *Chapter 7, Building a Shopping Cart Using Application State*.

The `@inject` directive is used to inject a dependency into a component. The following code injects `IJSRuntime` into the current component:

```
@inject IJSRuntime js
```

The `IJSRuntime` abstraction has two methods that we can use to invoke JavaScript functions:

- **InvokeAsync**
- **InvokeVoidAsync**

Both methods are asynchronous. The difference between these two methods is that one of them returns a value and the other does not. We can downcast an instance of `IJSRuntime` to an instance of `IJSInProcessRuntime` to run the method synchronously. Finally, we can invoke a .NET method from JavaScript by decorating the method with `JsInvokable`. We will look at examples of each of these methods later in this chapter.

However, before we can invoke a JavaScript method, we need to load the JavaScript into our application.

Loading JavaScript code

There are a few ways to load JavaScript code into a Blazor WebAssembly app. One way is to enter the JavaScript code directly into a `script` element in the body element of the `wwwroot/index.html` file. However, instead of entering the JavaScript code directly into the .html file, we recommend using an external JavaScript file for your JavaScript functions.

We can add an external file by referencing it in the `wwwroot./index.html` file. The following code references a file called `btwInterop.js` that is in the `wwwroot/scripts` folder:

```
<script src="scripts/bweInterop.js"></script>
```

A better way to organize scripts is to collocate an external JavaScript file with a specific component. To add a JavaScript file that is collocated with a specific component, create a JavaScript file in the same folder as the component with the same name as the component, but with a JavaScript file extension. For example, the MyComponent component that is defined in the MyComponent.razor file would use MyComponent.razor.js as its collocated JavaScript file.

For the component to reference the code in the JavaScript file, the file must be imported into the component during the OnAfterRenderAsync method of the component. In the following example, the import identifier is used to import a JavaScript file:

```
protected override async Task OnAfterRenderAsync(bool firstRender)
{
    if (firstRender)
    {
        module = await js.InvokeAsync<IJSObjectReference>
                ("import", "./Pages/MyComponent.razor.js");
    }
}
```

In the preceding code, the JavaScript file that is being imported is in the Pages folder and is named MyComponent.razor.js.

IMPORTANT NOTE

The collocated JavaScript files will be automatically moved to the wwwroot folder when the application is published. This approach is called JavaScript isolation and it makes downloading the JavaScript file lazy.

The preceding code uses the InvokeAsync method of IJSRuntime to invoke the JavaScript import function from .NET.

Invoking a JavaScript function from a .NET method

There are two different methods of IJSRutime that we can use to invoke JavaScript from .NET asynchronously:

- InvokeAsync
- InvokeVoidAsync

To invoke a JavaScript function from .NET synchronously, `IJSRutime` must be downcast to `IJSInProcessRuntime`.

InvokeAsync

The `InvokeAsync` method is an asynchronous method that is used to invoke a JavaScript function that returns a value.

This is the `InvokeAsync` method of `IJSRuntime`:

```
ValueTask<TValue> InvokeAsync<TValue>(string identifier,
                                      params object[] args);
```

In the preceding code, the first argument is the identifier for the JavaScript function, and the second argument is an array of JSON-serializable arguments. The second argument is optional. The `InvokeAsync` method returns a `ValueTask` of the `TValue` type. `TValue` is a JSON-deserialized instance of the JavaScript's return value.

In JavaScript, the `Window` object represents the browser's window. To determine the width and height of the current window, we use the `innerWidth` and `innerHeight` properties of the `Window` object.

The following JavaScript code includes a method called `getWindowSize` that returns the width and height of the `Window` object:

wwwroot/bweInterop.js

```
var bweInterop = {};
bweInterop.getWindowSize = function () {
    var size = {
        width: window.innerWidth,
        height: window.innerHeight
    }
    return size;
}
```

IMPORTANT NOTE

In this book, we will use the `bweInterop` namespace for our JavaScript code to both structure our code and minimize the risk of naming conflicts.

This is the definition of the WindowSize class that is used to store the size of the window in .NET:

```
public class WindowSize
{
    public int? Width { get; set; }
    public int? Height { get; set; }
}
```

The following Index component invokes the GetWindowSize method from the bweInterop.js file:

Pages/Index.razor

```
@page "/"
@inject IJSRuntime js


<PageTitle>Home</PageTitle>

@if (windowSize.Width != null)
{
    <h2>
        Window Size: @windowSize.Width x @windowSize.Height
    </h2>
}
<button @onclick="GetWindowSize">Get Window Size</button>

@code {
    private WindowSize windowSize = new WindowSize();
    private async Task GetWindowSize()
    {
        windowSize = await js.InvokeAsync<WindowSize>(
            "bweInterop.getWindowSize");
    }
}
```

In the preceding code, IJSRuntime is injected into the component. When the **Get Window Size** button is clicked, the GetWindowSize method uses the InvokeAsync method of IJSRuntime to invoke the getWindowSize JavaScript function. The GetWindowSize JavaScript function returns the width and height of the window to the windowSize property. Finally, the component regenerates its render tree and applies any changes to the browser's DOM.

This is a screenshot of the page after the **Get Window Size** button has been clicked:

Figure 5.1: Window size example

The InvokeSync method of IJSRuntime is used to call JavaScript functions that return a value. If we do not need to return a value, we can use the InvokeAsync method instead.

InvokeVoidAsync

The InvokeVoidAsync method is an asynchronous method that is used to invoke a JavaScript function that does not return a value.

This is the InvokeVoidAsync method of IJSRuntime:

```
InvokeVoidAsync(string identifier, params object[] args);
```

Just like the InvokeAsync method, the first argument is the identifier for the JavaScript function that is being called, and the second argument is an array of JSON-serializable arguments. The second argument is optional.

In JavaScript, the Document object represents the root node of the HTML document. The title property of the Document object is used to specify the text that appears in the browser's title bar. Assume that we want to update the browser's title as we navigate between the components in our Blazor WebAssembly app. To do that, we need to use JavaScript to update the title property.

The following JavaScript code exports a function called setDocumentTitle that sets the title property of the Document object to the value provided by the title argument:

Shared/Document.razor.js

```
export function setDocumentTitle(title) {
    document.title = title;
}
```

The preceding code uses an export statement to export the setDocumentTitle function.

IMPORTANT NOTE

The export statement in JavaScript is used to export functions from JavaScript to be imported into other programs.

The following Document component uses the setDocumentTitle JavaScript function to update the browser's title bar:

Shared/Document.razor

```
@inject IJSRuntime js

@code {
    [Parameter] public string Title { get; set; } = "Home";

    protected override async Task OnAfterRenderAsync
        (bool firstRender)
    {
        if (firstRender)
        {
            IJSObjectReference module =
                await js.InvokeAsync<IJSObjectReference>
                    ("import", "./Shared/Document.razor.js");

            await module.InvokeVoidAsync
                ("setDocumentTitle", Title);
        }
    }
}
```

In the preceding code, IJSRuntime is injected into the component. Then, the OnAfterRenderAsync method uses the InvokeAsync method to import the JavaScript code and the InvokeVoidAsync method to invoke the setDocumentTitle JavaScript function.

IMPORTANT NOTE

We are not using the bweInterop namespace in the collocated JavaScript code to emphasize that it is only referenced by one component.

The following markup uses the Document component to update the browser's title bar to Home – My App:

```
<Document Title="Home - My App" />
```

The following screenshot shows the resulting document title:

Figure 5.2: Updated document title

TIP

You can use the built-in PageTitle component to set the title of the page.

By default, JS interop calls are asynchronous. To make synchronous JS interop calls, we need to use IJSInProcessRuntime.

IJSInProcessRuntime

So far in this chapter, we have only looked at invoking JavaScript functions asynchronously. But we can also invoke JavaScript functions synchronously. We do that by downcasting IJSRuntime to IJSInProcessRuntime. IJSInProcessRuntime allows our .NET code to invoke JS interop calls synchronously. This can be advantageous because these calls have less overhead than their asynchronous counterparts.

These are the synchronous methods of `IJsInProcessRuntime`:

- `Invoke`
- `InvokeVoid`

The following code uses `IJSInProcessRuntime` to invoke a JavaScript function synchronously:

```
@inject IJSRuntime js

@code {
    private string GetGuid()
    {
        string guid =
            ((IJSInProcessRuntime)js).Invoke<string>("getGuid");

        return guid;
    }
}
```

In the preceding code, the `IJsRuntime` instance has been downcast to an `IJSInProcessRuntime` instance. The `Invoke` method of the `IJSInProcessRuntime` instance is used to invoke the `getGuid` JavaScript method.

The `IJSRuntime` abstraction provides methods to invoke JavaScript functions directly from .NET methods. They can be invoked either asynchronously or synchronously. Invoking a .NET method directly from a JavaScript function requires a special attribute.

Invoking a .NET method from a JavaScript function

We can invoke a public .NET method from JavaScript by decorating the method with the `JSInvokable` attribute.

The following .NET method is decorated with the `JSInvokable` attribute to enable it to be invoked from JavaScript:

```
private WindowSize windowSize = new WindowSize();

[JSInvokable]
public void GetWindowSize(WindowSize newWindowSize)
{
    windowSize = newWindowSize;
```

```
        StateHasChanged();
    }
```

In the preceding code, the windowSize property is updated each time the GetWindowSize method is invoked from JavaScript. After the windowSize property is updated, the component's StateHasChanged method is called to notify the component that its state has changed, and therefore, the component should be re-rendered.

IMPORTANT NOTE

The StateHasChanged method of a component is only called automatically for EventCallback methods. In other cases, it must be called manually to notify the UI that it may need to be re-rendered.

To invoke a .NET method from JavaScript, we must create a DotNetObjectReference class for JavaScript to use to locate the .NET method. The DotNetObjectReference class wraps a JS interop argument, indicating that the value should not be serialized as JSON but instead, should be passed as a reference.

IMPORTANT NOTE

To avoid memory leaks and allow garbage collection on a component that creates a DotNetObjectReference class, you must diligently dispose of each instance of DotNetObjectReference.

The following code creates a DotNetObjectReference instance that wraps the Resize component. The reference is then passed to the JavaScript method:

```
private DotNetObjectReference<Resize> objRef;

protected async override Task OnAfterRenderAsync(bool firstRender)
{
    if (firstRender)
    {
        objRef = DotNetObjectReference.Create(this);
        await js.InvokeVoidAsync(
            "bweInterop.registerResizeHandler",
```

```
            objRef);
    }
}
```

We can invoke a method in a .NET component from JavaScript using a reference to the component created with `DotNetObjectReference`. In the following JavaScript, the `registerResizeHandler` function creates the `resizeHandler` function that is called at initialization, and every time the window is resized.

bweInterop.js

```
bweInterop.registerResizeHandler = function (dotNetObjectRef) {
    function resizeHandler() {
        dotNetObjectRef.invokeMethodAsync('GetWindowSize',
            {
                width: window.innerWidth,
                height: window.innerHeight
            });
    };
    resizeHandler();
    window.addEventListener("resize", resizeHandler);
}
```

In the preceding example, the `invokeMethodAsync` function is used to invoke the `GetWindowSize` .NET method that was decorated with the `JSInvokable` attribute.

TIP

You can use either the `invokeMethod` function or the `invokeMethodAsync` function to invoke .NET instance methods from JavaScript.

This is the complete .NET code for the `Resize` component:

Resize.razor

```
@page "/resize"

@inject IJSRuntime js
@implements IDisposable
```

```
<PageTitle>Resize</PageTitle>

@if (windowSize.Width != null)
{
        <h2>
            Window Size: @windowSize.Width x @windowSize.Height
        </h2>
}

@code {
    private DotNetObjectReference<Resize> objRef;
    private WindowSize windowSize = new WindowSize();

    protected async override Task OnAfterRenderAsync(
        bool firstRender)
    {
        if (firstRender)
        {
            objRef = DotNetObjectReference.Create(this);
            await js.InvokeVoidAsync(
                "bweInterop.registerResizeHandler",
                    objRef);
        }
    }

    [JSInvokable]
    public void GetWindowSize(WindowSize newWindowSize)
    {
        windowSize = newWindowSize;
        StateHasChanged();
    }

    public void Dispose()
    {
        objRef?.Dispose();
    }
}
```

The preceding code for the `Resize` component displays the current width and height of the browser. As you resize the browser, the displayed values are automatically updated. Also, the `DotNetObjectReference` object is disposed of when the component is disposed. To test the `Resize` component, press *Ctrl+F5* to start the application without debugging. After the application starts, navigate to the `/resize` page and resize the window.

The `IJSRuntime` abstraction provides us with a way to invoke JavaScript functions from .NET and to invoke .NET methods from JavaScript.

We will be using JavaScript's Web Storage API to complete the project in this chapter. But before we can use it, we need to understand how it works.

Using local storage

The Web Storage API for JavaScript provides mechanisms for browsers to store key/value pairs. For each web browser, the size of data that can be stored in web storage is at least 5 MB per origin. The `localStorage` mechanism is defined in the Web Storage API for JavaScript. We need to use JS interop to access the application's local storage because the Web Storage API requires the use of JavaScript.

The application's local storage is scoped to a particular URL. If the user reloads the page or closes and reopens the browser, the contents of local storage are retained. If the user opens multiple tabs, each tab shares the same local storage. The data in local storage is retained until it is explicitly cleared, since it does not have an expiration date.

IMPORTANT NOTE

Data in a `localStorage` object that is created when using an *InPrivate* window or *Incognito* window is cleared when the last tab is closed.

These are the methods of `localStorage`:

- **key**: This method returns the name of the indicated key based on its position in `localStorage`.
- **getItem**: This method returns the value for the indicated key from `localStorage`.
- **setItem**: This method takes a key and value pair and adds them to `localStorage`.
- **removeItem**: This method removes the indicated key from `localStorage`.
- **clear**: This method clears `localStorage`.

IMPORTANT NOTE

sessionStorage is also defined in the Web Storage API. Unlike localStorage, which shares its value between multiple browser tabs, sesssionStorage is scoped to an individual browser tab. Therefore, if the user reloads the page, the data persists, but if the user closes the tab (or the browser), the data is cleared.

To view the contents of the application's local storage, open the browser's developer tools by pressing *F12* and selecting the **Application** tab. Select **Local Storage** in the **Storage** section of the menu on the left. The following screenshot shows the **Application** tab of the **DevTools** dialog in Microsoft Edge:

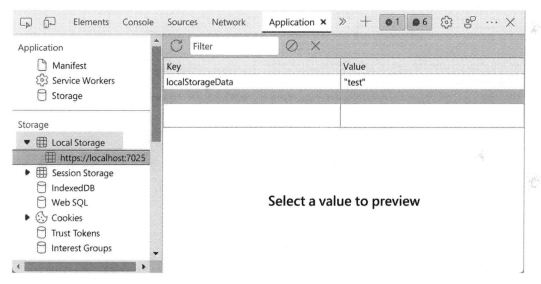

Figure 5.3: Local Storage

By using the Web Storage API, it is easy to store data in the browser and retrieve it. Now, let's get a quick overview of the project that we are going to build in this chapter.

Creating the local storage service

In this chapter, we will build a local storage service. The service will both write to and read from the application's local storage. We will use JS interop to accomplish this. We will use the InvokeVoidAsync method to write to local storage and the InvokeAsync method to read from local storage. Finally, we will create a component to test our service.

The test component will both read and write local storage. It will use JS interop to display the contents of local storage in a JavaScript alert box.

The following screenshot shows both the test component and the application's local storage. When the **Save to Local Storage** button is clicked, the value of the text in the **localStorageData** textbox is saved to local storage.

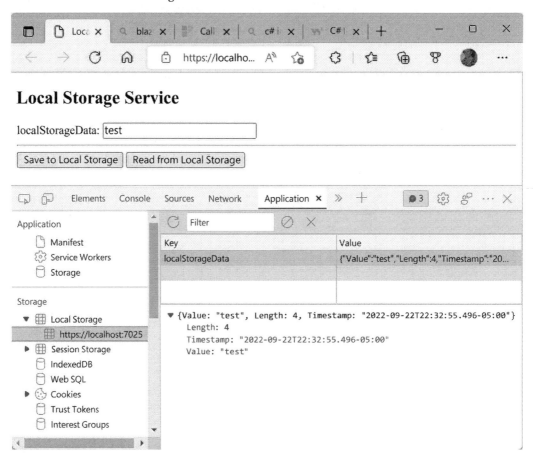

Figure 5.4: Local Storage Service test page

When the **Read from Local Storage** button is clicked, the value of **localStorageData** is displayed in a JavaScript alert box. The following screenshot shows a sample of an alert that is displaying the value in local storage:

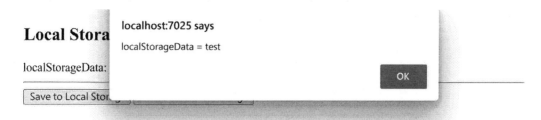

Figure 5.5: Read from Local Storage

The build time for this project is approximately 60 minutes.

Project overview

The LocalStorage project will be created by using Microsoft's **Blazor WebAssembly App Empty** project template to create an empty Blazor WebAssembly project. First, we will add a JavaScript file with the JavaScript functions that our service will need to use to update the application's local storage. Next, we will create the interface and class with the .NET methods that will invoke the JavaScript functions. Finally, we will test our service by adding a collocated JavaScript file.

Getting started with the project

We need to create a new Blazor WebAssembly app. We do this as follows:

1. Open Visual Studio 2022.

2. Click the **Create a new project** button.

3. Press *Alt+S* to enter the **Search for templates** textbox.

4. Enter Blazor and press the *Enter* key.

    The following screenshot shows the **Blazor WebAssembly App Empty** project template:

Figure 5.6: Blazor WebAssembly App Empty project template

5. Select the **Blazor WebAssembly App Empty** project template and click the **Next** button.

6. Enter LocalStorage in the **Project name** textbox and click the **Next** button.

This is a screenshot of the dialog used to configure our new project:

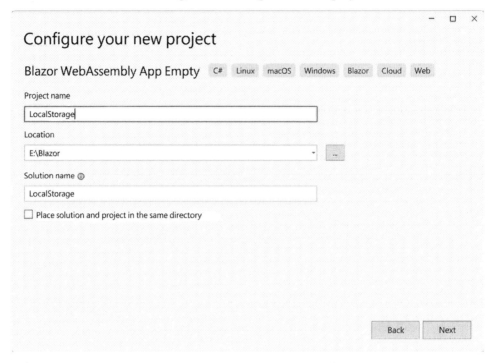

Figure 5.7: Configure your new project dialog

TIP

In the preceding example, we placed the LocalStorage project into the E:/ Blazor folder. However, the location of this project is not important.

7. Select **.NET 7.0** as the **Framework** version to use.

8. Check the **Configure for HTTPS** checkbox.

9. Uncheck the **ASP.NET Core Hosted** checkbox.

10. Uncheck the **Progressive Web Application** checkbox.

This is a screenshot of the dialog used to collect additional information about our new project:

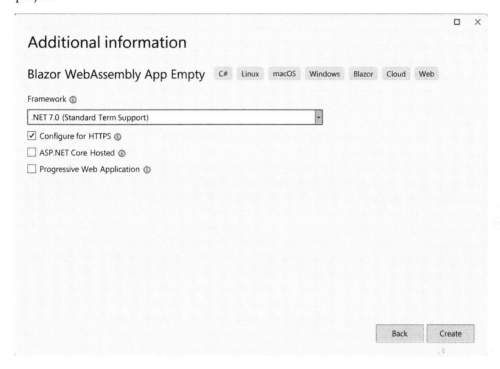

Figure 5.8: Additional information dialog

11.   Click the **Create** button.

We have created an empty LocalStorage Blazor WebAssembly project. Let's now start adding the JavaScript functions that we will need for reading and writing to local storage.

Writing JavaScript to access local storage

We need to write the JavaScript functions that will read to and write from the application's local storage. We do this as follows:

1.   Right-click the wwwroot folder and select the **Add, New Folder** option from the menu.

2.   Name the new folder scripts.

3.   Right-click the scripts folder and select the **Add, New Item** option from the menu.

4.   Enter javascript in the **Search** box.

5.   Select **JavaScript File**.

6. Name the JavaScript file bweInterop.js.

7. Click the **Add** button.

8. Enter the following JavaScript:

```
var bweInterop = {};

bweInterop.setLocalStorage = function (key, data) {
    localStorage.setItem(key, data);
}

bweInterop.getLocalStorage = function (key) {
    return localStorage.getItem(key);
}
```

The preceding JavaScript includes a setLocalStorage function that writes to local storage, and the getLocalStorage function, which reads from local storage.

9. Open the wwwroot/index.html file.

10. Add the following markup to the bottom of the body element:

```
<script src="scripts/bweInterop.js"></script>
```

IMPORTANT NOTE

In the wwwroot/index.html file, the script tag that references your custom Java-Script should be after the Blazor script reference.

Now we need to add the .NET code that will invoke these JavaScript functions. First, we will create the interface for our service.

Adding the ILocalStorageService interface

We need to create an interface for our service. We do this as follows:

1. Right-click the LocalStorage project and select the **Add**, **New Folder** option from the menu.

2. Name the new folder Services.

3. Right-click the **Services** folder and then select the **Add**, **New Item** option from the menu.

4. Enter `interface` in the **Search** box.

5. Select **Interface**.

6. Name the file `ILocalStorageService`.

7. Click the **Add** button.

8. Add the following code to the `ILocalStorageService` interface:

```
ValueTask SetItemAsync<T>(string key, T item);
ValueTask<T?> GetItemAsync<T>(string key);
```

The preceding methods will be used to set the value of local storage.

9. Open the `Program.cs` file.

10. Add the following using statement:

```
using LocalStorage.Services;
```

11. Add the following code after the code that registers `HttpClient`:

```
builder.Services.AddScoped
    <ILocalStorageService, LocalStorageService>();
```

The preceding code registers the `LocalStorageService` in the dependency injection container. For more information on dependency injection, refer to *Chapter 7, Building a Shopping Cart Using Application State*.

We have defined the abstract methods of the service and registered it with the application. Now it's time to create the `LocalStorageService` class.

Creating the LocalStorageService class

We need to create a new class based on the interface we just created. We do this as follows:

1. Right-click the **Services** folder and select the **Add, Class** option from the menu.

2. Name the new class `LocalStorageService`.

3. Update the `LocalStorageService` class to inherit from `ILocalStorageService`:

```
public class LocalStorageService : ILocalStorageService
```

4. Add the following code to the `LocalStorageService` class:

```
private IJSRuntime js;
public LocalStorageService(IJSRuntime JsRuntime)
```

```
{
    js = JsRuntime;
}
```

The preceding code defines the constructor for the `LocalStorageService` class.

5.   Add the `SetItemAsync` method to the `LocalStorageService` class:

```
public async ValueTask SetItemAsync<T>(string key, T item)
{
    await js.InvokeVoidAsync(
        "bweInterop.setLocalStorage",
        key,
        JsonSerializer.Serialize(item));
}
```

The `SetItemAsync` method invokes the `bweInterop.setLocalStorage` JavaScript function with a key and a serialized version of the item to be stored in `localStorage`.

6.   Update the `GetItemAsync` method to the following:

```
public async ValueTask<T?> GetItemAsync<T>(string key)
{
    var json = await js.InvokeAsync<string>
        ("bweInterop.getLocalStorage", key);
    return JsonSerializer.Deserialize<T>(json);
}
```

The `GetItemAsync` method invokes the `bweInterop.getLocalStorage` JavaScript function with a key. If `bweInterop.getLocalStorage` returns a value, that value is deserialized and returned.

We have completed our service. Now we need to test it.

Creating the DataInfo class

The `DataInfo` class will be used to hold the data that we read and write from the application's local storage:

1.   Right-click the `LocalStorage` project and select the **Add, New Folder** option from the menu.

2.   Name the new folder `Models`.

3.   Right-click the **Models** folder and select the **Add, Class** option from the menu.

4.   Name the new class `DataInfo`.

5.   Add the following properties to the `DataInfo` class:

```
public string? Value { get; set; }
public int Length { get; set; }
public DateTime Timestamp { get; set; }
```

The `DataInfo` class includes the data, information about the length of the data, and the date and time the data was updated.

Now that we have defined an object to hold our data, it's time to test writing data to the application's local storage.

Writing to local storage

We need to test writing to the application's local storage using our local storage service. We do this as follows:

1.   Open the `Pages/Index.razor` file.

2.   Delete the `H1` element.

3.   Add the following directive:

```
@using LocalStorage.Services
```

4.   Add the following markup:

```
<PageTitle>Local Storage Service</PageTitle>

<h2>Local Storage Service</h2>

localStorageData:
<input type="text" @bind-value="data" size="25" />
<hr />
<button @onclick="SaveToLocalStorageAsync">
    Save to Local Storage
</button>
```

The preceding markup adds a textbox to enter the data to be saved to the application's local storage and a button to call the `SaveToLocalStorageAsync` method.

5.   Right-click the **Pages** folder and select the **Add, Class** option from the menu.

6.   Name the new class `Index.razor.cs`.

7.   Change the class into a partial class by adding the `partial` keyword:

```
Public partial class Index
```

8.   Add the following to the code:

```
[Inject]
ILocalStorageService? localStorage { get; set; }

private string? data;

async Task SaveToLocalStorageAsync()
{
    var dataInfo = new DataInfo()
    {
        Value = data,
        Length = data!.Length,
        Timestamp = DateTime.Now
    };

    await localStorage!.SetItemAsync<DataInfo?>(
        "localStorageData",
        dataInfo);
}
```

The preceding code injects the `LocalStorageService` into the component and defines the `SaveToLocalStorageAsync` method. The `SaveToLocalStorageAsync` method uses **localStorageData** as the key when saving the data to `localStorage`.

9.   Press *Ctrl+F5* to start the application without debugging.

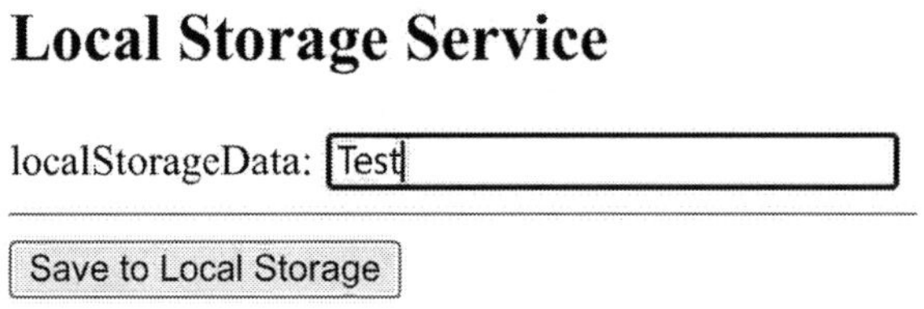

Local Storage Service

localStorageData: [Test|]

[Save to Local Storage]

Figure 5.9: Local Storage Service test page

10. Enter the word Test into the **localStorageData** textbox.

11. Click the **Save to Local Storage** button.

12. Press *F12* to open the browser's developer tools.

13. Select the **Application** tab.

14. Open Local Storage.

15. Enter a different word into the **localStorageData** textbox.

16. Click the **Save to Local Storage** button.

17. Verify that the application's local storage has been updated.

18. Close the browser.

We have used the Web Storage API to save data to the application's local storage. Next, we need to learn how to read from the application's local storage. Since we will be displaying the data in a JavaScript alert box, we need to add some JavaScript code to call the alert function.

Adding a collocated JavaScript file

We need to add a collocated JavaScript file to contain the JavaScript code that will call the alert function. We do this as follows:

1. Return to Visual Studio.

2. Right-click the **Pages** folder and select the **Add**, **New Item** option from the menu.

3. Enter javascript in the **Search** box.

4. Select **JavaScript File**.

5. Name the JavaScript file Index.razor.js.

6. Add the following JavaScript to the Index.razor.js file:

```
export function showLocalStorage(data) {
    alert(data);
}
```

The preceding code exports the showLocalStorage function that opens an alert box, containing the text that is specified by the data parameter.

7. Open the Pages/Index.razor.cs file.

8. Inject an instance of IJSRuntime into the Index component by adding the following code:

```
[Inject]
IJSRuntime js { get; set; }
```

9. Add the following property:

```
private IJSObjectReference? module;
```

10. Add the `OnAfterRenderAsync` method:

```
protected override async Task OnAfterRenderAsync(bool firstRender)
{
    if (firstRender)
    {
        module = await js.InvokeAsync<IJSObjectReference>
                ("import", "./Pages/Index.razor.js");
    }
}
```

The JavaScript functions that are in the `Pages/Index.razor.js` file can now be invoked from the `Index` component.

Reading from local storage

We need to test reading from the application's local storage using our local storage service. We do this as follows:

1. Open the `Pages/Index.razor` file.

2. Add the following button beneath the existing button:

```
<button @onclick="ReadFromLocalStorageAsync">
    Read from Local Storage
</button>
```

The preceding markup adds a button that calls the `ReadFromLocalStorageAsync` method.

3. Open the `Pages/Index.razor.cs` file.

4. Add the `ReadFromLocalStorageAsync` method:

```
async Task ReadFromLocalStorageAsync()
{
    if (module is not null)
    {
        DataInfo? savedData =
            await localStorage!.GetItemAsync
                <DataInfo>("localStorageData");
```

```
        string result =
            $"localStorageData = {savedData!.Value}";

        await module.InvokeVoidAsync
            ("showLocalStorage", result);
    }
}
```

The ReadFromLocalStorageAsync method uses the localStorageData key when accessing the application's local storage.

5. Press *Ctrl+F5* to start the application without debugging.

6. Click the **Read from Local Storage** button.

7. Verify that the contents of the alert box match the contents of the application's local storage.

The ReadFromLocalStorage method invoked the showLocalStorage function in the collocated JavaScript file. We have now completed the testing of our local storage service.

Summary

You should now be able to create a local storage service by using JS interop to invoke JavaScript functions from your Blazor WebAssembly application.

In this chapter, we explained why you may still need to use JavaScript and how to use the IJSRuntime abstraction to invoke JavaScript functions from .NET, both asynchronously and synchronously. Conversely, we explained how to invoke .NET methods from JavaScript functions. Finally, we explained how to store data in the browser by using the application's local storage.

After that, we used the Blazor WebAssembly App Empty project template to create a new project. We added a couple of JavaScript functions to read and write the application's local storage. Then, we added a class to invoke those JavaScript functions. In the last part of the chapter, we tested our local storage service by adding a collocated JavaScript file that opened a JavaScript alert box.

One of the biggest benefits of using Blazor WebAssembly is that all the code runs on the browser. This means that a web app built using Blazor WebAssembly can run offline. In the next chapter, we will leverage this advantage to create a progressive web app.

Questions

The following questions are provided for your consideration:

1. Can `IJSRuntime` be used to render a UI?
2. How would you add our local storage service to a Razor class library?
3. What are the benefits of using a collocated JavaScript file?
4. Do you think that you will still use JavaScript? If so, what will you use it for?
5. In what scenarios do you need to invoke JavaScript asynchronously rather than synchronously?

Further reading

The following resources provide more information regarding the topics covered in this chapter:

*   For more information on using JavaScript, refer to `https://www.w3schools.com/js`.
*   For more detailed information on JavaScript, refer to `https://developer.mozilla.org/en-US/docs/Web/javascript`.
*   For the JavaScript reference, refer to `https://developer.mozilla.org/en-US/docs/Web/JavaScript/Reference`.
*   For more information on `localStorage`, refer to `https://www.w3.org/TR/webstorage/#the-localstorage-attribute`.
*   For more information on Microsoft Edge (Chromium) Developer Tools, refer to `https://learn.microsoft.com/en-us/microsoft-edge/devtools-guide-chromium`.

6

Building a Weather App as a Progressive Web App (PWA)

As web developers, we develop amazing web apps of all kinds, but until recently there has been a divide between what a web app can do versus what a native app can do. A new class of apps called **Progressive Web Apps (PWAs)** is helping to bridge that divide by enabling us to add native-like capabilities, reliability, and installability to our web apps. A PWA is a web application that takes advantage of native app features while retaining all the features of a web app.

In this chapter, we will learn what defines a PWA, as well as how to create a PWA by adding a **manifest file** and a **service worker** to an existing web application.

The project that we create in this chapter will be a local 5-day weather forecast application that can be installed and run as a native application on Windows, macOS, iPhones, Android phones, and so on and can be distributed through the various app stores. We will use JavaScript's **Geo-location API** to obtain the location of the device and the **OpenWeather One Call API** to fetch the weather forecast for that location. We will convert the application into a PWA by adding a manifest file and a service worker. The service worker will use the **CacheStorage API** to cache information so that the PWA can work offline.

> *Native app, am I?*
>
> *Web application, am I?*
>
> *PWA!*

In this chapter, we will cover the following topics:

- Understanding PWAs
- Working with manifest files
- Working with service workers
- Using the `CacheStorage` API
- Using the `Geolocation` API
- Using the `OpenWeather One Call` API
- Creating a PWA

Technical requirements

To complete this project, you need to have Visual Studio 2022 installed on your PC. For instructions on how to install the free Community Edition of Visual Studio 2022, refer to *Chapter 1, Introduction to Blazor WebAssembly*.

We will be using an external weather API to access the weather forecast data for our project. The API that we will be using is the `OpenWeather One Call` API. This is a free API that is provided by `OpenWeather` (`https://openweathermap.org`). To get started with this API, you need to create an account and obtain an API key. If you do not want to create an account, you can use the `weather.json` file that we have provided in the GitHub repository for this chapter.

The source code for this chapter is available in the following GitHub repository: `https://github.com/PacktPublishing/Blazor-WebAssembly-by-Example-Second-Edition/tree/main/Chapter06`.

The Code in Action video is available here: `https://packt.link/Ch6`.

Understanding PWAs

A PWA is a web application that uses modern web capabilities to deliver a native app-like experience to users. PWAs look and feel like native applications because they run in their own app window instead of the browser's window, and they can be launched from the **Start** menu or taskbar. PWAs offer an offline experience and load instantly due to their use of caching. They can receive push notifications and are automatically updated in the background. Finally, although they do not require a listing in an app store for distribution, they can be distributed through the various app stores.

Many large companies, such as Pinterest, Starbucks, Trivago, and Twitter, have embraced PWAs. Companies are drawn to PWAs because they can develop them once and use them everywhere.

A PWA feels like a native application due to a combination of technologies. To convert a web app into a PWA, it must use HTTPS and include both a manifest file and a service worker.

HTTPS

To be converted into a PWA, the web app must use HTTPS and must be served over a secure network. This should not be a problem since most browsers will no longer serve pages over HTTP. Therefore, even if you are not planning to convert a Blazor WebAssembly app into a PWA, you should always be using HTTPS.

> **TIP**
>
> A **Secure Sockets Layer (SSL)** certificate is required to enable HTTPS. A great source for free SSL certificates is **Let's Encrypt** (`https://letsencrypt.org`). It is a free, automated, and open **Certificate Authority (CA)**.

Manifest files

A manifest file is a simple **JavaScript Object Notation (JSON)** document that contains an application's name, defaults, and startup parameters for when a web application is launched. It describes how an application looks and feels.

This is an example of a simple manifest file:

```
{
  "name": "My Sample PWA",
  "display": "standalone",
  "background_color": "#ffffff",
  "theme_color": "#03173d",
  "icons": [
    {
      "src": "icon-512.png",
      "type": "image/png",
      "sizes": "512x512"
    }
  ]
}
```

A manifest file must include the name of the application and at least one icon. We will look more closely at manifest files in the next section.

Service workers

A service worker is a JavaScript file that defines the offline experience for the PWA. It intercepts and controls how a web browser handles its network requests and asset caching.

This is the content of the `service-worker.js` file that is included in the `Blazor WebAssembly` PWA project template provided by Microsoft:

```
self.addEventListener('fetch', () => { });
```

It is only one line of code and—as you can see—it does not actually do anything. However, it counts as a service worker and is all that is technically needed to convert an application into a PWA. We will take a closer look at more robust service workers later in this chapter.

A PWA is a web app that can be installed on a device like a native application. If a web app uses HTTPS and includes both a manifest file and a service worker, it can be converted into a PWA. Let's take a closer look at manifest files.

Working with manifest files

A manifest file provides information about an app in JSON format. It is usually in the root folder of an application. The following code snippet shows how to add a manifest file named `manifest.json` to the `index.html` file:

```
<link href="manifest.json" rel="manifest" />
```

Here is a more robust manifest file that includes more fields than the previous example:

manifest.json

```
{
    "dir": "ltr",
    "lang": "en",
    "name": " 5-Day Weather Forecast",
    "short_name": "Weather",
    "scope": "/",
    "display": "standalone",
    "start_url": "./",
    "background_color": "transparent",
```

```json
    "theme_color": "transparent",
    "description": "This is a 5-day weather forecast.",
    "orientation": "any",
    "related_applications": [],
    "prefer_related_applications": false,
    "icons": [
      {
        "src": "icon-512.png",
        "type": "image/png",
        "sizes": "512x512"
      }
    ],
    "url": "https://bweweather.azurewebsites.net",
    "screenshots": [],
  "categories": ["weather"]
  }
```

As mentioned earlier, a manifest file must include the name of the application and at least one icon. Beyond that, everything else is optional, although we highly recommend that you include at least the description, short_name, and start_url in your manifest files.

These are the keys used in the preceding manifest.json file:

- dir: The base direction of name, short_name, and description. It is either ltr, rtl, or auto.

- lang: The primary language of name, short_name, and description.

- name: The name of the app. The maximum length is 45 characters.

- short_name: The short name of the app. The maximum length is 12 characters.

- scope: The navigation scope of the app.

- display: The way the app is displayed. The valid options are fullscreen, standalone, minimal-UI, or browser.

- start_url: The **Uniform Resource Locator** (**URL**) of the app.

- background_color: The color used for the app's background during installation on the splash screen.

- theme_color: The default theme color.

- description: A short description of the app.

- orientation: The default screen orientation. Some of the options are any, natural, landscape, and portrait.

- related_applications: Any related apps that the developer wishes to highlight. These are usually native apps.

- prefer_related_applications: A value notifying the user agent that the related application is preferred over a web app.

- icons: One or more images used by the app. This is usually the largest section of the file because many devices prefer images of different sizes.

- url: The address of the app.

- screenshots: An array of images of the app in action.

- categories: An array of strings representing the categories that the app belongs to.

The preceding list does not include all the keys that can be included in a manifest.json file. Also, more keys are still being added every year.

A manifest file controls how the PWA appears to the user and is required to convert a web app into a PWA. A service worker is also required to convert a web app into a PWA. Let's take a closer look at service workers.

Working with service workers

Service workers provide the magic behind PWAs. They are used for caching, background syncing, and push notifications. A service worker is a JavaScript file that intercepts and modifies navigation and resource requests. It gives us full control over which resources are cached and how our PWA behaves in different situations.

A service worker is simply a script that your browser runs in the background. It is separate from the app and has no **Document Object Model (DOM)** access. It runs on a different thread than the thread used by the main JavaScript that powers your app, so it is not blocking. It is designed to be fully asynchronous.

Service worker life cycle

When working with service workers, it is very important to understand their life cycle because offline support can add a significant amount of complexity to the web app. There are three steps in the life cycle of a service worker—**install, activate, and fetch**, as illustrated in the following diagram:

Figure 6.1: Service worker life cycle

Install

During the install step, the service worker usually caches some of the static assets of the website, such as a You are offline splash screen. If the files are cached successfully, the service worker is installed. However, if any of the files fail to download and cache, the service worker is not installed and does not move to the activate step.

If the service worker is not successfully installed, it will try to be installed the next time the web app is run. Therefore, the developer can be assured that if the service worker has been successfully installed, the cache contains all the static assets that were designated to be cached. After the install step is successfully completed, the activate step is initiated.

Activate

During the activate step, the service worker handles the management of the old caches. Since a previous installation may have created a cache, this is the app's opportunity to delete it. After the activate step is successfully completed, the service worker is ready to begin processing the fetch events.

Fetch

During the fetch step, the service worker controls all the pages that fall under its scope. It handles all the fetch events that occur when a network request is made from the PWA. The service worker will continue to fetch until it is terminated.

Updating a service worker

To update the service worker that is running for our website, we need to update the service worker's JavaScript file. Each time a user navigates to our site, the browser downloads the current service worker and compares it with the installed service worker. If they are different, it will attempt to replace the old service worker.

However, this does not happen immediately. The new service worker must wait until the old service worker is no longer in control before it can be activated. The old service worker will remain in control until all the open pages are closed. When the new service worker takes control, its activate event will fire.

Cache management is handled during the activate callback. The reason we manage the cache during the activate callback is that if we were to wipe out any old caches in the install step, the old service worker (which has control of all the current pages) would suddenly stop being able to serve files from that cache.

The following screenshot shows a service worker that is **waiting to activate**:

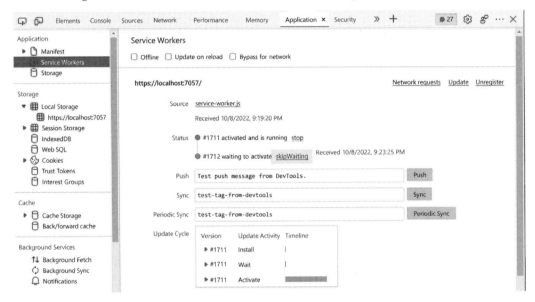

Figure 6.2: Service worker waiting to activate

TIP

The service worker will not be activated until the user has navigated away from the app in all tabs. Reloading the tab will not suffice, even if the app is only running in that one tab. However, you can activate a service worker that is **waiting to activate** by clicking the **skipWaiting** link. The **skipWaiting** link is highlighted in *Figure 6.2*.

Types of service workers

There are many different types of service workers, from the ridiculously simple to the more complex. The following diagram shows some of the different types of service workers, ordered from simple to complex:

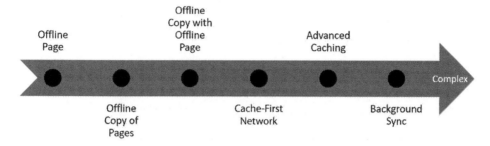

Figure 6.3: Types of service workers from simple to complex

Offline page

This is the simplest type of functioning service worker to create. All we need to create this type of service worker is an HTML page that indicates an application is offline. Whenever an application is unable to connect to a network, we simply display that HTML page.

Offline copy of pages

With this type of service worker, we store a copy of each page in the cache as our visitors view them. When the application is offline, it serves the pages from the cache. This approach may only work for applications with a limited number of pages because if a page that a user wants to view has not yet been viewed by that user, it will not yet be in the cache and the app will fail.

Offline copy with offline page

This type of service worker is an improved version of the offline copy of pages service worker. It combines the two previous types of service workers. With this type of service worker, we store a copy of each page in the cache as our visitors view them. When an application is offline, it serves the pages from the cache. If a page that a user wants to view is not in the cache, we display the HTML page that indicates the application is offline.

Cache-first network

This type of service worker always uses the cache first. If the requested page is in the cache, it serves that page before it requests the page from the server and updates the cache with the requested page. Using this service worker, we always serve the version of the page that is in the cache before requesting the page from the server, thus users are served the same data whether they are online or offline.

IMPORTANT NOTE

The cache-first network service worker is the type of service worker that is preferred by Microsoft.

Advanced caching

This type of service worker is a combination of each of the preceding types. With this type of service worker, we designate different files and routes to be cached using different rules. For example, some data, such as stock prices, should never be cached, while other data that does not change very often should be cached.

Background sync

This is the most complex type of service worker. It allows a user to continue to use an application to add and edit data when they are offline. Then, when they are back online, the application will sync their data with the network.

This is not a complete list of all the different types of service workers that are available. However, it should give you an idea of the power and flexibility of service workers and the importance of caching. All the service workers on our list rely on the CacheStorage API for caching.

Using the CacheStorage API

The CacheStorage API is used to cache request/response object pairs, where the request objects are the keys and the response objects are the values. It was designed to be used by service workers to provide offline functionality. A caches object is an instance of CacheStorage. It is a global object that is located in the window object.

We can use the following code to test if CacheStorage is available on the browser:

```
const hasCaches = 'caches' in self;
```

A `caches` object is used to maintain a list of caches for a particular web app. Caches cannot be shared with other web apps and they are isolated from the browser's HTTP cache. They are entirely managed through the JavaScript that we write.

These are some of the methods of `CacheStorage`:

- `delete(cacheName)`: This method deletes the indicated cache and returns `true`. If the indicated cache is not found, it returns `false`.
- `has(cacheName)`: This method returns `true` if the indicated cache exists and `false` otherwise.
- `keys`: This method returns a string array of the names of all the caches.
- `open(cacheName)`: This method opens the indicated cache. If it does not exist, it is created and then opened.

When we open an instance of `CacheStorage`, a `Cache` object is returned. These are some of the methods of a `Cache` object:

- `add(request)`: This method takes a request and adds the resulting response to the cache.
- `addAll(requests)`: This method takes an array of requests and adds all the resulting responses to the cache.
- `delete(request)`: This method returns `true` if it can find and delete the indicated request, and `false` otherwise.
- `keys()`: This method returns an array of keys.
- `match(request)`: This method returns the response associated with the matching request.
- `put(request, response)`: This method adds the request and response pair to the cache.

> **TIP**
>
> A `Cache` object does not get updated unless we explicitly request it to be updated. Also, these objects do not expire. We need to delete them as they become obsolete.

Service workers use the `CacheStorage` API to allow the PWA to continue to function when it is offline. Next, we will explain how to use the **Geolocation API**.

Using the Geolocation API

The Geolocation API for JavaScript provides a mechanism for us to obtain the location of a user. Using the Geolocation API, we can obtain the coordinates of a device that the browser is running on.

The Geolocation API is accessed through a navigator.geolocation object. When we make a call to the navigator.geolocation object, the user's browser asks the user for permission to access their location. If they accept, the browser uses the device's positioning hardware, such as the **Global Positioning System (GPS)** on a smartphone, to determine its location.

Before we attempt to use the navigator.geolocation object, we should verify that it is supported by the browser. The following code tests for the presence of geolocation support on the browser:

```
if (navigator.geolocation) {
    var position = await getPositionAsync();
} else {
    throw Error("Geolocation is not supported.");
};
```

For the project in this chapter, we will be using the getCurrentPosition method to retrieve the device's location. This method uses two callback functions. The success callback function returns a GeolocationPosition object, while the error callback function returns a GeolocationPositionError object. If the user denies us access to their position, it will be reported in the GeolocationPositionError object.

These are the properties of the GeolocationPosition object:

- coords.latitude: This property returns a double that represents the latitude of the device.
- coords.longitude: This property returns a double that represents the longitude of the device.
- coords.accuracy: This property returns a double that represents the accuracy of the latitude and the longitude, expressed in meters.
- coords.altitude: This property returns a double that represents the altitude of the device.
- coords.altitudeAccuracy: This property returns a double that represents the accuracy of the altitude, expressed in meters.
- coords.heading: This property returns a double that represents the direction in which the device is heading, expressed in degrees. If the device is stationary, the value is NaN.

- coords.speed: This property returns a double that represents the speed of the device, expressed in meters per second.
- timestamp: This property returns the date and time of the response.

The GeolocationPosition object always returns the coords.latitude, coords.longitude, coords.accuracy, and timestamp properties. The other properties are only returned if they are available.

By using JavaScript's Geolocation API, we can determine the latitude and longitude of a device. We need this information to use the OpenWeather One Call API to request a local weather forecast for our project.

Using the OpenWeather One Call API

The data source for the project in this chapter is a free API provided by OpenWeather. It is called the OpenWeather One Call API (https://openweathermap.org/api/one-call-api). This API can return current, forecast, and historical weather data. We will be using it to access the local forecast for the next 5 days. This is the format of an API call using the OpenWeather One Call API:

```
https://api.openweathermap.org/data/2.5/
onecall?lat={lat}&lon={lon}&appid={API key}
```

These are the parameters for the OpenWeather One Call API:

- lat: Latitude. This parameter is required.
- lon: Longitude. This parameter is required.
- appid: API key. This parameter is required. After you create an account, you can manage your API keys from the API keys tab.
- units: Units of measurement. This is set to Standard, Metric, or Imperial.
- exclude: Excluded data. This is used to simplify data that is returned. Since we will only be using the daily forecast, we will exclude current, per minute, and hourly data, and alerts for our project. This is a comma-delimited list.
- lang: Language of the output.

This is a fragment of the response from the OpenWeather One Call API:

weather.json fragment

```json
{
  "dt": 1616436000,
  "sunrise": 1616416088,
  "sunset": 1616460020,
  "temp": {
    "day": 58.5,
    "min": 54.75,
    "max": 62.6,
    "night": 61.29,
    "eve": 61.25,
    "morn": 54.75
  },
  "feels_like": {
    "day": 49.69,
    "night": 51.91,
    "eve": 50.67,
    "morn": 47.03
  },
  "pressure": 1011,
  "humidity": 85,
  "dew_point": 54.01,
  "wind_speed": 17.83,
  "wind_deg": 168,
  "weather": [
    {
      "id": 502,
      "main": "Rain",
      "description": "heavy intensity rain",
      "icon": "10d"
    }
  ],
  "clouds": 98,
  "pop": 1,
  "rain": 27.91,
  "uvi": 2.34
},
```

In the preceding JSON fragment, we have highlighted the fields that we are using in this chapter's project.

IMPORTANT NOTE

This project uses version 2.5 of the OpenWeather One Call API. They have recently released version 3.0 of the API. There is a small fee to use the new version of the API if you make over 1,000 API calls in a day.

The OpenWeather One Call API is a simple API that we will be using to obtain the daily forecast for a given location. Now, let's get a quick overview of the project that we are going to build in this chapter.

Creating a PWA

In this chapter, we will build a Blazor WebAssembly app to display a local 5-day weather forecast and then convert it into a PWA.

The web app we will build uses JavaScript's Geolocation API to determine the current latitude and longitude of the device. It uses the OpenWeather One Call API to obtain the local weather forecast and uses a variety of Razor components to display the weather forecast to the user. After we have completed the web app, we will convert it into a PWA by adding a logo, a manifest file, and a service worker. Finally, we will install, run, and uninstall the PWA.

This is a screenshot of the completed application:

Sunday, October 9, 2022	Monday, October 10, 2022	Tuesday, October 11, 2022	Wednesday, October 12, 2022	Thursday, October 13, 2022
broken clouds	scattered clouds	scattered clouds	moderate rain	clear sky
79 F° / 57 F°	86 F° / 65 F°	84 F° / 68 F°	87 F° / 69 F°	81 F° / 58 F°

Figure 6.4: 5-Day Weather Forecast application

The build time for this project is approximately 90 minutes.

Project overview

A WeatherForecast project will be created by using Microsoft's **Blazor WebAssembly App Empty** project template to create an empty Blazor WebAssembly project. First, we will use JavaScript interop with the Geolocation API to obtain the coordinates of the device. We will then use the OpenWeather One Call API to obtain a weather forecast for those coordinates. Next, we will create a couple of Razor components to display the forecast.

To convert the web app into a PWA, we will add a logo, a manifest file, and an offline page service worker. After testing the service worker, we will install, run, and uninstall the PWA.

Getting started with the project

We need to create a new Blazor WebAssembly app. We do this as follows:

1. Open Visual Studio 2022.
2. Click the **Create a new project** button.
3. Press *Alt+S* to enter the **Search for templates** textbox.
4. Enter Blazor and press the *Enter* key.

    The following screenshot shows the **Blazor WebAssembly App Empty** project template.

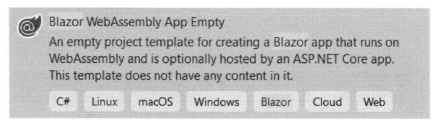

Figure 6.5: Blazor WebAssembly App Empty project template

5. Select the **Blazor WebAssembly App Empty** project template and click the **Next** button.
6. Enter WeatherForecast in the **Project name** textbox and click the **Next** button.

This is a screenshot of the dialog used to configure our new project:

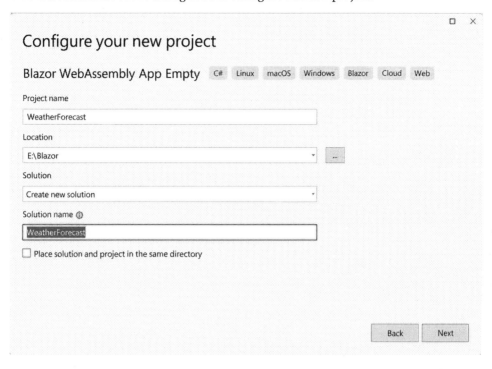

Figure 6.6: Configure your new project dialog

TIP

In the preceding example, we placed the WeatherForecast project into the E:/Blazor folder. However, the location of this project is not important.

7. Select **.NET 7.0** as the version of the **Framework** to use.

8. Check the **Configure for HTTPS** checkbox.

9. Uncheck the **ASP.NET Core Hosted** checkbox.

10. Uncheck the **Progressive Web Application** checkbox.

This is a screenshot of the dialog used to collect additional information about our new project:

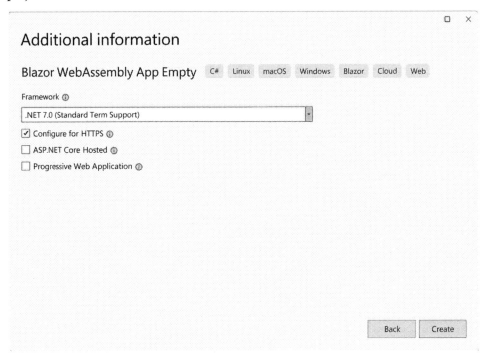

Figure 6.7: Additional information dialog

IMPORTANT NOTE

The reason that we are not checking the **Progressive Web Application** check-box is that we will be transforming the application into a PWA as part of this project.

11.   Click the **Create** button.

We have created an empty WeatherForecast Blazor WebAssembly project. Let's get started by adding the JavaScript function for determining the location of the device.

Add JavaScript to determine our location

We need to add the JavaScript function to determine our current latitude and longitude. We do this as follows:

1. Right-click the wwwroot folder and select the **Add, New Folder** option from the menu.

2. Name the new folder scripts.

3. Right-click the scripts folder and select the **Add, New Item** option from the menu.

4. Enter javascript in the **Search** box.

5. Select **JavaScript File**.

6. Name the file bweInterop.js.

TIP

In this book, we will be using the bweInterop namespace for our JavaScript code to both structure our code and minimize the risk of naming conflicts.

7. Click the **Add** button.

8. Enter the following JavaScript:

```javascript
var bweInterop = {};

bweInterop.getPosition = async function () {
    function getPositionAsync() {
        return new Promise((success, error) => {
            navigator.geolocation.getCurrentPosition
                (success, error);
        });
    }
    if (navigator.geolocation) {
        var position = await getPositionAsync();
        var coords = {
            latitude: position.coords.latitude,
            longitude: position.coords.longitude
        };
        return coords;
    } else {
```

```
        throw Error("Geolocation is not supported.");
    };
}
```

The preceding JavaScript code uses the `Geolocation` API to return the latitude and longitude of the device. If it is not allowed or it is not supported, an error is thrown.

9. Open the `wwwroot/index.html` file.

10. Add the following markup at the bottom of the body element:

```
<script src="scripts/bweInterop.js"></script>
```

We have created a JavaScript function that uses the `Geolocation` API to return our current latitude and longitude. Next, we need to invoke it from our web app.

Invoke the JavaScript function

We need to add a class to store our location and then we can invoke our `bweInterop.getPosition` function. We do this as follows:

1. Right-click the `WeatherForecast` project and select the **Add, New Folder** option from the menu.

2. Name the new folder `Models`.

3. Right-click the `Models` folder and select the **Add, Class** option from the menu.

4. Name the new class `Position`.

5. Add the following properties to the `Position` class:

```
public double Latitude { get; set; }
public double Longitude { get; set; }
```

This is the class that we will use to store our coordinates.

6. Open the `Pages/Index.razor` file.

7. Delete the `H1` element.

8. Add the following directives:

```
@using WeatherForecast.Models
@inject IJSRuntime js
```

9. Add the following markup:

```
<PageTitle>Weather Forecast</PageTitle>

@if (pos == null)
{
    <p><em>@message</em></p>
}
else
{
    <h2>
        Latitude: @pos.Latitude,
        Longitude: @pos.Longitude
    </h2>
}

@code {
    string message = "Loading...";
    Position? pos;
}
```

The preceding markup displays the value of the message field if the pos property is null. Otherwise, it displays the latitude and longitude from the pos property.

10. Add the following OnInitializedAsync method to the code block:

```
protected override async Task OnInitializedAsync()
{
    try
    {
        await GetPositionAsync();
    }
    catch (Exception)
    {
        message = "Geolocation is not supported.";
    };
}
```

The preceding code attempts to get our coordinates when the page initializes.

11. Add the following GetPositionAsync method to the code block:

```
private async Task GetPositionAsync()
{
    pos = await js.InvokeAsync<Position>(
        "bweInterop.getPosition");
}
```

The preceding code uses JavaScript interop to invoke the JavaScript function that we wrote that uses the Geolocation API to return our coordinates. For more information on JavaScript interop, refer to *Chapter 5, Building a Local Storage Service Using JavaScript Interoperability (JS Interop)*.

12. Press *Ctrl+F5* to start the application without debugging.

The following screenshot is an example of the dialog that will ask you for permission to access your location:

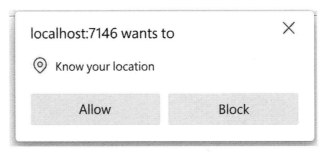

Figure 6.8: Geolocation permission dialog

13. Click the **Allow** button to allow the app to have access to your location.

The following screenshot is of the **Home** page of our Weather Forecast app:

Latitude: 33.1463, Longitude: 97.1334

Figure 6.9: Home page displaying our coordinates

You can disable the app's ability to access your location by using the **Location access allowed** dialog that is shown in the following screenshot:

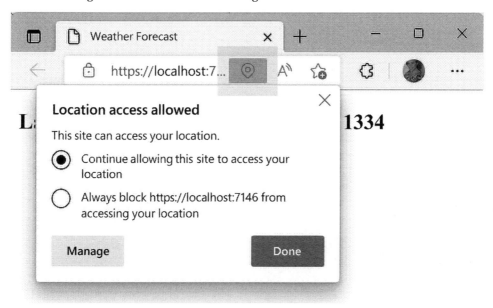

Figure 6.10: Location access allowed dialog

The **Location access allowed** dialog is accessed via the highlighted button on the browser's toolbar. You may want to toggle the permissions to see how that impacts the app.

14. Close the browser.

We have used the Geolocation API to display our latitude and longitude on the **Home** page. Next, we need to provide those coordinates to the OpenWeather One Call API.

Add an OpenWeather class

We need to add an OpenWeather class to capture the results from the OpenWeather One Call API. We do this as follows:

1. Return to Visual Studio.
2. Right-click the Models folder and select the **Add, Class** option from the menu.
3. Name the new class OpenWeather.
4. Click the **Add** button.

5. Add the following classes:

```
public class OpenWeather
{
    public Daily[] Daily { get; set; }
}
public class Daily
{
    public long Dt { get; set; }
    public Temp Temp { get; set; }
    public Weather[] Weather { get; set; }
}
public class Temp
{
    public double Min { get; set; }
    public double Max { get; set; }
}
public class Weather
{
    public string Description { get; set; }
    public string Icon { get; set; }
}
```

The preceding classes will be used to store the responses from the OpenWeather One Call API.

Now we need to add a component to display the responses. We will use Bootstrap to style our new component.

Install Bootstrap

We need to install Bootstrap in our web app. We do this as follows:

1. Right-click the wwwroot/css folder and select the **Add, Client-Side Library** option from the menu.

2. Enter bootstrap into the **Library** search textbox and press the *Enter* key.

3. Select **Choose specific files**.

4. Select only the css files, as shown in the following screenshot:

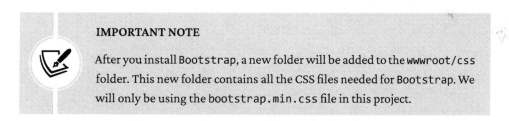

Figure 6.11: Add Client-Side Library dialog

5. Click the **Install** button.

> **IMPORTANT NOTE**
>
> After you install Bootstrap, a new folder will be added to the wwwroot/css folder. This new folder contains all the CSS files needed for Bootstrap. We will only be using the bootstrap.min.css file in this project.

Now that Bootstrap is installed, let's verify that it is working.

6. Open the wwwroot/index.html file.

7. Add the following markup to the head element before the link to the css/app.css stylesheet.

```
<link href="css/bootstrap/css/bootstrap.min.css"
      rel="stylesheet" />
```

8. Open the Pages/Index.razor page.

9. Add the following markup below the PageTitle component.

```
<div class="alert alert-info">
    Bootstrap is installed!
</div>
```

10. Press *Ctrl+F5* to start the application without debugging.

11. Verify that the top of the page is now blue.

12. Close the browser.

Now that Bootstrap is properly installed, we can add the new component.

Add a DailyForecast component

We need the new component to display each day's forecast. We do this as follows:

1. Right-click the WeatherForecast project and select the **Add**, **New Folder** option from the menu.

2. Name the new folder Shared.

3. Right-click the Shared folder and select the **Add, Razor Component** option from the menu.

4. Name the new component DailyForecast.

5. Click the **Add** button.

6. Replace the existing markup with the following markup:

```
<div class="card text-center">
    <div class="card-header">
        @Date
    </div>
    <div class="card-body">
        <img src="@IconUrl" />
        <h4 class="card-title">@Description</h4>
        <b>@((int)HighTemp) F&deg;</b> /
        @((int)LowTemp) F&deg;
    </div>
</div>

@code {


}
```

This component uses the Card component from Bootstrap to display the daily forecast.

7. Add the following code to the code block:

```
[Parameter] public long Seconds { get; set; }
[Parameter] public double HighTemp { get; set; }
[Parameter] public double LowTemp { get; set; }
[Parameter] public string? Description { get; set; }
[Parameter] public string? Icon { get; set; }

private string? Date;
private string? IconUrl;

protected override void OnInitialized()
{
    Date = DateTimeOffset
        .FromUnixTimeSeconds(Seconds)
        .LocalDateTime
        .ToLongDateString();

    IconUrl = String.Format(
        "https://openweathermap.org/img/wn/{0}@2x.png",
        Icon);
}
```

The preceding code defines the parameters that are used to display the daily weather forecast. The OnInitialized method is used to format the Date and IconUrl fields.

We have added a Razor component to display each day's weather forecast using the Card component from Bootstrap.

Fetch the forecast

We need to fetch the weather forecast. We can fetch the forecast by either calling the OpenWeather One Call API or using the weather.json file that is in GitHub. We do this as follows:

1. Open the Pages/Index.razor file.

2. Add the following using statements:

```
@using System.Text
@using WeatherForecast.Shared
```

3. Add the following directive:

```
@inject HttpClient Http
```

4. Add the following field to the top of the code block:

```
OpenWeather? forecast;
```

5. Add the GetForecastAsync method to the code block:

```
private async Task GetForecastAsync()
{


}
```

6. Add the following code to the GetForecastAsync method:

```
if (pos != null)
{
    string APIKey = "{Your API Key}";
    StringBuilder url = new StringBuilder();
    url.Append("https://api.openweathermap.org");
    url.Append("/data/2.5/onecall?");
    url.Append("lat=");
    url.Append(pos.Latitude);
    url.Append("&lon=");
    url.Append(pos.Longitude);
    url.Append("&exclude=");
    url.Append("current,minutely,hourly,alerts");
    url.Append("&units=imperial");
    url.Append("&appid=");
    url.Append(APIKey);
    forecast = await Http.GetFromJsonAsync<OpenWeather>
        (url.ToString());
}
```

IMPORTANT NOTE

You need to replace {Your_API_Key} with the API key that you obtained from OpenWeather. Also, it may take a couple of hours for your API key to become active.

The preceding method uses the OpenWeather One Call API with the coordinates obtained by the GetPositionAsync method to populate the forecast object.

If you cannot use the OpenWeather One Call API, use the following version of the GetForecastAsync method:

```
forecast = await Http.GetFromJsonAsync<OpenWeather>
    ("sample-data/weather.json");
```

The preceding version of the GetForecastAsync method uses a static file to populate the forecast object. It assumes that the weather.json file has been downloaded from the GitHub repository for this chapter and that it has been placed into the wwwroot/sample-data folder.

7. Update the OnInitializedAsync method to call the GetForecastAsync method and update the error message, like this:

```
try
{
    await GetPositionAsync();
    await GetForecastAsync();
}
catch (Exception)
{
    message = "Error encountered.";
};
```

Now that we have populated the forecast object, we can display the forecast.

Display the forecast

We need to add a collection of daily forecasts to the **Home** page. We do this as follows:

1. Remove the div element.

2. Replace the @if statement with the following markup:

```
@if (forecast == null)
{
    <p><em>@message</em></p>
}
else
{
```

```
<div class="card-group">
    @foreach (var item in forecast.Daily.Take(5))
    {
        <DailyForecast
            Seconds="@item.Dt"
            LowTemp="@item.Temp.Min"
            HighTemp="@item.Temp.Max"
            Description="@item.Weather[0].Description"
            Icon="@item.Weather[0].Icon" />
    }
</div>
}
```

The preceding markup loops through the forecast object five times. It uses the DailyForecast component to display the daily forecast.

3. Press *Ctrl+F5* to start the application without debugging.

4. Close the browser.

We have completed our Weather Forecast application. Now, we need to convert it into a PWA. To do that, we need to add a logo, a manifest file, and a service worker.

Add the logo

We need to add an image to be used as a logo for the app. We do this as follows:

1. Right-click the wwwroot folder and select the **Add, New Folder** option from the menu.

2. Name the new folder images.

3. Copy the Sun-512.png image from the GitHub repository for this chapter to the images folder.

At least one image must be included in the manifest file for the PWA to be installed. Now, we can add a manifest file.

Add a manifest file

To convert the web app into a PWA, we need to add a manifest file. We do this as follows:

1. Right-click the wwwroot folder and select the **Add, New Item** option from the menu.

2. Enter json in the **Search** box.

3. Select **JSON File**.

4. Name the file `manifest.json`.

5. Click the **Add** button.

6. Enter the following JSON code:

```json
{
    "lang": "en",
    "name": "5-Day Weather Forecast",
    "short_name": "Weather",
    "display": "standalone",
    "start_url": "./",
    "background_color": "#ffa500",
    "theme_color": "transparent",
    "description": "This is a 5-day weather forecast app",
    "orientation": "any",
    "icons": [
      {
        "src": "images/Sun-512.png",
        "type": "image/png",
        "sizes": "512x512"
      }
    ]
}
```

7. Open the `wwwroot/index.html` file.

8. Add the following markup to the bottom of the head element:

```html
<link href="manifest.json" rel="manifest" />
```

9. Add the following markup below the preceding markup:

```html
<link rel="apple-touch-icon"
      sizes="512x512"
      href="images/Sun-512.png" />
```

TIP

With iOS Safari, you must include the preceding link tag to instruct it to use the indicated icon or it will generate an icon by taking a screenshot of the page's content.

We have added a manifest file to our web app to control how it looks and behaves when it is installed. Next, we need to add a service worker.

Add a simple service worker

To finish converting the web app into a PWA, we need to add a service worker. We do this as follows:

1. Right-click the wwwroot folder and select the **Add, New Item** option from the menu.

2. Enter html in the **Search** box.

3. Select **HTML Page**.

4. Name the file offline.html.

5. Click the **Add** button.

6. Add the following markup to the body element:

    ```
    <h1>You are offline.</h1>
    ```

7. Right-click the wwwroot folder and select the **Add, New Item** option from the menu.

8. Enter javascript in the **Search** box.

9. Select JavaScript File.

10. Name the file service-worker.js.

11. Click the **Add** button.

12. Add the following constants:

    ```
    const OFFLINE_VERSION = 1;
    const CACHE_PREFIX = 'offline';
    const CACHE_NAME = '${CACHE_PREFIX}${OFFLINE_VERSION}';
    const OFFLINE_URL = 'offline.html';
    ```

    The preceding code sets the name of the current cache and the name of the file we will be using to indicate that we are offline.

13. Add the following event listeners:

    ```
    self.addEventListener('install',
        event => event.waitUntil(onInstall(event)));

    self.addEventListener('activate',
        event => event.waitUntil(onActivate(event)));
    ```

```
self.addEventListener('fetch',
    event => event.respondWith(onFetch(event)));
```

The preceding code designates the functions to be used for each of the following steps: install, activate, and fetch.

14. Add the following `onInstall` function:

```
async function onInstall(event) {
    console.info('Service worker: Install');
    const cache = await caches.open(CACHE_NAME);
    await cache.add(new Request(OFFLINE_URL));
}
```

The preceding function opens the indicated cache. If the cache does not yet exist, it creates the cache and then opens it. After the cache is open, it adds the indicated request/response pair to the cache.

15. Add the following `onActivate` function:

```
async function onActivate(event) {
    console.info('Service worker: Activate');
    const cacheKeys = await caches.keys();
    await Promise.all(cacheKeys
        .filter(key => key.startsWith(CACHE_PREFIX)
            && key !== CACHE_NAME)
        .map(key => caches.delete(key)));
}
```

The preceding code fetches the names of all the caches. All the caches that do not match the name of the indicated cache are deleted.

TIP

It is your responsibility to purge obsolete caches. Each browser has a limit as to the amount of storage that a web app can use. If you violate that limit, all of your caches may be deleted by the browser.

16. Add the following onFetch function:

```
async function onFetch(event) {
    if (event.request.method === 'GET') {
        try {
            return await fetch(event.request);
        } catch (error) {
            const cache = await
                caches.open(CACHE_NAME);
            return await cache.match(OFFLINE_URL);
        };
    };
}
```

In the preceding code, if the fetch fails, the cache is opened, and the previously cached offline page is served.

17. Open the wwwroot/index.html file.

18. Add the following markup to the bottom of the body element:

```
<script>
    navigator.serviceWorker.register('service-worker.js');
</script>
```

The preceding code registers the service worker.

We have added an offline page service worker that will display the offline.html page when the PWA is offline.

Test the service worker

We need to test that the service worker is allowing us to work offline. We do this as follows:

1. Press *Ctrl+F5* to start the application without debugging.

2. Click *F12* to open the Developer Tools interface.

3. Select the **Application** tab.

4. Select the **Manifest** option from the menu on the left to view the **App Manifest** details.

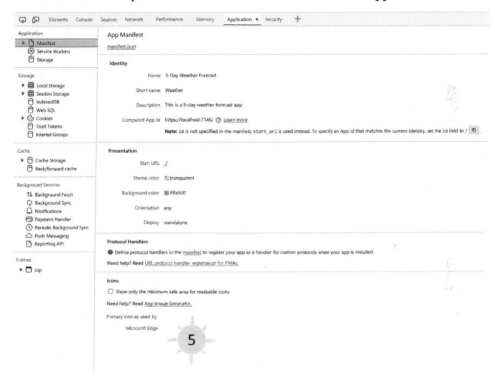

Figure 6.12: App Manifest details

5. Select the **Service Workers** option from the menu on the left to view the service worker that is installed for the current client, as illustrated in the following screenshot:

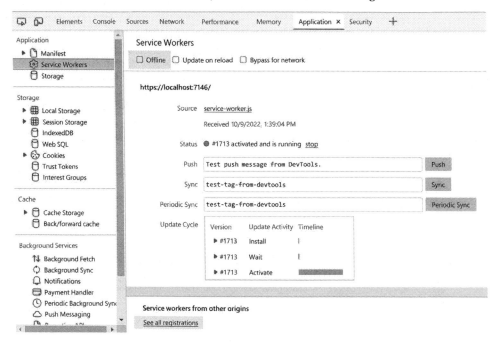

Figure 6.13: Service Workers dialog

In the preceding screenshot, we have highlighted both the **Offline** checkbox and the **See all registrations** link.

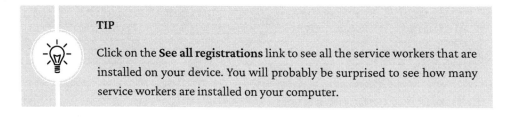

TIP

Click on the **See all registrations** link to see all the service workers that are installed on your device. You will probably be surprised to see how many service workers are installed on your computer.

6. Select the **Cache Storage** option from the menu on the left to view the caches.

7. Click on the **offline1** cache to view its contents, as illustrated in the following screenshot:

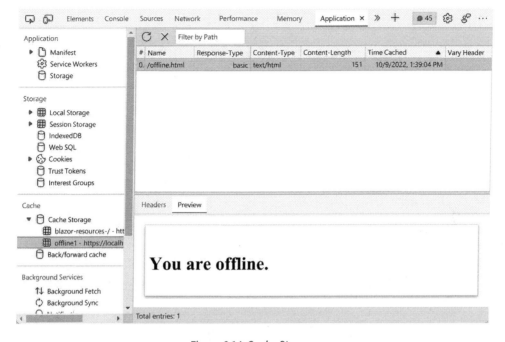

Figure 6.14: Cache Storage

8. Select the **Service Workers** option from the menu on the left.

9. Check the **Offline** checkbox on the **Service Workers** dialog.

> **TIP**
>
> The **Offline** checkbox is highlighted in Figure 16.13.

10. Refresh the browser, and you should see the following screen:

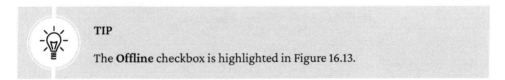

Figure 6.15: Offline page

The page that is displayed is from the browser's cache.

11. Uncheck the **Offline** checkbox on the **Service Workers** dialog.

12. Refresh the browser.

Since the web app is now back online, the **Offline** page is no longer displayed.

We have tested that the service worker enables our web app to work offline. Now, we can install the PWA.

Install the PWA

We need to test the PWA by installing it. We do this as follows:

1. Select the **App available. Install 5-Day Weather Forecast** menu option from the browser's menu:

Figure 6.16: Install 5-Day Weather Forecast option

> **TIP**
>
> On Chromium-based browsers, the **Install** button is on the URL bar. However, for other types of browsers, you will need to install the PWA from either the **Menu** button or the **Share** button.

2. Click the **Install** button in the **Install PWA** dialog:

Figure 6.17: Install PWA dialog

3. Click the **Allow** button in the **App installed** dialog.

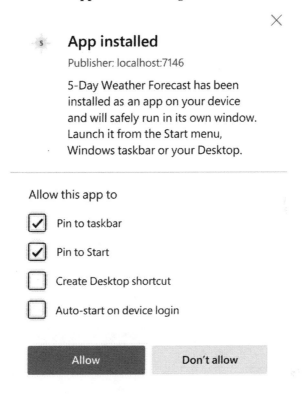

Figure 6.18: App installed dialog

Once installed, the PWA appears without an address bar. It appears on our taskbar, and we can run it from our **Start** menu. The following screenshot shows the PWA after it has been installed:

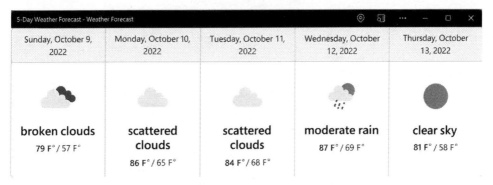

Figure 6.19: Installed PWA

4. Close the app.

5. Click the *Windows* key and search for the **5-Day Weather Forecast** app.

6. Open the **5-Day Weather Forecast** app.

When the application opens, its icon appears on the taskbar. We can pin it to the taskbar if we want.

We have successfully installed and run the PWA. It is just as easy to uninstall a PWA as it is to install one.

Uninstall the PWA

We need to uninstall the PWA. We do this as follows:

1. Close the **5-Day Weather Forecast** app.

2. Click the *Windows* key and search for the **5-Day Weather Forecast** app.

3. Right-click the **5-Day Weather Forecast** app and select the **Uninstall** option from the menu.

Figure 6.20: Uninstall the 5-Day Weather Forecast app

4. Click the **Uninstall** button.

Figure 6.21: Uninstall the 5-Day Weather Forecast app

We have uninstalled the PWA.

IMPORTANT NOTE

It may take a few seconds for the app to be removed from the taskbar.

Summary

You should now be able to convert a Blazor WebAssembly app into a PWA by adding a manifest file and a service worker.

In this chapter, we introduced PWAs. We explained how to convert a web app into a PWA by adding a manifest file and a service worker. We explained how to work with manifest files and service workers. We went into some detail explaining the different types of service workers and explained how to use the CacheStorage API to cache request/response pairs. Finally, we demonstrated how to use both the Geolocation API and the OpenWeather One Call API.

After that, we used the Blazor WebAssembly App Empty project template to create a new project. We added a JavaScript function that uses the Geolocation API to obtain our coordinates. We added some models to capture the coordinates and used JavaScript interop to invoke the JavaScript function. We used the OpenWeather One Call API to obtain the local 5-day weather forecast. We installed Bootstrap and created a Razor component to display each day's forecast.

In the last part of the chapter, we converted the Blazor WebAssembly app into a PWA by adding an image, a manifest file, and an offline page service worker. Finally, we installed, ran, and uninstalled the PWA. We can apply our new skills to convert our existing web apps into PWAs that combine the benefits of a web app with the look and feel of a native app.

In the next chapter, we will use **dependency injection (DI)** to build a shopping cart application.

Questions

The following questions are provided for your consideration:

1. Are service workers asynchronous or synchronous?
2. Can localStorage be used inside a service worker for data storage?
3. Can service workers manipulate the DOM?
4. Are PWAs secure?
5. Are PWAs platform-specific?
6. What are the differences between a PWA and a native app?

Further reading

The following resources provide more information concerning the topics in this chapter:

- For more information on the Geolocation API specification, refer to https://w3c.github.io/geolocation-api.
- For more information on using the Geolocation API, refer to https://developer.mozilla.org/en-US/docs/Web/API/Geolocation_API.
- For more information on the Weather API, refer to https://openweathermap.org/api.
- For more information on the Web Application Manifest specification, refer to https://www.w3.org/TR/appmanifest.
- For more information on the Service Worker specification, refer to https://w3c.github.io/ServiceWorker.
- For more information on using the CacheStorage API, refer to https://developer.mozilla.org/en-US/docs/Web/API/CacheStorage.
- For more examples of service workers, refer to the Workbox website at https://developers.google.com/web/tools/workbox.
- For more information on Microsoft's PWABuilder, refer to https://www.pwabuilder.com.
- For a PWA image generator, refer to https://www.pwabuilder.com/imageGenerator.
- For more information on Bootstrap, refer to https://getbootstrap.com/.

7

Building a Shopping Cart Using Application State

Sometimes, we need our applications to maintain their state between different pages. We can accomplish this by using **dependency injection (DI)**. DI is used to access services that are configured in a central location.

In this chapter, we will create a shopping cart. As we add and delete items from the shopping cart, the application will maintain a list of the items in the shopping cart. The contents of the shopping cart will be retained when we navigate to another page and then return to the page with the shopping cart. Also, the shopping cart's total will be displayed on all the pages.

Application state,

dependency injection

a team built on trust!

In this chapter, we will cover the following topics:

- Introducing the application state
- Understanding DI
- Creating the shopping cart project

Technical requirements

To complete this project, you need to have Visual Studio 2022 installed on your PC. For instructions on how to install the free Community Edition of Visual Studio 2022, refer to *Chapter 1, Introduction to Blazor WebAssembly.*

The source code for this chapter is available in the following GitHub repository: `https://github.com/PacktPublishing/Blazor-WebAssembly-by-Example-Second-Edition/tree/main/Chapter07`.

The Code in Action video is available here: `https://packt.link/Ch7`.

Introducing the application state

In a Blazor WebAssembly app, the browser's memory is used to hold the application's state. This means that when the user navigates between pages, the state is lost unless we preserve it. We will be using the `AppState` pattern to preserve the application's state.

In the `AppState` pattern, a service is added to a DI container to coordinate the state between related components. The service contains all the states that need to be maintained. Because the service is managed by the DI container, it can outlive individual components and retain the state of the application as the UI changes.

The service can be a simple class or a complex class. One service can be used to manage the state of multiple components across the entire application. One benefit of the `AppState` pattern is that it leads to a greater separation between presentation logic and business logic.

IMPORTANT NOTE

The application state that is held in the browser's memory is lost when the user reloads the page.

For the project in this chapter, we will use a DI service instance to preserve the application's state.

Understanding DI

DI is a technique in which an object accesses services that have been configured in a central location. The central location is the DI container. When using DI, each consuming class does not need to create its own instance of the injected class that it has a dependency on. It is provided by the framework and is called a service. In a Blazor WebAssembly application, the services are defined in the `program.cs` file.

We have already used DI in this book with the following services:

- `HttpClient`
- `IJSRuntime`
- `NavigationManager`

DI containers

When a Blazor WebAssembly application starts, it configures a DI container. The DI container is responsible for building the instances of the service and it lives until the user closes the tab in the browser that is running the web app. In the following example, the `CartService` implementation is registered for `ICartService`:

```
builder.Services.AddSingleton<ICartService, CartService>();
```

After a service has been added to a DI container, we use the @inject directive to inject the service into any classes that depend on it. The @inject directive takes two parameters, `Type` and `Property`:

- `Type`: This is the type of service.
- `Property`: This is the name of the property that is receiving the service.

The following example shows how to use the @inject directive to reference the `CartService` that was registered in the preceding code:

```
@inject ICartService cartService
```

Dependencies are injected after the component instance has been created, but before the `OnInitialized` or `OnInitializedAsync` life cycle events are executed. This means that you cannot use the injected class in the component's constructor, but you can use it in either the `OnInitialized` or `OnInitializedAsync` method.

The lifetime of each service is designated when it is registered.

Service lifetimes

The lifetime of a service that is injected using DI can be any of the following values:

- **Singleton**
- **Scoped**
- **Transient**

Singleton

If the service's lifetime is defined as Singleton, this means that a single instance of the class will be created and that instance will be shared throughout the application. Any components that use the service will receive an instance of the same service. In a Blazor WebAssembly application, this is true for the lifetime of the current application that is running in the current tab of the browser.

The following code will create a shared instance of the ICartService class:

```
builder.Services.AddSingleton<ICartService, CartService>();
```

This is the lifetime of the service that we will use to manage the application's state in this chapter's project.

Scoped

If the service's lifetime is defined as Scoped, this means that a new instance of the class will be created for each scope. Since a Blazor WebAssembly application's concept of the scope coincides with the life cycle of the application, Scoped-registered services are treated like Singleton services.

The following code will create a shared instance of the ICartService class:

```
builder.Services.AddScoped<ICartService, CartService>();
```

The instance created by the preceding code is identical to the instance created by using the AddSingleton method.

IMPORTANT NOTE

In the Blazor WebAssembly project templates provided by Microsoft, they use a Scoped service to create the HttpClient instance for data access. This is because Microsoft's project templates use the Scoped service lifetime for their services for symmetry with server-side Blazor.

Transient

If the service lifetime of the service is defined as Transient, this means that a new instance of the class will be created every time an instance of the service is requested. When using Transient services, the DI container acts as a factory that creates unique instances of the class. Once the instance is created and injected into the dependent component, the container has no further interest in it.

The following code will create a transient instance of the `OneUseService` class:

```
builder.Services.AddTransient<IOneUseService, OneUseService>();
```

The service's lifetime is defined in the DI container. A service instance can be either scoped or transient.

We can use DI to inject the same service instance into multiple components. DI is used by the `AppState` pattern to allow the application to maintain the state between components.

Now, let's get a quick overview of the project that we are going to build in this chapter.

Creating the shopping cart project

In this chapter, we will build a Blazor WebAssembly app that includes a shopping cart. We will be able to add and remove different products from the shopping cart. The cart's total will be displayed on each of the pages in the app.

The following is a screenshot of the completed application:

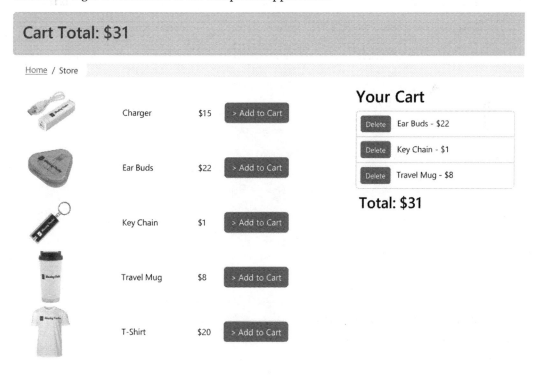

Figure 7.1: Shopping cart app

The build time for this project is approximately 60 minutes.

Project overview

The ShoppingCart project will be created by using Microsoft's **Blazor WebAssembly App Empty** project template to create an empty Blazor WebAssembly project. First, we will add logic to add and remove products from the shopping cart. Then, we will demonstrate that the cart's state is lost when we navigate between pages. To maintain the cart's state, we will register a service in the DI container that uses the AppState pattern. Finally, we will demonstrate that by injecting the new service into the relevant components, the cart's state is not lost.

Creating the shopping cart project

We need to create a new Blazor WebAssembly app. We do this as follows:

1. Open Visual Studio 2022.

2. Click on the **Create a new project** button.

3. Press *Alt+S* to enter the search for templates textbox.

4. Enter Blazor and press the *Enter* key.

    The following screenshot shows the **Blazor WebAssembly App Empty** project template.

Figure 7.2: Blazor WebAssembly App Empty project template

5. Select the **Blazor WebAssembly App Empty** project template and click on the **Next** button.

6. Enter ShoppingCart in the **Project name** textbox and click on the **Next** button.

This is a screenshot of the dialog used to configure our new project:

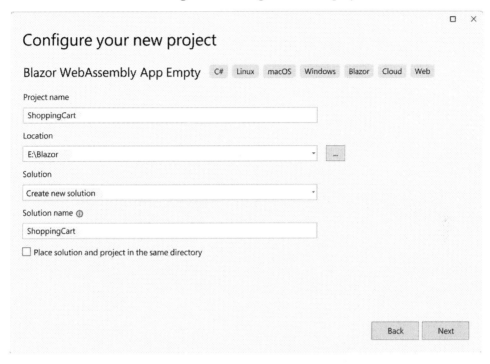

Figure 7.3: Configure your new project dialog

TIP

In the preceding example, we placed the ShoppingCart project into the E:/ Blazor folder. However, the location of this project is not important.

7.   Select **.NET 7.0** as the version of the **Framework** to use.

8.   Check the **Configure for HTTPS** checkbox.

9.   Uncheck the **ASP.NET Core Hosted** checkbox.

10. Uncheck the **Progressive Web Application** checkbox.

This is a screenshot of the dialog used to collect additional information about our new project:

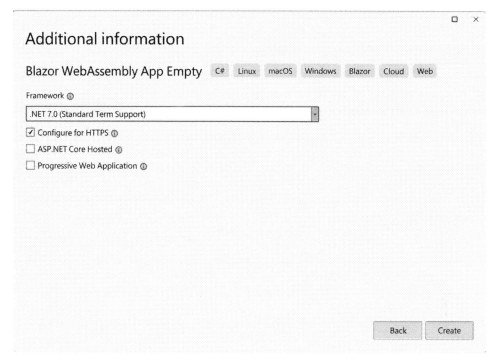

Figure 7.4: Additional information dialog

11. Click on the **Create** button.

We have created an empty ShoppingCart Blazor WebAssembly project. We will use Bootstrap to style our frontend.

Installing Bootstrap

We need to install Bootstrap into our web app. We do this as follows:

1. Right-click on the wwwroot/css folder and select the **Add**, **Client-Side Library** option from the menu.

2. Enter bootstrap into the **Library** search textbox and press the *Enter* key.

3. Select **Choose specific files**.

4. Select `css` files only, as shown in the following screenshot:

> **Add Client-Side Library**   ✕
>
> Provider: `cdnjs` ˅
>
> Library: `bootstrap@5.2.2`   ❶
>
> ○ Include all library files
> ◉ Choose specific files:
>
> ⊿ ■ 📁 Files:
>   ▷ ☑ 📁 css
>   ▷ ☐ 📁 js
>   ▷ ☐ 📁 scss
>
> Target Location: `wwwroot/css/bootstrap/`
>
>   Install   Cancel

Figure 7.5: Add Client-Side Library dialog

TIP

Although the preceding screenshot has version 5.2.2 of `Bootstrap` selected, you can use any version of `Bootstrap` to complete this project.

5. Click on the **Install** button.

IMPORTANT NOTE

After you install `Bootstrap`, a new folder will be added to the `wwwroot/css` folder. This new folder contains all the CSS files needed for `Bootstrap`. We will only be using the `bootstrap.min.css` file in this project.

6. Open the `wwwroot/index.html` file.

7. Add the following markup to the head element before the link to the `css/app.css` stylesheet:

```
<link href="css/bootstrap/css/bootstrap.min.css"
      rel="stylesheet" />
```

8. Open the `MainLayout.razor` file.

9. Update the main element to the following:

```
<main class="px-4">
    @Body
</main>
```

The preceding code uses Bootstrap to add padding around the body of the page.

10. Open the `Pages/Index.razor` file.

11. Delete the h1 element.

12. Add the following markup:

```
<PageTitle>Home</PageTitle>

<div class="bg-light">
    <ol class="breadcrumb">
        <li class="breadcrumb-item active">Home</li>
    </ol>
</div>

<h1 class="display-3">Welcome to Blazing Tasks!</h1>
<h2>
    The store is open for business.
</h2>
<button type="button" class="btn btn-danger mt-2">
    Start Shopping
</button>
```

The preceding code includes a breadcrumb that will be styled by using Bootstrap. A breadcrumb indicates the page's current location within a navigational hierarchy. The code also includes a button. However, the button does not yet do anything.

13. Press *Ctrl+F5* to start the application without debugging.

This is a screenshot of the **Home** page:

Figure 7.6: Home page of the ShoppingCart project

14. Click on the **Start Shopping** button to verify that nothing happens.

15. Close the browser.

When the user clicks the **Start Shopping** button, they should navigate to the **Store** page. However, the **Store** page does not yet exist.

Adding a Store component

We need to add a Store component. We do this as follows:

1. Right-click on the Pages folder and select the **Add, Razor Component** option from the menu.

2. Name the new component Store.

3. Click on the **Add** button.

4. Delete the H3 element.

5. Add the following markup before the code block:

```
@page "/store"

<PageTitle>Store</PageTitle>

<ol class="breadcrumb bg-light">
    <li class="breadcrumb-item"><a href="#">Home</a></li>
    <li class="breadcrumb-item active">Store</li>
</ol>
```

The preceding code includes a breadcrumb that we can use to navigate to the **Home** page.

6. Open the Pages/Index.razor file.

7. Add the following @inject directive:

```
@inject NavigationManager navigation
```

The NavigationManager service is provided by the framework to manage URI navigation.

8. Add the following code block:

```
@code{
    protected void OpenStore()
    {
        navigation.NavigateTo("store");
    }
}
```

In the preceding code, when OpenStore is called, the NavigationManager will navigate to the Store page. Since this is a SPA, the page will not need to be reloaded.

9. Add the following @onclick event to the **Start Shopping** button:

```
@onclick="OpenStore"
```

10. Press *Ctrl+F5* to start the application without debugging.

11. Click on the **Start Shopping** button to navigate to the **Store** page.

12. Click on the **Home** breadcrumb to return to the **Home** page.

13. Close the browser.

We have added the **Store** page. However, it is blank.

Adding a Product class

We need to add the products that are for sale. We do this as follows:

1. Right-click on the ShoppingCart project and select the **Add, New Folder** option from the menu.

2. Name the new folder Models.

3. Right-click on the Models folder and select the **Add, Class** option from the menu.

4. Name the new class Product.

5. Click on the **Add** button.

6. Add the following properties to the Product class:

```
public int ProductId { get; set; }
public string? ProductName { get; set; }
public int Price { get; set; }
public string? Image { get; set; }
```

7. Right-click on the wwwroot folder and select the **Add, New Folder** option from the menu.

8. Name the new folder sample-data.

9. Right-click on the sample-data folder and select the **Add, New Item** option from the menu.

10. Enter json in the **Search** box.

11. Select **JSON File**.

12. Name the file products.json.

13. Click on the **Add** button.

14. Update the file to the following:

```
[
  {
    "productId": 1,
    "productName": "Charger",
    "price": 15,
    "image": "charger.jpg"
  },
  {
    "productId": 2,
    "productName": "Ear Buds",
    "price": 22,
    "image": "earbuds.jpg"
  },
  {
    "productId": 3,
    "productName": "Key Chain",
    "price": 1,
    "image": "keychain.jpg"
  },
  {
```

```
      "productId": 4,
      "productName": "Travel Mug",
      "price": 8,
      "image": "travelmug.jpg"
    },
    {
      "productId": 5,
      "productName": "T-Shirt",
      "price": 20,
      "image": "tshirt.jpg"
    }
  ]
```

TIP

You can copy the products.json file from the GitHub repository.

15. Right-click on the wwwroot folder and select the **Add**, **New Folder** option from the menu.

16. Name the new folder images.

17. Copy the following images from the GitHub repository to the images folder: Charger.jpg, Earbuds.jpg, KeyChain.jpg, TravelMug.jpg, and Tshirt.jpg.

We have added a collection of products to our web app. Next, we need to finish the Store page.

Finishing the Store component

We need to add a list of the items that are for sale in our store, and we need to add the ability to select the items that we would like to purchase. We do this as follows:

1. Open the Pages/Store.razor file.

2. Add the following directives:

```
@using ShoppingCart.Models
@inject HttpClient Http
```

3. Add the following code to the code block:

```
public IList<Product>? products;
public IList<Product> cart = new List<Product>();
```

```
private int total;

protected override async Task OnInitializedAsync()
{
    products = await Http.GetFromJsonAsync<Product[]>
            ("sample-data/products.json");
}
```

The preceding code uses HttpClient to populate the list of products from the products. json file.

4. Add the following if statement before the code block:

```
@if (products == null)
{
    <p><em>Loading...</em></p>
}
else
{
    <h1 class="display-3">Products</h1>
    <div class="row">
        <div id="products" class="col-xl-4 col-lg-6">
        </div>
        <div id="cart" class="col-xl-3 col-lg-4">
        </div>
    </div>
}
```

The preceding code displays the **Loading...** message until the list of products is loaded. Once the list of products has loaded, it displays the products and the cart.

5. Add the following markup to the products element:

```
<table width="100%">
    @foreach (Product item in products)
    {
        <tr>
            <td>
                <img src="images/@item.Image" />
            </td>
```

```
                    <td class="align-middle">
                        @item.ProductName
                    </td>
                    <td class="align-middle">
                        $@item.Price
                    </td>
                    <td class="align-middle">
                        <button type="button"
                                class="btn btn-danger">
                            Add to Cart
                        </button>
                    </td>
                </tr>
        }
</table>
```

The preceding markup adds a table that displays all the products that are for sale.

6. Add the following markup to the cart element:

```
@if (cart.Any())
{
    <h2>Your Cart</h2>
    <ul class="list-group">
        @foreach (Product item in cart)
        {
            <li class="list-group-item p-2">
                <button type="button"
                        class="btn btn-sm btn-danger me-2">
                    Delete
                </button>
                @item.ProductName - $@item.Price
            </li>
        }
    </ul>
    <div class="p-2">
        <h3>Total: $@total</h3>
    </div>
}
```

The preceding markup displays all the items in our cart.

7. Add the AddProduct method to the code block:

```
private void AddProduct(Product product)
{
    cart.Add(product);
    total += product.Price;
}
```

The preceding code adds the indicated product to the cart and increments the total by the product's price.

8. Add the DeleteProduct method to the code block:

```
private void DeleteProduct(Product product)
{
    cart.Remove(product);
    total -= product.Price;
}
```

The preceding code removes the indicated product from the cart and decrements the total by the product's price.

9. Add the following @onlclick event to the **Add to Cart** button:

```
@onclick="@(() => AddProduct(item))"
```

10. The preceding code calls the AddProduct method when the button is clicked. For more information on handling events, refer to *Chapter 8, Building a Kanban Board Using Events*.

11. Add the following @onlclick event to the **Delete** button:

```
@onclick="@(()=>DeleteProduct(item))"
```

The preceding code calls the DeleteProduct method when the button is clicked.

We have finished updating the **Store** page. Now we need to test it.

Demonstrating that the application state has been lost

We need to run our web app in order to test the Store page. We do this as follows:

1. Press *Ctrl+F5* to start the application without debugging.
2. Click on the **Start Shopping** button.

3. Add a few products to the cart using the **Add to Cart** button.

4. Delete a product from the cart using the **Delete** button.

5. Select the **Home** option on the navigation menu.

6. Return to the **Store** page by clicking on the **Start Shopping** button.

7. Confirm that the cart is now empty.

    When we navigate between the pages in our web app, the state is lost.

8. Close the browser.

We can maintain the state by using DI to enable the AppState pattern. We will add a CartService to our project that we will manage using DI.

Creating the the ICartService interface

We need to create an ICartService interface. We do this as follows:

1. Return to Visual Studio.

2. Right-click on the ShoppingCart project and select the **Add, New Folder** option from the menu.

3. Name the new folder Services.

4. Right-click on the Services folder and select the **Add, New Item** option from the menu.

5. Enter interface in the **Search** box.

6. Select **Interface**.

7. Name the file ICartService.

8. Click on the **Add** button.

9. Enter the following code:

```
IList<Product> Cart { get; }
int Total { get; }
event Action OnChange;
void AddProduct(Product product);
void DeleteProduct(Product product);
```

IMPORTANT NOTE

Visual Studio will automatically add the following using statement:

using ShoppingCart.Models;

We have created the ICartService interface. Now we need to create a class that inherits from it.

Creating the CartService class

We need to create the CartService class. We do this as follows:

1. Right-click the Services folder and select the **Add, Class** option from the menu.

2. Name the class CartService.

3. Click on the **Add** button.

4. Update the class to the following:

```
public class CartService : ICartService
{
    private List<Product> cart = new();
    private int total;

    public IList<Product> Cart
    {
        get => cart;
    }
    public int Total
    {
        get => total;
    }

    public event Action? OnChange;
}
```

The CartService class inherits from the ICartService interface.

5. Add the NotifyStateChanged method to the class:

```
private void NotifyStateChanged() => OnChange?.Invoke();
```

In the preceding code, the OnChange event is invoked when the NotifyStateChanged method is called.

6. Add the AddProduct method to the class:

```
public void AddProduct(Product product)
{
    cart.Add(product);
```

```
        total += product.Price;
        NotifyStateChanged();
    }
```

The preceding code adds the indicated product to the list of products and increments the total. It also calls the `NotifyStateChanged` method.

7. Add the `DeleteProduct` method to the class:

```
public void DeleteProduct(Product product)
{
    cart.Remove(product);
    total -= product.Price;
    NotifyStateChanged();
}
```

The preceding code removes the indicated product from the list of products and decrements the total. It also calls the `NotifyStateChanged` method.

We have completed the `CartService` class. Now we need to register `CartService` in the DI container.

Registering CartService in the DI container

We need to register `CartService` in the DI container before we can inject it into our `Store` component. We do this as follows:

1. Open the `Program.cs` file.

2. Add the following code after the code that registers `HttpClient`:

```
builder.Services.AddScoped<ICartService, CartService>();
```

We have registered `CartService`. Now we need to update the `Store` page to use it.

Injecting CartService into the Store component

We need to inject the `CartService` into the `Store` component. We do this as follows:

1. Open the `Pages\Store.razor` file.

2. Add the following directives:

```
@using ShoppingCart.Services
@inject ICartService cartService
```

3.   Update the @onclick event of the **Add to Cart** button to the following:

```
@onclick="@(() => cartService.AddProduct(item))"
```

The preceding markup uses cartService to add products to the cart.

4.   Update the cart element to the following:

```
@if (cartService.Cart.Any())
{
    <h2>Your Cart</h2>
    <ul class="list-group">
        @foreach (Product item in cartService.Cart)
        {
                <li class="list-group-item p-2">
                <button class="btn btn-sm btn-danger me-2">
                    Delete
                </button>
                @item.ProductName - $@item.Price
            </li>
        }
    </ul>
    <div class="p-2">
        <h3>Total: $@cartService.Total</h3>
    </div>
}
```

The preceding code replaces references to the cart property with references to the cartService.

5.   Add the following @onclick event to the **Delete** button:

```
@onclick="@(() =>cartService.DeleteProduct(item))"
```

The preceding markup uses cartService to delete products from the cart.

6.   Delete the cart property, the total property, the AddProduct method, and the DeleteProduct method from the code block.

7.   Press *Ctrl+F5* to start the application without debugging.

8.   Click on the **Start Shopping** button.

9.   Add a few products to the cart using the **Add to Cart** button.

10. Delete a product from the cart using the **Delete** button.

11. Select the **Home** option on the navigation menu.

12. Return to the **Store** page by clicking on the **Start Shopping** button.

13. Confirm that the cart is not empty.

We have confirmed that CartService is working. Now we need to add the cart total to all the pages.

Adding the cart total to all the pages

To view the cart total on all the pages, we need to add the cart total to a component that is used on all the pages. Since the MainLayout component is used by all the pages, we will add the cart total to it. We do this as follows:

1. Return to Visual Studio.

2. Open the Shared\MainLayout.razor file.

3. Add the following @using directive:

   ```
   @using ShoppingCart.Services
   ```

4. Add the following @inject directive:

   ```
   @inject ICartService cartService
   ```

5. Add the following markup above the main element:

   ```
   <div class="alert alert-primary">
       <h2>Cart Total: $@cartService.Total</h2>
   </div>
   ```

6. Press *Ctrl+F5* to start the application without debugging.

7. Add a few items to the cart.

8. Confirm that the **Cart Total** field at the top of the page does not update.

The cart total at the top of the page is not being updated as we add new items to the cart. We need to deal with this.

Using the OnChange method

We need to notify the component when it needs to be updated. We do this as follows:

1. Return to Visual Studio.

2. Open the Shared\MainLayout.razor file.

3. Add the following @implements directive:

```
@implements IDisposable
```

4. Add the following @code block:

```
@code{
    protected override void OnInitialized()
    {
        cartService.OnChange += StateHasChanged;
    }
    public void Dispose()
    {
        cartService.OnChange -= StateHasChanged;
    }
}
```

In the preceding code, the component's StateHasChanged method is subscribed to the cartService.OnChange method in the OnInitialized method and unsubscribed in the Dispose method.

5. Press *Ctrl+F5* to start the application without debugging.

6. Add a few products to the cart using the **Add to Cart** button.

7. Confirm that the **Cart Total** field at the top of the page updates.

8. Delete a product from the cart using the **Delete** button.

9. Confirm that the **Cart Total** field at the top of the page updates.

10. Select the **Home** option on the navigation menu.

11. Confirm that the **Cart Total** field is correctly displayed at the top of the **Home** page.

We have updated the component to call the StateHasChanged method whenever the OnChange method of CartService is invoked.

TIP

Do not forget to unsubscribe from the event when you dispose of the component.

You must unsubscribe from the event to prevent the StateHasChanged method from being invoked every time the cartService.OnChange event is raised. Otherwise, your application will experience resource leaks.

Summary

You should now be able to use DI to apply the `AppState` pattern to a Blazor WebAssembly app.

In this chapter, we introduced the application state and DI. We explained how to use a DI container and how to inject a service into a component. We also discussed the differences between the singleton, scoped, and transient service lifetimes.

After that, we used the **Blazor WebAssembly App Empty** project template to create a new project. We installed `Bootstrap` to style the frontend. We added a `Store` component to the project and demonstrated that the application state is lost when we navigate between pages. To maintain the application's state, we registered the `CartService` service in the DI container. Finally, we demonstrated that by using the `AppState` pattern, we can maintain the shopping cart's state.

We can apply our new skills with DI to maintain the application state for any Blazor WebAssembly app.

In the next chapter, we will build a Kanban board using events.

Questions

The following questions are provided for your consideration:

1. Can `localStorage` be used to maintain the cart's state when the page is reloaded?
2. Why don't we need to call the `StateHasChanged` method in the `Store` component?
3. How would you update the cart to allow for the addition of more than one of each type of product at a time?
4. When using DI, what is the difference between the various service lifetimes?

Further reading

The following resources provide more information concerning the topics covered in this chapter:

*   For more information on DI, refer to `https://learn.microsoft.com/en-us/aspnet/core/fundamentals/dependency-injection?view=aspnetcore-7.0`.
*   For more information on events, refer to `https://learn.microsoft.com/en-us/dotnet/csharp/programming-guide/events/`.

Join our community on Discord

Join our community's Discord space for discussions with the author and other readers:

`https://packt.link/BlazorWASM2e`

8

Building a Kanban Board Using Events

As developers, we strive to make our applications as dynamic as possible. For that, we use **events**. Events are messages sent by an object to indicate that an action has occurred. Razor components can handle many different types of events.

In this chapter, we will learn how to handle different types of events in a Blazor WebAssembly app. We will learn how to use lambda expressions and how to prevent default actions. We will also learn how to use both **arbitrary parameters** and **attribute splatting** to simplify how we assign attributes to components.

The project that we create in this chapter will be a Kanban board that uses the drag-and-drop API. Kanban boards visually depict work at various stages of a process. Our Kanban board will be comprised of three Dropzone components, with each one representing a different stage. Finally, we will use arbitrary parameters and attribute splatting to create a component to add new tasks to our Kanban board.

Events need handling.

Built-in event arguments

lambda expressions.

In this chapter, we will cover the following topics:

- Event handling
- Attribute splatting
- Arbitrary parameters
- Creating the Kanban board project

Technical requirements

To complete this project, you need to have Visual Studio 2022 installed on your PC. For instructions on how to install the free Community Edition of Visual Studio 2022, refer to *Chapter 1, Introduction to Blazor WebAssembly*.

The source code for this chapter is available in the following GitHub repository: `https://github.com/PacktPublishing/Blazor-WebAssembly-by-Example-Second-Edition/tree/main/Chapter08`.

The Code in Action video is available here: `https://packt.link/Ch8`.

Event handling

Razor components handle events by using an HTML element attribute named `@on{EVENT}`, where `EVENT` is the name of the event.

The following code calls the `OnClickHandler` method when the **Click Me** button is clicked:

```
<button type="button" @onclick="OnClickHandler">
    Click Me
</button>


@code {
    private void OnClickHandler()
    {
        // ...
    }
}
```

Event handlers automatically trigger a UI render. Therefore, we do not need to call `StateHasChanged` when processing them. Event handlers can reference any arguments that are associated with the event. Also, they can be used to call both synchronous and asynchronous methods.

The following code calls the asynchronous `OnChangeHandlerAsync` method when the checkbox is changed:

```
<input type="checkbox" @onchange="OnChangedHandlerAsync" />Is OK?

@code {
    bool isOk;
    private async Task OnChangedHandlerAsync(ChangeEventArgs e)
    {
        isOk = (bool)e.Value!;
        // await ...
    }
}
```

In the preceding code, the `ChangeEventArgs` class is used to supply information about the change event. The `ChangeEventArgs` class only had one property. It is the `Value` property and for this object, it is either `true` or `false`.

TIP

The event arguments are optional and should only be included if they are used by the method.

The `ChangeEventArgs` class inherits from the `EventArgs` class. All of the `EventArgs` classes that are supported by the ASP.NET Core framework are also supported by the Blazor WebAssembly framework. This is a list of the supported `EventArgs`:

- `ClipboardEventArgs`
- `DragEventArgs`
- `ErrorEventArgs`
- `EventArgs`
- `FocusEventArgs`
- `ChangeEventArgs`
- `KeyboardEventArgs`
- `MouseEventArgs`
- `PointerEventArgs`

- WheelEventArgs
- ProgressEventArgs
- TouchEventArgs

The EventArgs class is inherited by each of the preceding classes. We can create our own custom event data class by creating a class that derives from the EventArgs class.

So far, we have looked at ways to call a method without any arguments or with arguments that are automatically supplied by the event. However, sometimes we need to provide our own arguments.

Lambda expressions

When we need to provide arguments to a method, we can use a lambda expression. Lambda expressions are used to create anonymous functions. They use the => operator to separate the parameters from the body of the expression.

There are two forms that the body of a lambda expression can use. They can either use an expression or a statement block for their body. In the following example, the first button uses an expression and the second button uses a statement block:

```
<h1>@message</h1>

<button type="button"
        @onclick="@(() => SetMessage("Blazor is Awesome!"))">
    Who Is Awesome?
</button>

<button type="button"
        @onclick="@(() => { @message = "Blazor Rocks!"; })">
    Who Rocks?
</button>

@code{
    private string? message;
    private void SetMessage(string newMessage)
    {
        message = newMessage;

    }
}
```

In the preceding code, when the **Who Is Awesome?** button is clicked, the lambda expression calls the SetMessage method to update the value of the message field. When the **Who Rocks?** button is clicked, the statement lambda expression uses a statement to update the value of the message field.

> **TIP**
>
> If the body of a statement lambda only includes one statement, the parentheses are optional. Also, although you can include any number of statements in the body of a statement lambda, we recommend limiting the number of statements to two or three at most.

Preventing default actions

Occasionally, we need to prevent the default action associated with an event. We can do that by using the @on{EVENT}:preventDefault directive attribute, where EVENT is the name of the event.

For example, when dragging an element, the default behavior prevents it from being dropped into another element. However, for the Kanban board project in this chapter, we will need to drop items into various dropzones. Therefore, we will need to prevent that default behavior.

The following code prevents the ondragover default behavior from occurring. By preventing the default behavior, we will be allowed to drop elements into the div element that is being used as the dropzone:

```
<div class="dropzone"
    dropzone="true"
    ondragover="event.preventDefault();">
</div>
```

Focusing an element

There are times when we need to programmatically give focus to an HTML element. In those cases, we use the FocusAsync method of the ElementReference type. The ElementReference is identified by adding an @ref attribute to the HTML element that we want to give focus to. To assign focus to the HTML element a field of type ElementReference must be defined.

The following code adds the value of the input element to the list of tasks and sets the focus back to the input element each time the button is clicked:

Focus.razor

```
@page "/focus"

<input type="text" @ref="taskInput" @bind-value="@taskName" />
<button type="button" @onclick="OnClickHandlerAsync">
    Add Task
 </button>

@foreach (var item in tasks)
{
    <div>@item</div>
}

@code {
    private string? taskName;
    private ElementReference taskInput;
    private List<string> tasks = new();

    private async Task OnClickHandlerAsync()
    {
        tasks.Add(taskName!);
        taskName = "";
        await taskInput.FocusAsync();
    }
}
```

In the preceding code, taskInput is defined as an ElementReference. It is associated with the input element via the @ref attribute. In the OnClickHandlerAsync event, the FocusAsync method is called. The result is that each time the button is clicked, the focus is returned to the input element.

IMPORTANT NOTE

Since the FocusAsync method relies on the DOM, it only works on elements after they have been rendered.

The Blazor WebAssembly framework makes it easy for us to access events by using the @on{EVENT} attribute. All the EventArgs that we are used to using in the ASP.NET framework are supported. We use lambda expressions to provide arguments for the methods that are called by the event. We use the preventDefault directive attribute to prevent default actions. Finally, the FocusAsync method of the ElementReference type is used to programmatically assign focus to an HTML element.

When working with components, we usually need to supply multiple attributes. Using attribute splatting, we can avoid assigning the attributes directly in the HTML markup.

Attribute splatting

When a child component has many parameters, it can be tedious to assign each of the values in HTML. To avoid having to do that, we can use attribute splatting.

With attribute splatting, the attributes are captured in a dictionary and then passed to the component as a unit. One attribute is added per dictionary entry. The dictionary must implement IEnumerable<KeyValuePair<string,object>> or IReadOnlyDictionary<string, object> with string keys. We reference the dictionary using the @attributes directive.

This is the code for a component called BweButton that has a bunch of different parameters:

BweButton.razor

```
<button type="@Type"
        class="@Class"
        disabled="@Disabled"
        title="@Title"
        @onclick="@ClickEvent">
    @ChildContent
</button>

@code {
  [Parameter] public string? Class { get; set; }
  [Parameter] public bool Disabled { get; set; }
  [Parameter] public string? Title { get; set; }
  [Parameter] public string? Type { get; set; }
  [Parameter] public EventCallback ClickEvent { get; set; }
  [Parameter] public RenderFragment? ChildContent { get; set; }
}
```

This is sample markup to render a `BweButton` component without using attribute splatting:

```
<BweButton Class="button button-red"
           Disabled="false"
           Title="This is a red button"
           Type="button"
           ClickEvent="OnClickHandler">
    Submit
</BweButton>
```

This is the button that is rendered by the preceding markup:

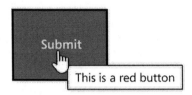

Figure 8.1: Rendered BweButton

This is the CSS that we are using to style the buttons in this section:

```
.button {
    color: white;
    cursor: pointer;
    padding: 2em;
}

.button-red {
    background-color: red;
}

.button-black {
    background-color: black;
}
```

In the preceding CSS, all the elements in the `button` class will have white text and 2em of padding. The elements in the `button-red` class will have a background color of red, and the elements in the `button-black` class will have a background color of black.

By using attribute splatting, we can simplify the preceding markup to the following:

```
<BweButton @attributes="InputAttributes"
           ClickEvent="OnClickHandler">
    Submit
</BweButton>
```

This is the definition of InputAttributes used by the preceding markup:

```
public Dictionary<string, object> InputAttributes { get; set; } =
    new ()
    {
        { "Class", "button button-red"},
        { "Disabled", false},
        { "Title", "This is a red button" },
        { "Type", "submit" }
    };
```

The preceding code defines the InputAttributes that are passed to BweButton. The resulting button is identical to the previous one where we set the attributes directly without using InputAttributes.

The real power of attribute splatting is realized when it is combined with arbitrary parameters.

Arbitrary parameters

In the preceding example, we used explicitly defined parameters to assign the button's attributes. A much more efficient way of assigning values to attributes is to use arbitrary parameters. An arbitrary parameter is a parameter that is not explicitly defined by the component. The Parameter attribute has a CaptureUnmatchedValues property that is used to allow the parameter to capture values that don't match any of the other parameters.

This is a new version of our button called BweButton2. It uses arbitrary parameters:

BweButton2.razor

```
<button @attributes="InputAttributes" >
    @ChildContent
</button>

@code {
```

```
[Parameter(CaptureUnmatchedValues = true)]
public Dictionary<string, object>? InputAttributes{get; set;}


[Parameter]
public RenderFragment? ChildContent { get; set; }
}
```

The preceding code includes a parameter named `InputAttributes` that has its `CaptureUnmatchedValues` property set to true.

IMPORTANT NOTE

A component can only have one parameter with its `CaptureUnmatchedValues` property set to `true`.

This is the updated markup used to render the new version of our button:

```
<BweButton2 @attributes="InputAttributes2"
            @onclick="OnClickHandler"
            class="button button-black">
    Submit
</BweButton2>
```

This is the definition of `InputAttributes2` used by the preceding markup:

```
public Dictionary<string, object> InputAttributes2 { get; set; } =
    new()
    {
        { "class", "button button-red" },
        { "title", "This is another button" },
        { "name", "btnSubmit" },
        { "type", "button" },
        { "myAttribute", "123"}
    };
```

Although none of the attributes in the dictionary have been explicitly defined in the new version of our button, BweButton2 is still rendered. In the preceding example, the class attribute is set twice.

This is the button that is rendered by the preceding code:

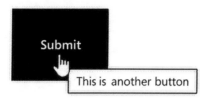

Figure 8.2: Rendered BweButton2 using arbitrary parameters

The reason the button is now black is due to the position of the @attributes directive in the button's markup. When attributes are splatted onto an element, they are processed from left to right. Therefore, if there are duplicate attributes assigned, the one that appears later in the order will be the one that is used.

Arbitrary parameters are used to allow previously undefined attributes to be rendered by the component. This is useful with components that support a large variety of customizations, such as a component that includes an input element.

Now, let's get a quick overview of the project that we are going to build in this chapter.

Creating the Kanban board project

The Blazor WebAssembly application that we are going to build in this chapter is a Kanban board. The Kanban board will have three dropzones: High Priority, Mid Priority, and Low Priority. We will be able to drag and drop tasks between the dropzones and add additional tasks. As each task is dragged to a different dropzone, the badge indicator on the task will be updated to match the dropzone's priority.

The following is a screenshot of the completed application:

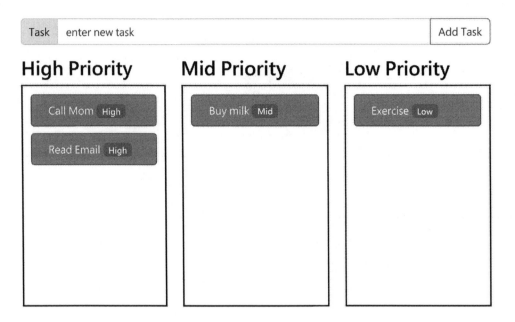

Figure 8.3: Kanban board app

The build time for this project is approximately 45 minutes.

Project overview

The KanbanBoard project will be created by using Microsoft's **Blazor WebAssembly App Empty** project template to create an empty Blazor WebAssembly project. First, we will add Bootstrap to the project. Then, we will create both the TaskItem class and a Dropzone component. We will add three of the Dropzone components to the Home page to create the Kanban board. Finally, we will add the NewTask component so that we are able to add new tasks to the Kanban board.

Create the Kanban board project

We need to create a new Blazor WebAssembly app. We do this as follows:

1. Open Visual Studio 2022.

2. Click the **Create a new project** button.

3. Press *Alt+S* to enter the search for templates textbox.

4. Enter Blazor and press the *Enter* key.

The following screenshot shows the **Blazor WebAssembly App Empty** project template.

Figure 8.4: Blazor WebAssembly App Empty project template

5. Select the **Blazor WebAssembly App Empty** project template and click the **Next** button.

6. Enter KanbanBoard in the **Project name** textbox and click the **Next** button.

This is a screenshot of the dialog used to configure our new project:

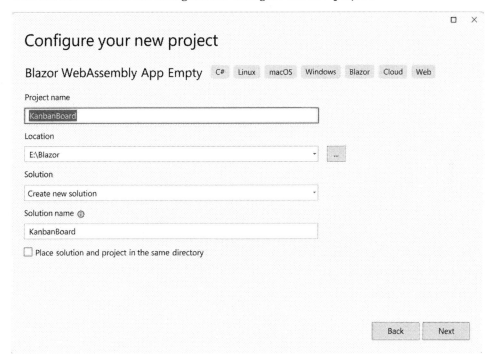

Figure 8.5: Configure your new project dialog

TIP

In the preceding example, we placed the KanbanBoard project into the E:/ Blazor folder. However, the location of this project is not important.

7. Select **.NET 7.0** as the version of the **Framework** to use.

8. Check the **Configure for HTTPS** checkbox.

9. Uncheck the **ASP.NET Core Hosted** checkbox.

10. Uncheck the **Progressive Web Application** checkbox.

This is a screenshot of the dialog used to collect additional information about our new project:

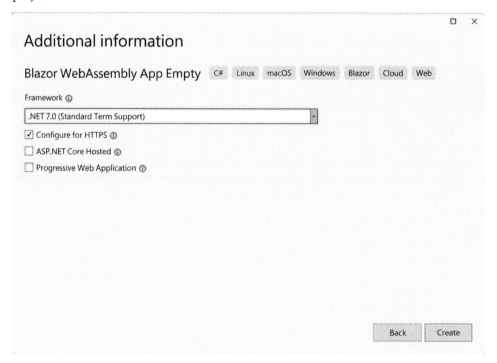

Figure 8.6: Additional information dialog

11. Click the **Create** button.

We have created an empty KanbanBoard Blazor WebAssembly project. We will use Bootstrap's grid system to lay out our board.

Install Bootstrap

We need to install Bootstrap into our web app. We do this as follows:

1. Right-click the wwwroot/css folder and select the **Add, Client-Side Library** option from the menu.

2. Enter bootstrap into the **Library** search textbox and press the *Enter* key.

3. Select **Choose specific files**.

4. Select only the **css** files as shown in the following screenshot.

Add Client-Side Library   ✕

Provider: cdnjs ⌄

Library: bootstrap@5.2.2   ⓘ

○ Include all library files

◉ Choose specific files:

▲ ■ 📁 Files:
  ▷ ✓ 📁 css
  ▷ ☐ 📁 js
  ▷ ☐ 📁 scss

Target Location: wwwroot/css/bootstrap/

                                        Install   Cancel

Figure 8.7: Add Client-Side Library dialog

TIP

Although the preceding screenshot has version 5.2.2 of Bootstrap selected, you can use any version of Bootstrap to complete this project.

5. Click the **Install** button.

IMPORTANT NOTE

After you install Bootstrap, a new folder will be added to the wwwroot/css folder. This new folder contains all the CSS files needed for Bootstrap. We will only be using the bootstrap.min.css file in this project.

6. Open the wwwroot/index.html file.

7. Add the following markup to the head element before the link to the css/app.css stylesheet:

```
<link href="css/bootstrap/css/bootstrap.min.css"
        rel="stylesheet" />
```

8. Open the MainLayout.razor file.

9. Update the main element to the following:

```
<main class="container">
    @Body
</main>
```

The preceding code adds a container around the body of the page. In this project, we will be using Bootstrap's grid system to lay out our content. It relies on a series of containers, rows, and columns. We will add the rows and columns later.

We will use the Kanban board to prioritize our tasks. But first, we need a way to define our tasks.

Add the classes

We need to add a TaskPriority enum and a TaskItem class. We do this as follows:

1. Right-click the KanbanBoard project and select the **Add**, **New Folder** option from the menu.

2. Name the new folder Models.

3. Right-click the Models folder and select the **Add**, **Class** option from the menu.

4. Name the new class TaskPriority.

5. Click the **Add** button.

6. Replace the class with the following TaskPriority enum:

```
public enum TaskPriority
{
    High,
    Mid,
    Low
}
```

7. Right-click the Models folder and select the **Add**, **Class** option from the menu.

8. Name the new class TaskItem.

9. Click the **Add** button.

10. Add the following properties to the TaskItem class:

```
public string? TaskName { get; set; }
public TaskPriority Priority { get; set; }
```

We have added the TaskPriority enum and the TaskItem class to represent the tasks on the Kanban board. Next, we need to create the dropzones.

Create the Dropzone component

We need to add a Dropzone component. We do this as follows:

1. Right-click the KanbanBoard project and select the **Add, New Folder** option from the menu.

2. Name the new folder Shared.

3. Right-click the Shared folder and select the **Add, Razor Component** option from the menu.

4. Name the new component Dropzone.

5. Click the **Add** button.

6. Remove the h3 element.

7. Add the following @using directive:

```
@using KanbanBoard.Models
```

8. Add the following parameters to the code block:

```
[Parameter]
public List<TaskItem> TaskItems { get; set; } = new();

[Parameter]
public TaskPriority Priority { get; set; }

[Parameter]
public EventCallback<TaskPriority> OnDrop { get; set; }

[Parameter]
public EventCallback<TaskItem> OnStartDrag { get; set; }
```

In the preceding code, the TaskItems parameter is used to keep track of the tasks that have been dropped into the Dropzone. The Priority parameter is used to indicate the priority of the tasks that are in the Dropzone.

The `OnDrop` event indicates the event that is invoked when a task is dropped into the `Dropzone`, and the `OnStartDrag` event indicates the event that is invoked when a task is dragged from the `Dropzone`.

9. Add the following markup:

```
<div class="col">
    <h2 style="">@Priority.ToString() Priority</h2>
    <div class="dropzone"
         ondragover="event.preventDefault();"
         @ondrop="OnDropHandler">

        @foreach (var item in TaskItems
            .Where(q => q.Priority == Priority))
            {

            }
    </div>
</div>
```

The preceding markup labels the `Dropzone` by its priority and allows elements to be dropped into it by preventing the default value of the ondragover event. The `OnDropHandler` method is called when an element is dropped into the `Dropzone`. Finally, it loops through all the items in the `TaskItems` class with the matching `Priority`.

10. Add the following markup within the @foreach loop:

```
<div class="draggable"
    draggable="true"
    @ondragstart="@(() => OnDragStartHandler(item))">

    @item.TaskName
    <span class="badge text-bg-secondary">
        @item.Priority
    </span>

</div>
```

The preceding markup makes the `div` element draggable by setting the `draggable` attribute to `true`. The `OnDragStartHandler` method is called when the element is dragged.

11. Add the following `OnDropHandler` method to the code block:

```
private void OnDropHandler()
{
    OnDrop.InvokeAsync(Priority);
}
```

The preceding code invokes the `OnDrop` method.

12. Add the following `OnDragStartHandler` method to the code block:

```
private void OnDragStartHandler(TaskItem task)
{
    OnStartDrag.InvokeAsync(task);
}
```

The preceding code invokes the `OnStartDrag` method.

We have added a `Dropzone` component. Now we need to add some styling to the component.

Add a stylesheet

We will add a stylesheet to the `Dropzone` component using CSS isolation. We do this as follows:

1. Right-click the `Shared` folder and select the **Add, New Item** option from the menu.

2. Enter `css` in the **Search** box.

3. Select **Style Sheet**.

4. Name the style sheet `Dropzone.razor.css`.

5. Click the **Add** button.

6. Enter the following styles:

```
.draggable {
    margin-bottom: 10px;
    padding: 10px 25px;
    border: 1px solid #424d5c;
    background: #ff6a00;
```

```
        color: #ffffff;
        border-radius: 5px;
        cursor: grab;
}

    .draggable:active {
        cursor: grabbing;
    }

.dropzone {
    padding: .75rem;
    border: 2px solid black;
    min-height: 20rem;
}
}
```

TIP

You can copy the Dropzone.razor.css file from the GitHub repository.

7. Open the wwwroot/index.html file.

8. Uncomment the following link element at the bottom of the head element:

```
<link href="KanbanBoard.styles.css" rel="stylesheet" />
```

We have finished styling the Dropzone component. Now we can put the Kanban board together.

Create the Kanban board

We need to add three Dropzone components to create our Kanban board, one for each of the three types of tasks. We do this as follows:

1. Open the _Imports.razor file.

2. Add the following using statements:

```
@using KanbanBoard.Models
@using KanbanBoard.Shared
```

3. Open the Pages\Index.razor file.

4. Remove the h1 element.

5. Add the following markup:

```
<PageTitle>Kanban Board</PageTitle>

<div class="row">
    <Dropzone Priority="TaskPriority.High"
            TaskItems="TaskItems"
            OnDrop="OnDrop"
            OnStartDrag="OnStartDrag" />

    <Dropzone Priority="TaskPriority.Mid"
            TaskItems="TaskItems"
            OnDrop="OnDrop"
            OnStartDrag="OnStartDrag" />

    <Dropzone Priority="TaskPriority.Low"
            TaskItems="TaskItems"
            OnDrop="OnDrop"
            OnStartDrag="OnStartDrag" />
</div>
```

The preceding code adds three Dropzone components, one for each priority.

6. Add the following code block:

```
@code {
    public TaskItem? CurrentItem;
    List<TaskItem> TaskItems = new();

    protected override void OnInitialized()
    {
        TaskItems.Add(new TaskItem
        {
            TaskName = "Call Mom",
            Priority = TaskPriority.High
        });

        TaskItems.Add(new TaskItem
        {
```

```
            TaskName = "Buy milk",
            Priority = TaskPriority.Mid
        });

        TaskItems.Add(new TaskItem
        {
            TaskName = "Exercise",
            Priority = TaskPriority.Low
        });
    }
}
```

The preceding code initializes the `TaskItems` object with three tasks.

7. Add the `OnStartDrag` method to the code block:

```
private void OnStartDrag(TaskItem item)
{
    CurrentItem = item;
}
```

The preceding code sets the value of `CurrentItem` to the item that is currently being dragged. We will use this value when the item is subsequently dropped. The `Dropzone` component invokes this method when the `@ondragstart` event is triggered.

8. Add the `OnDrop` method to the code block:

```
private void OnDrop(TaskPriority priority)
{
    CurrentItem!.Priority = priority;
}
```

The preceding code sets the `Priority` property of the `CurrentItem` to the priority associated with the `Dropzone` that `CurrentItem` is dropped into. The `Dropzone` component invokes this method when the `@ondrop` event is triggered.

9. Press *Ctrl+F5* to start the application without debugging.

10. Drag all the tasks to the **High Priority** dropzone.

After you drop each task into the **High Priority** dropzone, verify that the badge on the task is updated to **High**.

We have created a very simple Kanban board with three items. Let's add the ability to add more items through the UI.

Create the NewTask component

We need to add a NewTask component. We do this as follows:

1. Return to Visual Studio.

2. Right-click the Shared folder and select the **Add, Razor Component** option from the menu.

3. Name the new component NewTask.

4. Click the **Add** button.

5. Remove the h3 element.

6. Add the following markup:

```
<div class="row pt-3" >
    <div class="input-group mb-3">
        <label class="input-group-text"
          for="inputTask">
            Task
        </label>

        <input @ref="taskInput"
               type="text"
               id="inputTask"
               class="form-control"
               @bind-value="@taskName"
               @attributes="InputParameters" />

        <button type="button"
                class="btn btn-outline-secondary"
                @onclick="OnClickHandlerAsync">
            Add Task
        </button>
    </div>
</div>
```

The preceding markup includes a label, a textbox, and a button. The textbox includes an @ref attribute that we will use later to set focus to the textbox.

This is a screenshot of the `NewTask` component that we are working on:

Figure 8.8: NewTask component

7. Add the following code to the code block:

```
private string? taskName;
private ElementReference taskInput;

[Parameter(CaptureUnmatchedValues = true)]
public Dictionary<string, object>?
    InputParameters{ get; set; }

[Parameter]
public EventCallback<string> OnSubmit { get; set; }
```

The preceding code defines a parameter, `InputParameters`, that will be used for attribute splatting.

8. Add the `OnClickHandlerAsync` method to the code block:

```
private async Task OnClickHandlerAsync()
{
    if (!string.IsNullOrWhiteSpace(taskName))
    {
        await OnSubmit.InvokeAsync(taskName);
        taskName = null;
        await taskInput.FocusAsync();
    }
}
```

The preceding code invokes the `OnSubmit` method, sets the `taskName` field to `null`, and sets the focus to the `taskInput` object.

We have now created the `NewTask` component. Next, we need to start using it.

Use the NewTask component

We need to add the NewTask component to the Home page. We do this as follows:

1. Open the Pages\Index.razor file.

2. Add the following markup below the PageTitle component:

```
<NewTask OnSubmit="AddTask"
        @attributes="InputAttributes" />
```

3. Add the following code to the code block:

```
public Dictionary<string, object> InputAttributes = new ()
{
    { "maxlength", "25" },
    { "placeholder", "enter new task" },
    { "title", "This textbox is for adding your tasks." }
};
```

In the preceding code, properties are being set without being explicitly defined.

4. Add the AddTask method to the code block:

```
private void AddTask(string taskName)
{
    var taskItem = new TaskItem()
        {
            TaskName = taskName,
            Priority = TaskPriority.High
        };
    TaskItems.Add(taskItem);
}
```

The preceding code sets the priority of the new item to High and adds it to the TaskItems object.

5. Press *Ctrl+F5* to start the application without debugging.

6. Enter a new task and click the **Add Task** button.

When the **Add Task** button of the NewTask component is clicked, the AddTask method is invoked. The textbox is cleared, and the focus is returned to the textbox.

7. Enter another new task and click the **Add Task** button.

8. Drag and drop the tasks to change their priorities.

We have added the ability to add new tasks to the Kanban board.

Summary

You should now be able to handle events in your Blazor WebAssembly app. Also, you should be comfortable with using attribute splatting and arbitrary parameters.

In this chapter, we introduced event handling. We explained how to use EventArgs and how to use lambda expressions to provide arguments to a method. We also explained how to prevent default actions and how to use the @ref attribute to programmatically set the focus to a particular element. Finally, we introduced both attribute splatting and arbitrary parameters.

After that, we used the **Blazor WebAssembly App Empty** project template to create a new project and added Bootstrap to the project. Next, we added a Dropzone component to the project and used it to create a Kanban board. Finally, we added the ability to add tasks to the Kanban board while demonstrating both attribute splatting and arbitrary parameters.

Now that you know how to handle different types of events in your Blazor WebAssembly app, you can create more responsive applications. And, since you can use a dictionary to pass both explicitly declared attributes and implicit attributes to a component, you can create components faster since you do not need to explicitly define each parameter.

In the next chapter, we will create an application that can upload and read an Excel file.

Questions

The following questions are provided for your consideration:

1. How can you update the Kanban board to allow the user to delete a task?

2. Why would you want to include an attribute in the dictionary used for attribute splatting that is not defined on the component, either explicitly or implicitly?

3. What is the base class of the DragEventArgs class?

Further reading

The following resources provide more information concerning the topics covered in this chapter:

- For more information on **Document Object Model (DOM)** events, refer to `https://developer.mozilla.org/en-US/docs/Web/Events`.

- For more information on the `EventArgs` class, refer to `https://learn.microsoft.com/en-us/dotnet/api/system.eventargs`.

- For more information on the `DragEventArgs` class, refer to `https://learn.microsoft.com/en-us/dotnet/api/microsoft.aspnetcore.components.web.drageventargs`.

9

Uploading and Reading an Excel File

There are many different scenarios that require a web app to allow users to upload local files. Also, there are just as many different types of files that a user may need to upload.

In this chapter, we will learn how to upload different types of files by using the **InputFile** component. We will learn how to upload image files and how to resize the images that are uploaded. We will also learn how to perform virtualization by using the **Virtualize** component to only render the visible data. Finally, we will learn how to read a Microsoft Excel file by using the **Open XML SDK**.

The project that we create in this chapter will be an Excel reader that will allow us to upload an Excel file and view its contents in a table, using virtualization.

Decipher the parts

to read an Excel file –

not complicated!

In this chapter, we will cover the following topics:

- Uploading files
- Using virtualization
- Reading Excel files
- Creating the Excel reader project

Technical requirements

To complete this project, you need to have Visual Studio 2022 installed on your PC. For instructions on how to install the free Community Edition of Visual Studio 2022, refer to *Chapter 1, Introduction to Blazor WebAssembly*.

The source code for this chapter is available in the following GitHub repository: `https://github.com/PacktPublishing/Blazor-WebAssembly-by-Example-Second-Edition/tree/main/Chapter09`.

The Code in Action video is available here: `https://packt.link/Ch9`.

Uploading files

The `InputFile` component is a built-in Blazor component that is used to upload files into a Blazor app. It renders an HTML `input` element of type `file` and supplies a stream for the contents of the file. It is in the `Microsoft.AspNetCore.Components.Forms` namespace.

The `OnChange` event of the `InputFile` component is used to set the callback that gets invoked when a file is selected. This is an example of an `InputFile` component that invokes the `OnChangeHandler` method when a file is selected:

```
<InputFile OnChange="OnChangeHandler"
           accept="image/png, image/jpeg" />
```

This is the resulting HTML markup from the preceding example:

```
<input accept="image/png, image/jpeg" type="file" _bl_2="">
```

In the preceding HTML markup, the _bl_2 attribute is used for Blazor's internal processing, but everything else is a typical `input` element. The `accept` attribute is used to filter the types of files that are displayed in the **Select File** dialog.

The following screenshot shows how the preceding markup is rendered:

Choose File   No file chosen

Figure 9.1: Rendered InputFile component

When the **Choose File** button of the `InputFile` component is clicked, the **Select File** dialog opens to allow the user to select a file. This is a screenshot of the **Select File** dialog:

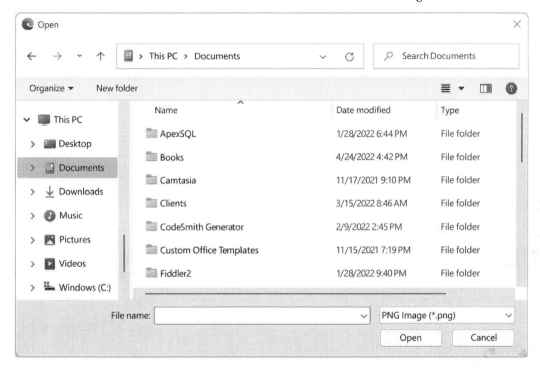

Figure 9.2: Select File dialog

IMPORTANT NOTE

Although we have indicated that only files of type `image/png` and `image/jpg` should be accepted, the **Select File** dialog allows the user to select **All files (*.*)** via the file type selector. Therefore, there is never any guarantee concerning the type of file that the user has selected.

The InputFileChangeEventArgs class is used to supply information about the OnChange event being raised. The following code sets the selectedFile field to the value of the File property of the InputFileChangeEventArgs object, provided to the OnChangeHandler method:

```
IBrowserFile? selectedFile;

private void OnChangeHandler(InputFileChangeEventArgs e)
{
    selectedFile = e.File;
}
```

The File property represents the uploaded file and is of type IBrowserFile.

These are the properties of the IBrowserFile interface:

- ContentType – the MIME type of the file
- LastModified – the last modified date of the file
- Name – the name of the file
- Size – the size of the file in bytes

IMPORTANT NOTE

You should never trust a file that is uploaded from the internet. You should treat it as a potential security risk to your app, server, and network. The ContentType, LastModified, Name, and Size properties can all be manipulated to cause your system harm and cannot be trusted.

The IBrowserFile interface only has one method. It is the OpenReadStream method that is used to read the uploaded file. By default, the maximum size of the stream is 500 KB. However, the maxAllowedSize parameter can be used to increase the maximum size of the stream. In the following example, the maximum size of the stream is set to the value of MAXFILESIZE:

```
var stream = await file.OpenReadStream(MAXFILESIZE);
```

Resizing images

Images can be quite large. Sometimes we need to restrict the size of images that are allowed to be uploaded into an application. In those cases, we can use the RequestImageFileAsync method to resize the image. These are the parameters of the RequestImageFileAsync method:

- Format – the format of the new image
- MaxWidth – the maximum width of the new image
- MaxHeight – the maximum height of the new image

IMPORTANT NOTE

The RequestImageFileAsync method does not verify that the image is a valid one. Therefore, any results should be treated as untrustworthy.

When using the RequestImageFileAsync method, the image is resized using the provided dimensions while preserving the aspect ratio of the original image. The following UploadImage component resizes the uploaded image:

UploadImage.razor

```
@page "/uploadImage"

@using Microsoft.AspNetCore.Components.Forms

<PageTitle>Upload Image</PageTitle>

<h1>Upload Image</h1>

<InputFile OnChange="OnChangeHandler"
    accept="image/png, image/jpeg" />

@if (@image != null)
{
    <p>Old file size: @uploadedFile!.Size.ToString("N0") bytes</p>
    <p>New file size: @resizedFile!.Size.ToString("N0") bytes</p>
    <img src="data:@uploadedFile.ContentType;base64,@image" />
}

@code {
    IBrowserFile? uploadedFile;
    IBrowserFile? resizedFile;
    string? image;
```

```
async Task OnChangeHandler(InputFileChangeEventArgs e)
{
    uploadedFile = e.File;
    resizedFile = await uploadedFile.RequestImageFileAsync(
            uploadedFile.ContentType,
            100,
            100
    );

    var buffer = new byte[resizedFile.Size];
    var stream = await resizedFile.OpenReadStream()
                                  .ReadAsync(buffer);
    image = Convert.ToBase64String(buffer);
}
}
```

The preceding code uses the RequestImageFileAsync method to resize the image to 100 x 100 pixels. It uses the OpenReadStream method to read the file, which is then encoded into a Base64 string. Finally, the image's original size, the resized image's new size, and the resized image itself are all rendered when the value of the image property is no longer null.

TIP

Although our example reads the file directly into memory, we recommend that you copy the stream directly into a file on disk or upload the file to an external service, such as Azure Blob Storage.

This is a screenshot that uses the **Upload Image** page to upload a very large photo, taken on a trip we took to St John, USVI:

Upload Image

Choose File │ StJohn.JPG

Old file size: 6,413,880 bytes

New file size: 4,719 bytes

Figure 9.3: Upload Image results

In the preceding example, we were able to reduce the size of the file from 6,413,880 bytes to 4,719 bytes.

Handling multiple files

By default, the InputFile component only allows for a single file to be selected. However, the InputFile component can be used to upload multiple files by using the multiple attribute, as shown in the following example:

```
<InputFile OnChange="OnChange" multiple />
```

When using the multiple attribute, the FileCount property of InputFileChangeEventArgs is used to determine the number of files that have been uploaded. When allowing for the upload of multiple files, instead of using the File property to access the files, we use the GetMultipleFiles method of InputFileChangeEventArgs to loop through the list of files that have been uploaded.

In the following example, the GetMultipleFiles method is used to return the list of files that were selected. The list of files is then looped through using a foreach loop:

```
async Task OnChange(InputFileChangeEventArgs e)
{
    var files = e.GetMultipleFiles();
    foreach (var file in files)
    {
    // do something
    }
}
```

IMPORTANT NOTE

You cannot add files to the list of files that have been selected. Each time InputFile is used, the previous list of files is replaced by the new list of files.

The InputFile component can be used to upload one or more files at a time to a Blazor WebAssembly app by using the multiple attribute.

The InputFile component can be used to upload many different types of files, such as Excel files and image files. By using the RequestImageFileAsync method, we can resize the images that are uploaded. We can use the multiple attribute to allow users to upload multiple files.

Using virtualization

There are times when we need to work with a large collection of items. In those cases, it is not efficient to render each item. It is much more efficient to only render a subset of the items. This technique is called **virtualization**.

The built-in Virtualize component is used to render the visible items of a collection. Specifically, it is used when we are using a loop to render a collection of items and using scrolling to limit the number of items visible at any given moment. The Virtualize component calculates the list of visible items and only renders those items. Since it does not render items that are invisible, it is more performant than using a method that renders every item in the collection. It can be found in the Microsoft.AspNetCore.Components.Web.Virtualization namespace.

IMPORTANT NOTE

When using the `Virtualize` component, all the items must be the same height in pixels.

The `Virtualize<TItem>` class includes the following properties:

- `ItemContent` – the item template. It is only required when using the `Placeholder` property.
- `Items` – the collection of items. This property cannot be used in conjunction with the `ItemsProvider` method.
- `ItemSize` – the height of each item in pixels. The default is 50 pixels.
- `ItemsProvider` – the function that asynchronously retrieves the collection of items. This property cannot be used in conjunction with the `Items` method.
- `OverscanCount` – the number of items that should be rendered before and after the visible region. When scrolling, this will help to reduce the amount of rendering. The default is 3.
- `Placeholder` – the content that is rendered while the component is waiting for the items to be provided by `ItemsProvider`. This property cannot be used in conjunction with the `Items` method.
- `SpacerElement` – the type of element used to display each item. The default is `div`.

Near our home, there is a weather station that continuously records the current temperature and humidity. There are thousands of data points collected every day.

This is the `Weather` class used to collect the data from the weather station:

```
public class Weather
{
    public DateTime Date { get; set; }

    public int Temperature { get; set; }

    public int Humidity { get; set; }
}
```

The following code will display each of the data points using a `foreach` loop:

```
@using Microsoft.AspNetCore.Components.Web.Virtualization

<div style="height:200px;overflow-y:scroll">
    @foreach (Weather weather in weatherHistory)
    {
        <p>
            @weather.Date.ToShortTimeString():
            Temp:@weather.Temperature
            Humidity:@weather.Humidity
        </p>
    }
</div>
```

In the preceding code, although the `foreach` loop is within a `div` element that limits the number of rows that are displayed, the UI still needs to render all the rows before returning control to the user. Since the collection of `Weather` objects contains thousands of records, the user will experience some lag while waiting for the UI to render all the rows. We can use the `Virtualize` component to only render the data that is being displayed.

Rendering Local Data

The following code uses the `Virtualize` component instead of a `foreach` loop to render the data from memory:

```
<div style="height:200px;overflow-y:scroll">
    <Virtualize Items="@weatherHistory" Context="weather">
        <p>
            @weather.Date.ToShortTimeString():
            Temp:@weather.Temperature
            Humidity:@weather.Humidity
        </p>
    </Virtualize>
</div>
```

The preceding code will allow the page to load faster because only the rows that are visible within the `div` element are rendered. The `Virtualize` component calculates the number of items that can fit inside the container and only renders those items. As the user scrolls through the items, the `Virtualize` component determines which items need to be rendered and renders them.

Rendering Remote Data

The following code uses the `ItemsProvider` method to fetch the list of items to be rendered from a remote data source:

```
<div style="height:200px;overflow-y:scroll">
    <Virtualize ItemsProvider="@LoadWeather"
                Context="weather"
                ItemSize="10"
                OverscanCount="2">
        <ItemContent>
            <p>
                @weather.Date.ToShortTimeString():
                Temp:@weather.Temperature
                Humidity:@weather.Humidity
            </p>
        </ItemContent>
        <Placeholder>
            <p><em>Loading  Weather...</em></p>
        </Placeholder>
    </Virtualize>
</div>
```

In the preceding example, the `LoadWeather` method is invoked when the `Virtualize` component needs to update the list of `Weather` objects that are being rendered.

This is a simple implementation of the `LoadWeather` method:

```
private async ValueTask<ItemsProviderResult<Weather>>
    LoadWeather(ItemsProviderRequest request)
{
    return new ItemsProviderResult<Weather>(
        await FetchWeather(request.StartIndex, request.Count),
        totalCount);
}

private async Task<IEnumerable<Weather>>
    FetchWeather(int start, int count)
{
```

```
    // call a service
}
```

In the preceding code, the `LoadWeather` method takes `ItemsProviderRequest` and returns `ItemsProviderResult`. The important thing to note is that `ItemsProviderRequest` includes both a `StartIndex` property and a `Count` property. `StartIndex` is the start index of the data requested and `Count` is the number of items requested.

In this chapter's project, we will read the values from an Excel spreadsheet that is uploaded into our application. Therefore, we need to learn how to read from an Excel spreadsheet.

Reading Excel files

We can read and write to Microsoft Excel files using the `Open XML SDK`. It provides the tools for us to work with not only Excel files but also Word and PowerPoint files. To use the `Open XML SDK`, we need to add the `DocumentFormat.OpenXml` NuGet package to our project.

Modern Excel files with the XLSX file extension are made up of a compressed collection of XML files. To view the individual files, change the file extension from XLSX to ZIP and view the files using a `.zip` viewer. You can also extract the files.

When using the `Open XML SDK`, the Excel document is represented with the `SpreadsheetDocument` class. This is the hierarchy of the elements in the class:

- `workbook` – the root element of the document
- `sheets` – the container for the sheets
- `sheet` – the pointer to the sheet definition file
- `worksheet` – the sheet definition that contains the sheet data
- `sheetData` – the data
- `row` – a row of data
- `c` – a cell within a row of data
- `v` – the value of a cell

To demonstrate the format of an Excel file, we have created a sample Excel file titled `Sample.xlsx`. The sample workbook includes two worksheets. The first worksheet is titled **Numbers** and the second one is titled **Welcome**. The **Numbers** worksheet includes two rows of numbers, and the **Welcome** worksheet includes the string **Hello World** in cell A1.

This is a screenshot of the `Sample.xlsx` file:

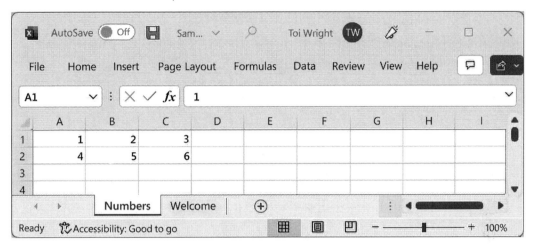

Figure 9.4: Sample.xlsx

 IMPORTANT NOTE

You can download a copy of `Sample.xlsx` from the GitHub repository.

If we change the filename of `Sample.xlsx` to `Sample.zip` and extract all the files, this is the resulting file structure:

Figure 9.5: File structure of Sample.zip

If you are familiar with Microsoft Excel, the files under the x1 folder will look familiar to you. The x1 folder contains a workbook.xml file and a worksheets folder, with a file for each sheet.

The workbook.xml file lists all the sheets in the workbook. The following markup from the workbook.xml file shows the contents of the sheets element:

```
<sheets>
    <sheet name="Numbers" sheetId="1" r:id="rId1"/>
    <sheet name="Welcome" sheetId="2" r:id="rId2"/>
</sheets>
```

This is the code to loop through all the sheets in the given SpreadsheetDocument:

```
private List<string> ReadSheetList(SpreadsheetDocument doc)
{
    List<string> mySheets = new();

    WorkbookPart wbPart = doc.WorkbookPart;
    Sheets sheets = wbPart.Workbook.Sheets;
    foreach (Sheet item in sheets)
    {
        mySheets.Add(item.Name);
    }
    return mySheets;
}
```

The worksheets folder contains one file that corresponds to each of the sheets identified in the sheets element of the workbook.xml file. In our example, they are named sheet1.xml and sheet2.xml. The following markup from the sheets1.xml file shows the contents of the sheetData element for the Numbers worksheet:

```
<sheetData>
    <row r="1" spans="1:3" x14ac:dyDescent="0.25">
        <c r="A1"><v>1</v></c>
        <c r="B1"><v>2</v></c>
        <c r="C1"><v>3</v></c>
    </row>
    <row r="2" spans="1:3" x14ac:dyDescent="0.25">
        <c r="A2"><v>4</v></c>
        <c r="B2"><v>5</v></c>
```

```
        <c r="C2"><v>6</v></c>
    </row>
</sheetData>
```

As you can see, sheetData is made up of a collection of rows. Each row has several cells, and each cell has a value.

The following markup from the sheets2.xml file shows the contents of the sheetData element for the Welcome worksheet:

```
<sheetData>
    <row r="1" spans="1:1" x14ac:dyDescent="0.25">
        <c r="A1" t="s"><v>0</v></c>
    </row>
</sheetData>
```

We are expecting the value of the A1 cell to be **Hello World**. However, it has the value of 0 (zero) instead. The reason for this is that all the strings are stored in the sharedStrings.xml file, and only the index to the location of the string within the sharedStrings.xml file is included in sheetData. Each unique string is only included once in the sharedStrings.xml file.

This is the data from the sharedStrings.xml file:

```
<sst count="1" uniqueCount="1">
    <si><t>Helllo World</t></si>
</sst>
```

The following code loops through each of the sheets in SpreadsheetDocument and returns the value of the first cell in the first row of each sheet:

```
private List<string> ReadFirstCell(SpreadsheetDocument doc)
{
    List<string> A1Value = new();

    WorkbookPart wbPart = doc.WorkbookPart;
    var stringTable = wbPart
        .GetPartsOfType<SharedStringTablePart>()
        .FirstOrDefault();

    Sheets sheets = wbPart.Workbook.Sheets;
    foreach (Sheet item in sheets)
```

```
    {
        WorksheetPart wsPart =
            (WorksheetPart)(wbPart.GetPartById(item.Id));
        SheetData sheetData = wsPart
            .Worksheet.Elements<SheetData>().First();
        Row row = sheetData.Elements<Row>().First();
        Cell cell = row.Elements<Cell>().First();

        string value = cell.CellValue.Text;
        if (cell.DataType != null)
        {
            if (cell.DataType.Value == CellValues.SharedString)
            {
                value = stringTable
                    .SharedStringTable
                    .ElementAt(int.Parse(value)).InnerText;
            }
        }
        A1Value.Add(value);
    }
    return A1Value;
}
```

You have learned how to read an Excel file by using the Open XML SDK. The Open XML SDK is very powerful. It can be used not only to read Excel files but also to both create new Excel files and update existing ones. It can also be used to create, read, and update both Word and PowerPoint files.

Now, let's get a quick overview of the project that we are going to build in this chapter.

Creating the Excel reader project

The Blazor WebAssembly application that we are going to build in this chapter is an Excel file reader. We will use the InputFile component to upload an Excel file. Then, we will use the Open XML SDK to loop through the rows of one of the worksheets in the Excel file. Finally, we will use the Virtualize component to render the data from the Excel file in an HTML table.

The following is a screenshot of the completed application:

| Choose File | SummerOlympics.xlsx |

File Name: SummerOlympics.xlsx
File Size: 47,223 bytes
Content type: application/vnd.openxmlformats-officedocument.spreadsheetml.sheet

| Read file |

Rows: 1345

Year	Country	Gold	Silver	Bronze
1896	Great Britain	2	3	2
1896	Hungary	2	1	3
1896	France	5	4	2
1896	United States	11	7	2
1896	Germany	6	5	2
1896	Austria	2	1	2
1896	Mixed team	1	0	1
1896	Greece	10	18	19

Figure 9.6: Excel reader app

The build time for this project is approximately 45 minutes.

Project overview

The ExcelReader project will be created by using Microsoft's **Blazor WebAssembly App Empty** project template to create an empty Blazor WebAssembly project. First, we will add the Open XML SDK to the project. Then, we will add a model to capture the information that we are reading from the Excel file. We will use an InputFile component to upload the Excel file. We will use the Open XML SDK to read the Excel file. Finally, we will use the Virtualize component to display the data from the Excel file.

Create the Excel reader project

We need to create a new Blazor WebAssembly app. We do this as follows:

1.   Open Visual Studio 2022.

2.	Click the **Create a new project** button.

3.	Press *Alt+S* to enter the **search for templates** textbox.

4.	Enter Blazor and press the *Enter* key.

	The following screenshot shows the **Blazor WebAssembly App Empty** project template:

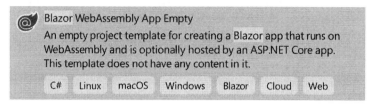

Figure 9.7: Blazor WebAssembly App Empty project template

5.	Select the **Blazor WebAssembly App Empty** project template and click the **Next** button.

6.	Enter ExcelReader in the **Project name** textbox and click the **Next** button.

	This is a screenshot of the dialog used to configure our new project:

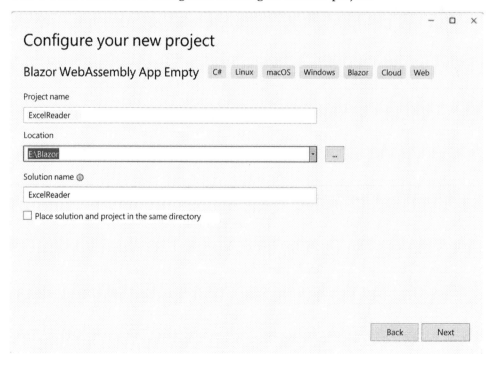

Figure 9.8: Configure your new project dialog

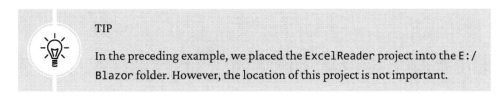

TIP

In the preceding example, we placed the ExcelReader project into the E:/
Blazor folder. However, the location of this project is not important.

7. Select **.NET 7.0** as the version of the **Framework** to use.

8. Check the **Configure for HTTPS** checkbox.

9. Uncheck the **ASP.NET Core Hosted** checkbox.

10. Uncheck the **Progressive Web Application** checkbox.

This is a screenshot of the dialog used to collect additional information about our new
project:

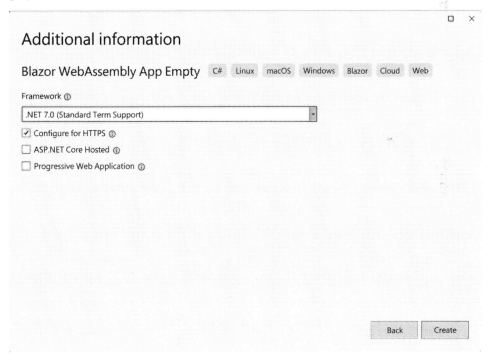

Figure 9.9: Additional information dialog

11. Click the **Create** button.

We have created an empty ExcelReader Blazor WebAssembly project. We will use the Open XML SDK to read the Microsoft Excel file.

Install the Open XML SDK

We need to install the Open XML SDK into our web app. We do this as follows:

1. Select **Tools, NuGet Package Manager, Package Manager Console** from the Visual Studio menu to open the **Package Manager Console**.

2. Enter the following command:

```
Install-Package DocumentFormat.OpenXml
```

3. Press the *Enter* key.

The Open XML SDK is now installed.

Now we need to add a class to contain the information that we will read from the Excel file.

Add the Medals class

The Excel file that we will upload will include a count of medals that were awarded to each country in each of the summer Olympic Games since 1896. We need to add a Medals class to collect that information. We do this as follows:

1. Right-click the **ExcelReader** project and select the **Add, New Folder** option from the menu.

2. Name the new folder Models.

3. Right-click the **Models** folder and select the **Add, Class** option from the menu.

4. Name the new class Medals.

5. Click the **Add** button.

6. Add the following properties to the Medals class:

```
public int Year { get; set; }
public string? Country { get; set; }
public int Gold { get; set; }
public int Silver { get; set; }
public int Bronze { get; set; }
```

We have added the Medals class to capture the data from the Excel file. Next, we need to add the ability to upload the Excel file that we want to read.

Upload the Excel file

We will use the InputFile component to both select and upload the Excel file. We do this as follows:

1. Open the Pages/Index.razor file.

2. Remove the h1 element.

3. Add the following using statement:

    ```
    @using Microsoft.AspNetCore.Components.Forms;
    ```

4. Add the following markup:

    ```
    <PageTitle>Excel Reader</PageTitle>

    <InputFile OnChange="@SelectFile" accept=".xlsx" />

    @if (file != null)
    {
        if (errorMessage == null)
        {
            <p>
                <div>File Name: @file.Name</div>
                <div>
                    File Size: @file.Size.ToString("N0") bytes
                </div>
                <div>Content type: @file.ContentType</div>
            </p>

            <button type="button">Read file</button>
        }

        <p>@errorMessage</p>
    }

    @code {

    }
    ```

The preceding markup includes an `InputFile` component and an `if` statement. If `file` is not null, the file's name, size, and content type are displayed.

5.   Add the following code to the code block:

```
IBrowserFile? file;
int MAXFILESIZE = 50000;
string? errorMessage;

private void SelectFile(InputFileChangeEventArgs e)
{
    file = e.File;

    errorMessage = null;
    if ((file.Size >= MAXFILESIZE) ||
    (file.ContentType != "application/vnd.openxmlformats-
officedocument.spreadsheetml.sheet"))
    {
        errorMessage = "Invalid file";
    }
}
```

The preceding code checks the size and content type of the file and displays an error message if they are invalid. It is a good practice to always set a maximum file size since the larger the file, the more resources are required to process it.

6.   Press *Ctrl+F5* to start the application without debugging.

7.   Click the **Choose file** button.

8.   Select the `SummerOlympics.xlsx` file and click the **Open** button.

The following screenshot shows the results:

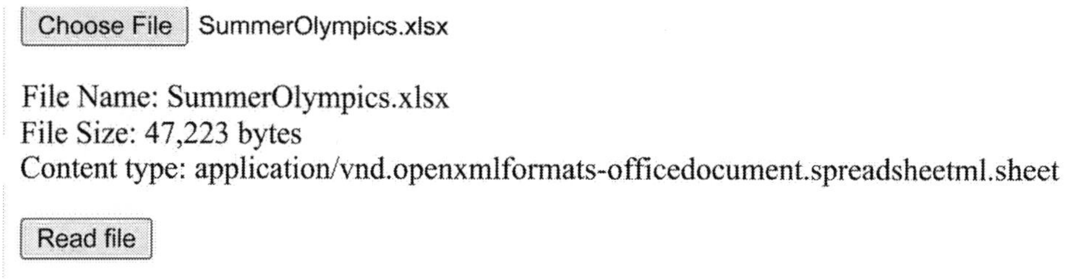

Choose File   SummerOlympics.xlsx

File Name: SummerOlympics.xlsx
File Size: 47,223 bytes
Content type: application/vnd.openxmlformats-officedocument.spreadsheetml.sheet

Read file

Figure 9.10: Select SummerOlympics.xlsx

IMPORTANT NOTE

You must download the `SummerOlympics.xlsx` file from the GitHub repository. It includes two worksheets: `olympic_hosts` and `olympic_medals`. We
will be working with the `olympic_medals` worksheet. It includes the medal
count by country and year for the summer Olympics.

9. Click the **Read file** button.

10. Verify that nothing happens.

We have successfully uploaded the Excel file, but when we click the **Read file** button, nothing
happens. Now we need to write the code to read the data from the Excel file.

Read the Excel file

We will use the `SpreadsheetDocument` class to read the data from the Excel file. We do this as
follows:

1. Return to Visual Studio.

2. Open the `Pages\Index.razor` file.

3. Add the following using statements:

```
@using DocumentFormat.OpenXml;
@using DocumentFormat.OpenXml.Packaging;
@using DocumentFormat.OpenXml.Spreadsheet;
```

4. Add the following fields to the code block:

```
bool loaded;
int rowCount;
```

The `loaded` field will be used to toggle the markup used to display the data, and the
`rowCount` field will be used to hold the number of rows in the Excel file.

5. Add the following `ReadFile` method to the code block:

```
private async Task ReadFile()
{
    try
    {
```

```
            var stream = new MemoryStream();
            await file.OpenReadStream(MAXFILESIZE)
                        .CopyToAsync(stream);

            SpreadsheetDocument doc =
                    SpreadsheetDocument.Open(stream, false);

            WorkbookPart wbPart = doc.WorkbookPart;

            var sheet = wbPart.Workbook
                    .Descendants<Sheet>()
                    .Where(s => s.Name == "olympic_medals")
                    .FirstOrDefault();

            WorksheetPart wsPart =
                    (WorksheetPart)(wbPart.GetPartById(sheet.Id));

            SheetData sheetData =
                    wsPart.Worksheet.Elements<SheetData>().First();

            rowCount = sheetData.Elements<Row>().Count();

            loaded = true;
        }
        catch (Exception)
        {
            errorMessage = "Invalid Excel file";
        }
    }
```

The preceding code sets the value of rowCount to the number of rows in the olympic_ medals worksheet.

6. Update the Read file button to the following:

```
<button type="button" @onclick="ReadFile">
    Read file
</button>
```

When the **Read file** button is clicked, the ReadFile method will be invoked.

7. Add the following if statement after the Read file button:

```
if (!loaded)
{
    <p><em>Loading...</em></p>
}
else
{
    <p>Rows: @rowCount</p>
}
```

The preceding code will display rowCount after the file has been loaded.

8. Press *Ctrl+F5* to start the application without debugging.

9. Click the **Choose file** button.

10. Select the SummerOlympics.xlsx file and click the **Open** button.

11. Click the **Read file** button.

12. Verify that the correct number of rows is displayed.

We have read the number of rows in the olympic_medals worksheet in the SummerOlympics. xlsx file. Next, we will populate a collection of medals by looping through each of the rows in the worksheet.

Populate the medals collection

We need to loop through all the rows to populate the collection of medals. We do this as follows:

1. Return to Visual Studio.

2. Open the Pages\Index.razor file.

3. Add the following using statements:

```
@using ExcelReader.Models;
@using System.Collections.ObjectModel;
```

4. Add the following field to the code block:

```
Collection<Medals> allMedals = new();
```

The allMedals field will be used to hold the data that is read from the Excel file.

5.   After the code that set rowCount, add the following code in the ReadFile method:

```
var stringTable = wbPart
    .GetPartsOfType<SharedStringTablePart>()
    .FirstOrDefault();

foreach (Row r in sheetData.Elements<Row>())
{
    if (r.RowIndex! == 1)
    {
        continue;
    };

    int col = 1;
    var medals = new Medals();
    foreach (Cell c in r.Elements<Cell>())
    {

        string value = c.InnerText;

        if (c.DataType != null)
        {
            if (c.DataType.Value ==
                CellValues.SharedString)
            {
                value = stringTable.SharedStringTable
                    .ElementAt(int.Parse(value))
                    .InnerText;
            }
        }

        switch (col)
        {
            case 1:
                medals.Year = int.Parse(value);
                break;
```

```
                    case 2:
                        medals.Country = value;
                        break;
                    case 3:
                        medals.Gold = int.Parse(value);
                        break;
                    case 4:
                        medals.Silver = int.Parse(value);
                        break;
                    case 5:
                        medals.Bronze = int.Parse(value);
                        break;
                    default:
                        break;
                }

                col = col + 1;
            }

        allMedals.Add(medals);
    }
```

The first thing that the preceding code does is load stringTable. Then, it determines the value of the cell and updates the appropriate property of the Medals object, based on the column that is being read. If the cell is of type SharedString, it determines its value by using stringTable.

6. Press *Ctrl+F5* to start the application without debugging.

7. Click the **Choose file** button.

8. Select the SummerOlympics.xlsx file and click the **Open** button.

9. Click the **Read file** button.

10. Verify that the correct number of rows is still displayed.

We are reading all the rows into the collection of medals, but we are not rendering them. Next, we need to render them to the screen.

Render the Medals collection

We need to add the `Virtualize` component to the `Home` page to render the data. We do this as follows:

1. Open the `Pages\Index.razor` file.

2. Add the following using statement:

    ```
    @using Microsoft.AspNetCore.Components.Web.Virtualization
    ```

3. Add the following markup below the p element that is displaying `rowCount`:

    ```
    <div style="height:200px;overflow-y:scroll" tabindex="-1">
        <table width="450">
            <thead style="position: sticky; top: 0; background-color:
    silver">
                <tr>
                    <th>Year</th>
                    <th width="255">Country</th>
                    <th>Gold</th>
                    <th>Silver</th>
                    <th>Bronze</th>
                </tr>
            </thead>
            <tbody>
                <Virtualize Items="@allMedals"
                            SpacerElement="tr">
                    <tr>
                        <td align="center">@context.Year</td>
                        <td>@context.Country</td>
                        <td align="center">@context.Gold</td>
                        <td align="center">
                            @context.Silver
                        </td>
                        <td align="center">
                            @context.Bronze
                        </td>
                    </tr>
    ```

```
                </Virtualize>
            </tbody>
        </table>
    </div>
```

The preceding markup uses the Virtualize component to display each of the objects in the collection.

4. Press *Ctrl+F5* to start the application without debugging.

5. Click the **Choose file** button.

6. Select the SummerOlympics.xlsx file and click the **Open** button.

7. Click the **Read file** button.

8. Scroll through the list of items.

We have added the ability to display all the items from a collection, using the Virtualize component.

Summary

You should now be able to upload files into your Blazor WebAssembly app. You should be able to use virtualization to render your pages faster when you are working with a large dataset. Finally, you should be comfortable with working with Microsoft Excel files.

In this chapter, we explained how to upload files and how to resize image files. We explained how to use virtualization. Finally, we introduced the Open XML SDK and explained how to use it to read Excel files.

After that, we used the **Blazor WebAssembly App Empty** project template to create a new project and added the Open XML SDK to the project. Next, we added an InputFile component to upload an Excel file to the app. We used the Open XML SDK to read the number of rows in a particular worksheet. Then, we looped through all the rows in the selected worksheet and stored their values in a collection. Finally, we used the Virtualize component to display all the items in the collection.

Now that you know how to upload files to your web app, your users can provide data to your application in a variety of different formats. In this project, we used an Excel file, but you can easily extrapolate what you have learned to use other types of files.

In the next chapter, we will use SQL Server to build a task manager using the ASP.NET Web API.

Questions

The following questions are provided for your consideration:

1. The `SummerOlypics.xlsx` file contains two worksheets. How can you join the data from the two worksheets before displaying it?

2. What are some of the benefits of resizing an image?

3. Is it a good practice to always include `Placeholder` when using the `Virtualize` component?

4. Can the `Open XML SDK` be used to create a new Excel file?

5. How can you avoid reading an entire file into memory when using the `InputFile` component?

Further reading

The following resources provide more information concerning the topics covered in this chapter:

- For more information on security best practices when uploading files, refer to `https://learn.microsoft.com/en-us/aspnet/core/mvc/models/file-uploads`.

- For the `Virtualize` component source code in GitHub, refer to `https://github.com/dotnet/aspnetcore/blob/main/src/Components/Web/src/Virtualization/Virtualize.cs`.

- For more information on the `Open XML SDK`, refer to `https://learn.microsoft.com/en-us/office/open-xml/open-xml-sdk`.

- For more information on the Open XML specification, refer to `https://www.ecma-international.org/publications-and-standards/standards/ecma-376/`.

10

Using Azure Active Directory to Secure a Blazor WebAssembly Application

Security is important. Most applications require each user to provide their credentials before they can access all the functionality supplied by the application. Managing usernames, passwords, roles, and groups can be tedious and complicated. Using **Azure Active Directory (Azure AD)** makes it easy. Azure AD is an identity provider in the cloud.

The project that we create in this chapter will allow the user to view the claims provided by the token that is returned from Azure AD after the user is authenticated by Azure AD. We will be using the **Microsoft Authentication Library (MSAL)** to acquire **JSON Web Tokens (JWTs)** from Azure AD. We will be using **Open ID Connect (OIDC)** endpoints to authenticate users. OIDC is a simple identity layer built on the industry standard OAuth 2.0 protocol. It allows clients to verify the identity of a user based on the authentication performed by an identity provider, such as Duende Identity Server or Azure AD.

In this chapter, we will learn the difference between authentication and authorization. We will learn how to use the `RemoteAuthenticationView` component to handle the various actions required during each stage of authentication. We will also learn how to use the `CascadingAuthenticationState` component to share the authentication state with each of its children. Finally, we will learn how to control what is rendered to the user by using the `Authorize` attribute and the `AuthorizeView` component.

The project that we create in this chapter will be a claims reader. It will allow users who belong to a particular group within Azure AD to view the contents of the token that is returned from Azure AD after authentication. If the user is not authenticated or does not belong to the appropriate group, they will receive a warning message.

> *Who are you? And what*
>
> *are you authorized to do?*
>
> *Your identity.*

In this chapter, we will cover the following topics:

- Understanding the difference between authentication and authorization
- Working with authentication
- Controlling the user interface using authorization
- Creating the claims viewer project

Technical requirements

To complete this project, you need to have Visual Studio 2022 installed on your PC. For instructions on how to install the free Community Edition of Visual Studio 2022, refer to *Chapter 1, Introduction to Blazor WebAssembly*. Since we will be using Azure AD for authentication, you will need an account on Microsoft Azure. If you do not have an account on Microsoft Azure, refer to *Chapter 1, Introduction to Blazor WebAssembly*, to create a free account.

The source code for this chapter is available in the following GitHub repository: `https://github.com/PacktPublishing/Blazor-WebAssembly-by-Example-Second-Edition/tree/main/Chapter10`.

The Code in Action video is available here: `https://packt.link/Ch10`.

Understanding the difference between authentication and authorization

Authentication and authorization are the two sides of the same security coin. Authentication is the process of obtaining credentials from a user to verify the identity of the user. Authorization is the process of checking the privileges for the user to access specific resources.

Authentication always precedes authorization.

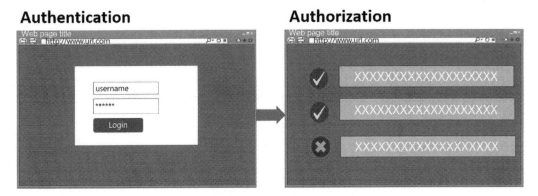

Figure 10.1: Authentication vs Authorization

The preceding image illustrates the difference between authentication and authorization. The left-hand side of the image shows a sample login screen that is used to determine who the user is. The right-hand side of the image shows the list of groups or roles that the user does or does not belong to, which is used to determine what the user can do.

Authentication

Blazor provides the **RemoteAuthenticatorView** component to make creating the various authentication pages easier. This component persists and controls state across authentication operations.

This is a high-level explanation of how authentication works:

1. An anonymous user attempts to log in or requests a page with the `Authorize` attribute applied.
2. The user is redirected to the `/authentication/login` page.
3. The user enters their credentials.
4. If they are authenticated, they are redirected to the `/authentication/login-callback` page.
5. However, if they are not authenticated, they are redirected to the `/authentication/login-failed` page.

This is the code for a sample Authentication component that relies on the RemoteAuthenticatorView component to handle the various authentication actions:

Authentication.razor

```
@page "/authentication/{action}"

@using Microsoft.AspNetCore.Components.WebAssembly.Authentication

<RemoteAuthenticatorView Action="@Action">
    <LoggingIn>
        Please sign in to your account ...
    </LoggingIn>
</RemoteAuthenticatorView>

@code{
    [Parameter] public string? Action { get; set; }
}
```

In the preceding code, the Action property is determined by the route, and the LoggingIn property is used to define the UI that is rendered while the user is logging in. The LoggingIn property is a RenderFragment. We do not need to provide the LoggingIn property since there is a default one defined by the RemoteAuthenticatorView component. We have only included it as an example. All the properties of the RemoteAuthenticatorView component that are of type RenderFragment have default values provided for them by the framework.

In the preceding code, only two of the properties of the RemoteAuthenticatorView component are defined. However, there are quite a few more properties available.

These are the properties of the RemoteAuthenticatorView class:

- Action: the current action. The options are LogIn, LogInCallback, LogInFailed, LogOut, LogOutCallback, LogOutFailed, LogOutSucceeded, Profile, and Register.

- ApplicationPaths: the paths to the various authentication pages. Since we will be using the default values for each path, we will not be using this property.

- AuthenticationState: the authentication state. It is persisted during the authentication operation. It is of type TAuthenticationState.

- CompletingLoggingIn: the UI to display when LogInCallback is being handled. It is a RenderFragment.

- `CompletingLogOut`: the UI to display when `LogOutCallback` is being handled. It is a `RenderFragment`.

- `LoggingIn`: the UI to display when `LogIn` is being handled. It is a `RenderFragment`.

- `LogInFailed`: the UI to display when `LogInFailed` is being handled. It is a `RenderFragment`.

- `LogOut`: the UI to display when `LogOut` is being handled. It is a `RenderFragment`.

- `LogOutFailed`: the UI to display when `LogOutFailed` is being handled. It is a `RenderFragment`.

- `LogOutSucceeded`: the UI to display when `LogOutSucceeded` is being handled. It is a `RenderFragment`.

- `OnLogInSucceeded`: the event callback that is invoked when the log-in operation succeeds.

- `OnLogOutSucceeded`: the event callback that is invoked when the logout operation succeeds.

- `Registering`: the UI to display when `Register` is being handled. It is a `RenderFragment`.

- `UserProfile`: the UI to display when `Profile` is being handled. It is a `RenderFragment`.

Using the `RemoteAuthenticatorView` component makes it easy to handle the authentication process.

Authorization

In Blazor WebAssembly applications, the authorization checks are all handled on the client. Since a malicious user can change the behavior of the client-side code, our authorization checks can be compromised. Therefore, we will only be using authorization to handle differences in the user interface that vary depending on the rights of the user.

TIP

Never trust the client!

Real security can only be enforced by using a backend server. We cannot authenticate our users on the client, nor can we reliably authorize their actions on the client.

Authentication and authorization work together to secure our applications. Authentication is used to determine who the user is, while authorization is used to determine what they can do.

In addition to the `RemoteAuthenticatorView` component, Blazor WebAssembly provides some other built-in components to help us work with authentication.

Working with authentication

The CascadingAuthenticationState component and the AuthorizeRouteView component work together to make authentication simpler. The CascadingAuthenticationState component is responsible for cascading the user's authentication state to all its descendants. It is typically used to wrap the Router component.

In the following example, the App component relies on the CascadingAuthenticationState component to provide the user's authentication state to all the routable components:

 IMPORTANT NOTE

Sometimes we refer to routable components as pages.

App.razor

```
@inject NavigationManager Navigation

<CascadingAuthenticationState>
    <Router AppAssembly="@typeof(App).Assembly">
        <Found Context="routeData">
        </Found>
        <NotFound>
            <PageTitle>Not found</PageTitle>
            <LayoutView Layout="@typeof(MainLayout)">
                <p>Sorry, there's nothing here.</p>
            </LayoutView>
        </NotFound>
    </Router>
</CascadingAuthenticationState>
```

In the preceding markup, the Found attribute contains the following AuthorizeRouteView component:

```
<AuthorizeRouteView RouteData="@routeData"
                    DefaultLayout="@typeof(MainLayout)">
    <NotAuthorized>
        @if (context.User.Identity?.IsAuthenticated != true)
        {
```

```
                    Navigation.NavigateToLogin($"authentication/login");
        }
        else
        {
            <p>
                ERROR: You are not authorized to access
                this page.
            </p>
        }
    </NotAuthorized>
</AuthorizeRouteView>
<FocusOnNavigate RouteData="@routeData" Selector="h1" />
```

In the preceding code, the Router component is used to route the requests. If a valid route is found, it uses the AuthorizeRouteView component instead of the RouteView component to determine if the user is authorized to view the page. If they are not authorized and they have not yet been authenticated, it redirects the user to the /authentication/login page. However, if they are not authorized and they have been authenticated, it renders the error message.

Since the App component is using the CascadingAuthenticationState component, the Task<AuthenticationState> cascading parameter is supplied to each page. The following code uses it to populate the userName field:

```
[CascadingParameter]
private Task<AuthenticationState> authStateTask { get; set; }

private string userName;

protected override async Task OnInitializedAsync()
{
    var authState = await authStateTask;
    var user = authState.User;

    if (user.Identity.IsAuthenticated)
    {
        userName = user.Identity.Name;
    };
}
```

In the preceding code, the `authStateTask` parameter is used to cascade the value of the `AuthenticationState` from the `CascadingAuthenticationState` component.

Blazor WebAssembly uses the built-in DI service called `AuthenticationStateProvider` to determine whether the user is logged in. The `AuthenicationStateProvider` class provides information about the authentication state of the current user. The `User` property of the `AuthenicationStateProvider` provides the **ClaimsPrincipal** for the current user. The `ClaimsPrincipal` is simply the claims-based identity of the user.

By using the built-in components, we can confirm the identity of the user. Next, we need to determine what the user is authorized to do.

Controlling the user interface using authorization

After a user is authenticated, authorization rules are used to control what the user can see and do. The `Authorize` attribute and the `AuthorizeView` component are used to control the user interface.

The Authorize attribute

The `Authorize` attribute is used to require that the user is authorized to view the page that is decorated with the attribute. It should only be used on routable components. The following component includes the `Authorize` attribute:

Secure.razor

```
@page "/secure"

@using Microsoft.AspNetCore.Authorization
@attribute [Authorize]

<h2>Secure Page</h2>
Congratulations, you have been authenticated!
```

When an unauthenticated user tries to navigate to a page with the `Authorize` attribute, they are automatically redirected to the `/authentication/login` page.

TIP

You can require authentication for every page by adding the `Authorize` attribute to the `_Imports.razor` file. However, if you do that, you must add the `AllowAnonymous` attribute to the `Authentication` component or your users won't be able to log in.

The `Authorize` component supports role-based and policy-based authorization. If the user has been authenticated and they try to navigate to a page that includes either role-based or policy-based authorization, and they do not meet the requirements, they will receive the message provided by the App component. In the preceding sample App component, the message is as follows:

```
ERROR: You are not authorized to access this page
```

This example uses the `Roles` parameter for role-based authorization:

```
@page "/secure"
@attribute [Authorize(Roles = "admin, siteadmin")]
```

In the preceding example, only users who are in either the `admin` or `siteadmin` role can access this page.

This example uses the `Policy` parameter for policy-based authorization:

```
@page "/secure"
@attribute [Authorize(Policy = "content-admin")]
```

In the preceding example, only users who meet the requirements of the `content-admin` policy can access the page.

The `Authorize` attribute should only be used on routable components since authorization is not performed for child components within a page.

For example, if we create a routable component called `Secure` and secure it using either role-based or policy-based authorization, the user cannot navigate to the page if their credentials do not meet the requirements. However, if we place the same component in another page that the user is authorized to view, they can see the content of the `Secure` component.

To only authorize the display of certain parts of a page, use the `AuthorizeView` component.

The AuthorizeView component

The `AuthorizeView` component is used to control the parts of the user interface that are displayed based on what the user is authorized to view.

IMPORTANT NOTE

By default, non-authenticated users are not authorized to view any content.

The `AuthorizeView` class has the following properties:

- `Authorized`: the content that is rendered if the user is authorized. It is a `RenderFragment`.
- `Authorizing`: the content that is rendered as the user is being authenticated. It is a `RenderFragment`.
- `NotAuthorized`: the content that is rendered if the user is not authorized. It is a `RenderFragment`.
- `Policy`: the policy that determines if the content can be rendered.
- `Roles`: a comma-delimited list of the roles that are allowed to render the content.

Unlike the `RemoteAuthenticatorView` component, the framework does not provide default values for the `RenderFragments` used by the `AuthorizeView` component.

The following code uses the `AuthorizeView` component to create a `LoginDisplay` component:

LoginDisplay.razor

```
@using Microsoft.AspNetCore.Components.Authorization
@using Microsoft.AspNetCore.Components.WebAssembly.Authentication

@inject NavigationManager Navigation

<AuthorizeView>
    <Authorized>
        Hello, @context.User.Identity?.Name!
        <button @onclick="BeginLogout">Log out</button>
    </Authorized>
    <NotAuthorized>
        <a href="authentication/login">Log in</a>
    </NotAuthorized>
    <Authorizing>
        Please be patient. We are trying to authorize you.
    </Authorizing>
</AuthorizeView>

@code{
    private void BeginLogout(MouseEventArgs args)
    {
        Navigation.NavigateToLogout("authentication/logout");
    }
}
```

The preceding example provides both the Authorized template and the NotAuthorized template. If the user is authorized, their name is displayed, and the **Log out** button is rendered. If the user is not authorized, the **Log in** link is rendered.

The AuthorizeView component supports role-based and policy-based authorization. If the user has been authenticated and they try to navigate to a page that includes either role-based or policy-based authorization, and they meet the requirements, the UI in the Authorized template will be rendered; otherwise, the UI in the NotAuthorized template will be rendered.

This example uses the Roles parameter for role-based authorization:

```
<AuthorizeView Roles="admin, siteadmin">
    <p>
        You can only view this content if you are an admin or
        siteadmin.
    </p>
</AuthorizeView>
```

In the preceding example, only users who are in either the admin or siteadmin role will have the indicated text rendered.

This example uses the Policy parameter for policy-based authorization:

```
<AuthorizeView Policy="content-admin">
    <p>
        You can only view this content if you satisfy
        the "content-admin" policy.
    </p>
</AuthorizeView>
```

In the preceding example, only users who meet the requirements of the content-admin policy will have the indicated text rendered.

The AuthorizeView component can be used in the NavMenu component. However, although a component does not appear in the NavMenu, that does not prevent the user from navigating directly to the component. So, you must always set authorization rules at the component level.

TIP

Never rely on the NavMenu component to hide components from unauthorized users.

We can use the `Authorize` attribute and the `AuthorizeView` component to force the user to be authenticated and to hide portions of the user interface.

Now, let's get a quick overview of the project that we are going to build in this chapter.

Creating the claims viewer project

The Blazor WebAssembly application that we are going to build in this chapter is a claims viewer. First, we will add the application to Azure AD. After we have added the application, we will add a group and a user to Azure AD. We will add the required NuGet packages and configure the project to use MSAL authentication. Next, we will add components for authentication and login display. We will also add the following routable components: **Secure** and **WhoAmI**. Finally, we will add and test an authentication policy.

The following is a screenshot of the **WhoAmI** component from the completed application:

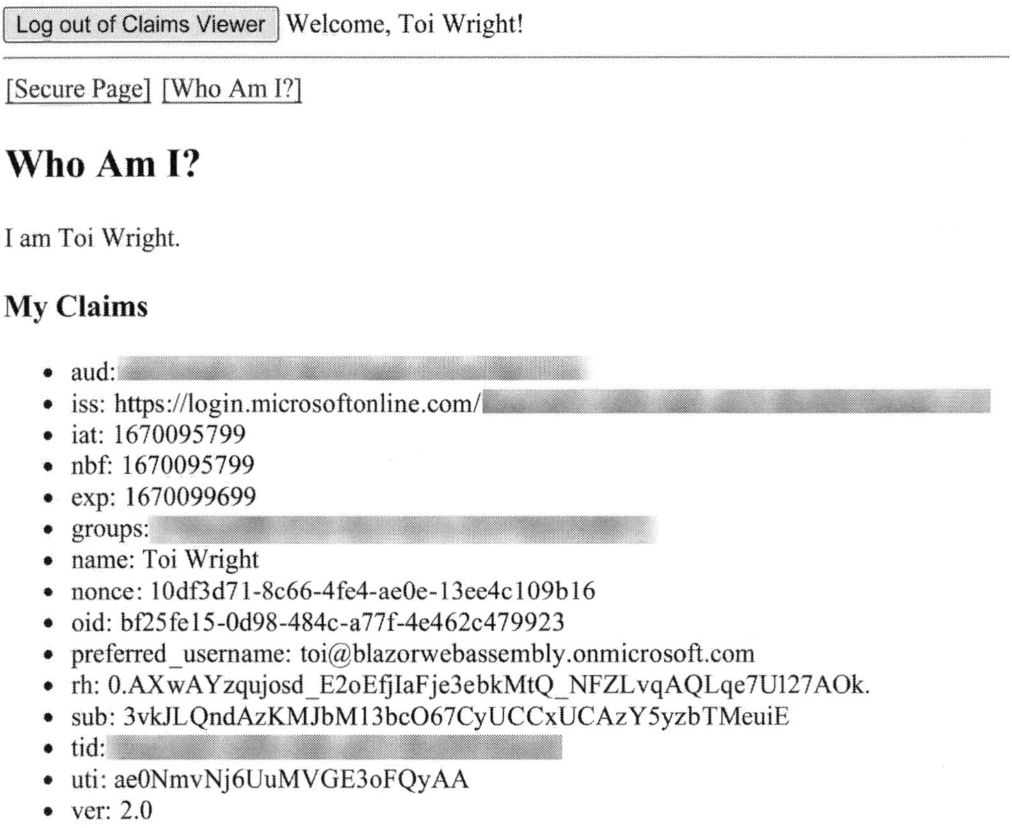

| Log out of Claims Viewer | Welcome, Toi Wright!

[Secure Page] [Who Am I?]

Who Am I?

I am Toi Wright.

My Claims

- aud:
- iss: https://login.microsoftonline.com/
- iat: 1670095799
- nbf: 1670095799
- exp: 1670099699
- groups:
- name: Toi Wright
- nonce: 10df3d71-8c66-4fe4-ae0e-13ee4c109b16
- oid: bf25fe15-0d98-484c-a77f-4e462c479923
- preferred_username: toi@blazorwebassembly.onmicrosoft.com
- rh: 0.AXwAYzqujosd_E2oEfjIaFje3ebkMtQ_NFZLvqAQLqe7Ul27AOk.
- sub: 3vkJLQndAzKMJbM13bcO67CyUCCxUCAzY5yzbTMeuiE
- tid:
- uti: ae0NmvNj6UuMVGE3oFQyAA
- ver: 2.0

Figure 10.2: The WhoAmI component from Claims Viewer

The build time for this project is approximately 60 minutes.

Project overview

The ClaimsViewer project will be created by using Microsoft's **Blazor WebAssembly App Empty** project template to create an empty Blazor WebAssembly project. After we have created our project, we will configure Azure AD by adding the application, a new group, and a new user to our Azure AD tenant. Then, we will add the required NuGet packages and update our project's settings. Next, we will add an authentication component and a login display component. We will also add a component to display the contents of our claims. Finally, we will add and test an authentication policy.

IMPORTANT NOTE

Since Microsoft is constantly updating the Azure Portal, some of the screens in the Azure Portal may no longer match the information in this chapter.

Create the claims viewer project

We need to create a new Blazor WebAssembly app. We do this as follows:

1. Open Visual Studio 2022.

2. Click the **Create a new project** button.

3. Press *Alt+S* to enter the **Search for templates** textbox.

4. Enter Blazor and press the *Enter* key.

    The following screenshot shows the **Blazor WebAssembly App Empty** project template:

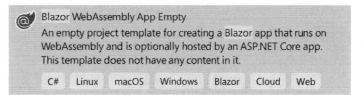

Figure 10.3: Blazor WebAssembly App Empty project template

5. Select the **Blazor WebAssembly App Empty** project template and click the **Next** button.

6. Enter ClaimsViewer in the **Project name** textbox and click the **Next** button.

This is a screenshot of the dialog used to configure our new project:

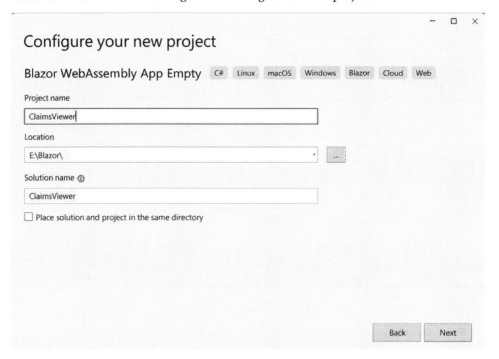

Figure 10.4: Blazor WebAssembly App Empty Project Template

TIP

In the preceding example, we placed the ClaimsViewer project into the E:/ Blazor folder. However, the location of this project is not important.

7. Select **.NET 7.0** as the version of the Framework to use.

8. Check the **Configure for HTTPS** checkbox.

9. Uncheck the **ASP.NET Core Hosted** checkbox.

10. Uncheck the **Progressive Web Application** checkbox.

This is a screenshot of the dialog used to collect additional information about our new project:

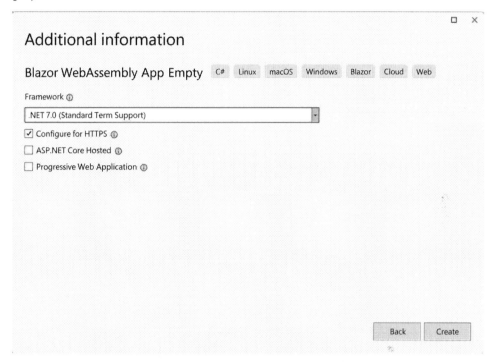

Figure 10.5: Additional information dialog

11. Click the **Create** button.

We have created an empty ClaimsViewer Blazor WebAssembly project. We will use Azure AD to provide the identity services.

Add the application to Azure AD

We need to register the application in Azure AD and add an appsettings.json file to the project. We do this as follows:

1. Right-click the wwwroot folder and select the **Add, New Item** option from the menu.

2. Enter json in the **Search** box.

3. Select **App Settings File**.

4. Name the new item appsettings.json.

5. Click the **Add** button.

6. Replace all the text in the file with the following:

```
{
  "AzureAd": {
    "Authority": "https://login.microsoftonline.com/{Directory
(tenant) ID}",
    "ClientId": "{Application (client) ID}",
    "ValidateAuthority": true
  }
}
```

After we add the application to Azure AD, we will replace the {Directory (tenant) ID} and the {Application (client) ID} placeholders used in the preceding code.

7. Navigate to the Azure Portal, `https://portal.azure.com`.

8. Open your `Azure Active Directory` resource.

IMPORTANT NOTE

An instance of `Azure Active Directory` was automatically created when you signed up for a Microsoft Cloud service subscription.

9. Select **App registration** from the **Add** menu.

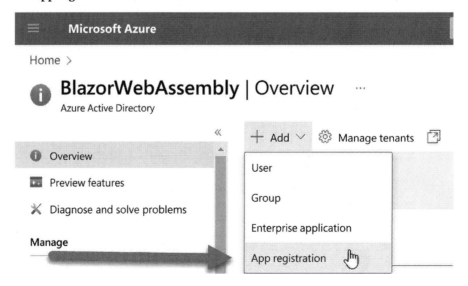

Figure 10.6: App registration in Azure AD

10. For the user-facing display name, enter `ClaimsViewer`.

11. For the supported account types, select the **Accounts in this organizational directory only** option.

12. For the redirect URI, select **Single-page application (SPA)** as the platform and enter the following text for the URI:

```
https://localhost:5001/authentication/login-callback
```

The following screenshot shows the completed **Register an application** dialog:

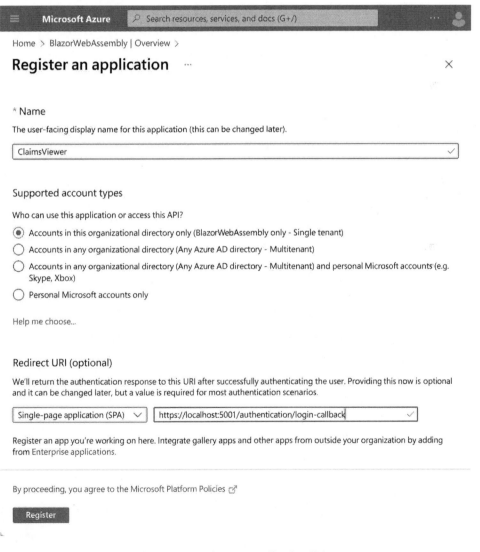

Figure 10.7: Register an application dialog

13. Click the **Register** button.

The following screenshot highlights the information that we need to copy to the appsettings.json file in our project:

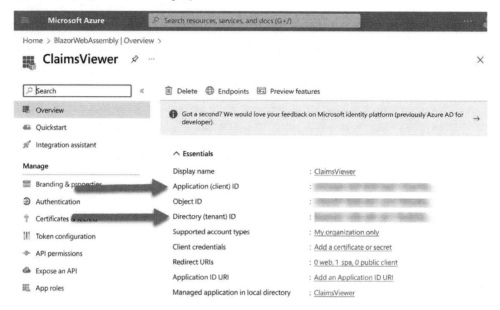

Figure 10.8: ClaimsViewer app in Azure AD

14. Return to Visual Studio.

15. Open the appsettings.json file.

16. Replace the **{Directory (tenant) ID}** placeholder with the value of Directory (tenant) ID from Azure AD.

17. Replace the **{Application (client) ID}** placeholder with the value of Application (client) ID from Azure AD.

To test our application, we need to add at least one user. Also, later in this project, we will need to use a group to enable policy-based authentication. So, let's add a user and a group.

Add a user and a group to Azure AD

Before we exit the Azure Portal, let's create a new group and add a new user to that group. We do this as follows:

1. Return to your Azure Active Directory tenant.

2. Select **Groups** from the menu.

3. Select **New group** from the top menu.

4. For the **Group type**, leave **Security** selected.

5. For the **Group name**, enter ViewAll.

6. For the **Group description**, enter Members can view all of the claims.

    The following screenshot shows the completed **New Group** dialog:

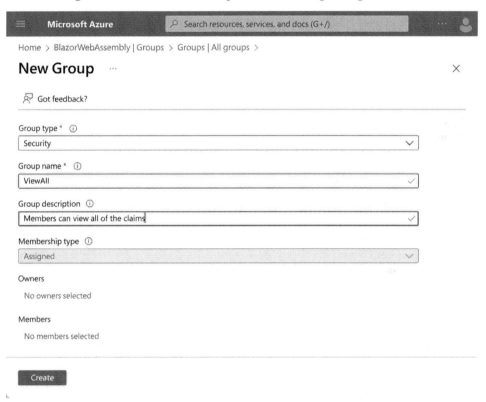

Figure 10.9: New Group dialog in Azure AD

7. Click the **Create** button.

You should now see the new group. If you do not see the new group, select the **Refresh** option from the top menu. The following screenshot highlights the information that we will need to complete this project:

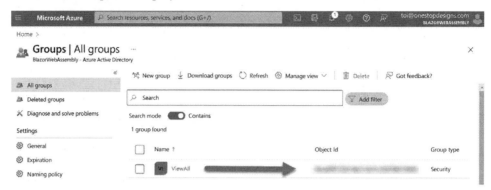

Figure 10.10: Groups in Azure AD

8. Copy the **Object Id** for your new group and save it for later.

    We will need the Object Id of the group when we add an authentication policy to our project.

9. Return to your Azure Active Directory tenant.

10. Select **App registrations** from the menu.

11. Click on the **ClaimsViewer** application.

12. Select **Token configuration** from the menu.

13. Click the **Add groups claim** option.

14. Check the **Security groups** checkbox.

15. Click the **Add** button.

16. Return to your **Azure Active Directory** resource.

17. Select **Users** from the menu.

18. Select **Create new user** from the **New user** top menu as shown in the following screenshot:

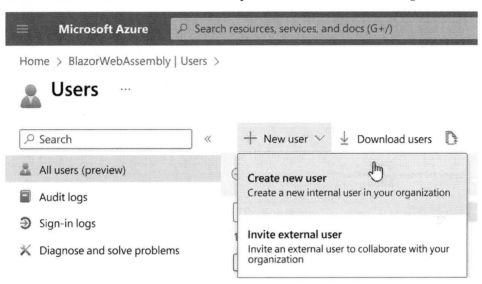

Figure 10.11: Create new user in Azure AD

19. Enter a **Username** and **Name** for the new user.

20. Enter a **Password**.

21. Add the **ViewAll** group.

22. Click the **Create** button.

You should now see your new user. If you do not see your new user, select the **Refresh** option from the top menu.

You have added a new user to Azure AD that is a member of the **ViewAll** group. We have finished setting up Azure AD. Now we can return to Visual Studio.

Add the required NuGet packages

We need to add three NuGet packages to our application. We do this as follows:

1. Return to Visual Studio.

2. Select **Tools, NuGet Package Manager**, and **Package Manager Console** from the Visual Studio menu to open the **Package Manager Console**.

3. Enter the following command:

    ```
    Install-package Microsoft.AspNetCore.Authorization
    ```

4. Press the *Enter* key.

    You have installed the ASP.NET Core authorization classes.

5. Enter the following command:

    ```
    Install-package Microsoft.AspNetCore.Components.Authorization
    ```

6. Press the *Enter* key.

    You have installed authentication and authorization classes for Blazor applications.

7. Enter the following command:

    ```
    Install-package Microsoft.Authentication.WebAssembly.Msal
    ```

8. Press the *Enter* key.

    You have installed the Microsoft Authentication Library. It is used to acquire security tokens from the Microsoft identity platform. The tokens can be used to both authenticate users and access Web APIs.

9. Open the _Imports.razor file.

10. Add the following using statements:

    ```
    @using Microsoft.AspNetCore.Authorization
    @using Microsoft.AspNetCore.Components.Authorization
    @using Microsoft.AspNetCore.Components.WebAssembly.Authentication
    ```

All the required NuGet packages have been installed. Now we need to update some of the project's settings.

Enable authentication

We need to update some of the project's files to enable authentication. We do this as follows:

1. Open the wwwroot/index.html file.

2. Add the following `script` element above the existing `script` element:

```
<script
src="_content/Microsoft.Authentication.WebAssembly.Msal/
AuthenticationService.js">
</script>
```

3. Open the `Properties/launchSettings.json` file.

4. Add the following to `iisSettings`:

```
    "windowsAuthentication": false,
    "anonymousAuthentication": true,
```

5. Open the `Program.cs` file.

6. Add the following code above the last line in the file:

```
builder.Services.AddMsalAuthentication(options =>
{
    builder.Configuration.Bind("AzureAd",
        options.ProviderOptions.Authentication);

    options.ProviderOptions.LoginMode = "redirect";
});
```

In the preceding code, the application is instructed to reference the **AzureAd** section of the `appsetting.json` file for the parameters that are required to authenticate the app. The value of `LoginMode` can be either popup or `redirect`. We are using `redirect` because the popup login dialog is not modal and can easily get hidden behind other windows.

7. Open the `App.Razor` file.

8. Add the following directive:

```
@inject NavigationManager Navigation
```

9. Surround the `Router` element with the following `CascadingAuthenticationState` element:

```
<CascadingAuthenticationState>
</CascadingAuthenticationState>
```

10. Replace the `RouteView` element with the following `AuthorizeRouteView` element:

```
<AuthorizeRouteView RouteData="@routeData"
    DefaultLayout="@typeof(MainLayout)">
    <NotAuthorized>
        @if (context.User.Identity?.IsAuthenticated !=
            true)
        {
            Navigation.NavigateTo($"authentication/login");
        }
        else
        {
            <p>
                You are not authorized to access
                this resource.
            </p>
        }
    </NotAuthorized>
</AuthorizeRouteView>
```

In the preceding code, if the user is not authorized and they have not been authenticated, they are redirected to the `authentication/login` page. However, if they are not authorized and they have been authenticated, the error message is rendered.

We have enabled authentication in our application. Now we need to add an `Authentication` component.

Add an Authentication component

We need to add an `Authentication` component to handle our authentication actions. We do this as follows:

1. Right-click the `Pages` folder and select the **Add, Razor Component** option from the menu.

2. Name the new component `Authentication`.

3. Replace all the text in the file with the following:

```
@page "/authentication/{action}"

@using Microsoft.AspNetCore.Components.WebAssembly.Authentication
```

```
<RemoteAuthenticatorView Action="@Action" />

@code {
    [Parameter] public string? Action { get; set; }
}
```

By leveraging the power of the RemoteAuthenticatorView component, we were able to create an Authentication component with only a few lines of code. Now let's add a way for the users to log in and out of our application.

Add a LoginDisplay component

We will add a LoginDisplay component to log the users in and out of our application. We do this as follows:

1. Right-click the ClaimsViewer project and select the **Add**, **New Folder** option from the menu.

2. Name the new folder Shared.

3. Right-click the Shared folder and select the **Add**, **Razor Component** option from the menu.

4. Name the new component LoginDisplay.

5. Replace all the text in the file with the following:

```
@inject NavigationManager Navigation

<AuthorizeView>
    <Authorized>
        <button @onclick="BeginLogout">
            Log out of Claims Viewer
        </button>
        Welcome, @context.User.Identity?.Name!
    </Authorized>
    <NotAuthorized>
        <button @onclick="BeginLogin">
            Log in to Claims Viewer
        </button>
    </NotAuthorized>
</AuthorizeView>


<hr />
```

```
@code {


}
```

The preceding markup includes an AuthorizeView component. If the user has been authenticated, the **Log out of Claims Viewer** button is rendered. If the user has not been authenticated, the **Log in to Claims Viewer** button is rendered.

6. Add the following code to the code block:

```
private void BeginLogin(MouseEventArgs args)
{
    Navigation
        .NavigateToLogin($"authentication/login");
}


private void BeginLogout(MouseEventArgs args)
{
    Navigation
        .NavigateToLogout($"authentication/logout", $"/");
}
```

Both the BeginLogin method and the BeginLogout method redirect the user to the Authentication page. The BeginLogin method sets the action parameter to login, and the BeginLogout method sets the action parameter to logout and includes a value for the ReturnUrl. In this example, the ReturnUrl is the Home page.

7. Open the _Imports.razor file.

8. Add the following using statement:

```
@using ClaimsViewer.Shared
```

9. Open the MainLayout.razor file.

10. Update the main element to the following:

```
<main style="padding:10px">
    <LoginDisplay />
    <a href="/secure">[Secure Page]</a>
    <a href="/whoami">[Who Am I?]</a>
```

```
        @Body
    </main>
```

Since we have added the `LoginDisplay` component to the `MainLayout` component, it will appear on every page of our application.

Now that the users can log in and log out, let's test our application by adding the `Authorize` attribute to a routable component.

Add a Secure component

We will add the routable `Secure` component to demonstrate the `Authorize` attribute. We do this as follows:

1. Right-click the `Pages` folder and select the **Add, Razor Component** option from the menu.

2. Name the new component `Secure`.

3. Replace all the text in the file with the following:

```
@page "/secure"

@attribute [Authorize]

<h2>Secure Page</h2>
Congratulations, you have been authenticated!
```

4. Open the `Pages/Index.razor` page.

5. Replace the contents of the h1 element with the following:

```
Welcome to the Claims Viewer app.
```

6. Press *Ctrl+F5* to start the application without debugging.

7. Click the **Log in to Claims Viewer** button.

8. Enter your credentials and click the **Sign in** button.

The first time you sign in, you will receive the following dialog:

 Microsoft

toi@blazorwebassembly.onmicrosoft.com

Permissions requested

ClaimsViewer
App info

This application is not published by Microsoft.

This app would like to:

∨   View your basic profile

∨   Maintain access to data you have given it access to

Accepting these permissions means that you allow this app to use your data as specified in their terms of service and privacy statement. You can change these permissions at https://myapps.microsoft.com. Show details

Does this app look suspicious? Report it here

Terms of use   Privacy & cookies   · · ·

Figure 10.12: Permissions requested dialog

9.   Click the **Accept** button.

After you click the **Accept** button, you will receive the following dialog:

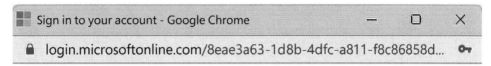

Microsoft

toi@blazorwebassembly.onmicrosoft.com

Help us protect your account

Microsoft has enabled Security Defaults to keep your account secure. Learn more about the benefits of Security Defaults

Skip for now (14 days until this is required)

Use a different account

Learn more

Next

Terms of use   Privacy & cookies   · · ·

Figure 10.13: Security Defaults dialog

10. Click the **Skip for now** link.

IMPORTANT NOTE

Do not click the **Next** button on the preceding dialog unless you want to use Microsoft Authenticator.

11. Click the **Yes** button when asked if you want to stay signed in.

    You are now authenticated. Notice that the LoginDisplay has been updated to display the **Log out of Claims Viewer** button and the user's name.

12. Click the **Secure Page** link.

IMPORTANT NOTE

If you have not yet been authenticated when you click the **Secure Page** link, you will be forced to log in because the page includes an Authenticate attribute.

13. Click the **Log out of Claims Viewer** button.
14. Pick the account to sign out of.
15. Close the browser.

We have demonstrated the Authorize attribute. Now let's use the AuthorizeView component again.

Add a WhoAmI component

We need to create the WhoAmI component that will be used to display information about the user. We will use the AuthorizeView component to render different information based on the user's authentication status. We do this as follows:

1. Return to Visual Studio.
2. Right-click the Pages folder and select the **Add, Razor Component** option from the menu.
3. Name the new component WhoAmI.
4. Replace all the text in the file with the following:

```
@page "/whoami"
@using System.Security.Claims;
```

```
<h1>Who Am I?</h1>

<AuthorizeView>
    <NotAuthorized>
        <div>
            <b>WARNING: You are not authenticated!</b>
            You must log in to Claims Viewer.
        </div>
    </NotAuthorized>
    <Authorized>
        I am @myName
    </Authorized>
</AuthorizeView>

@code {

}
```

The preceding code renders the name of the user if they have been authenticated. If the user has not yet been authenticated, the warning message is rendered instead.

5. Add the following code to the code block:

```
[CascadingParameter]
private Task<AuthenticationState>?
authStateTask
{ get; set; }

private string? myName;
private List<Claim>? myClaims;

protected override async Task OnInitializedAsync()
{
    var authState = await authStateTask!;
    var user = authState.User;

    if (user.Identity!.IsAuthenticated)
```

```
    {
        myName = user.Identity.Name;
        myClaims = user.Claims.ToList();
    };
}
```

In the preceding code, the value of authStateTask is cascading from the App component.

6. Press *Ctrl+F5* to start the application without debugging.

7. Click the **Who Am I** link.

    The AuthorizeView component is rendering the text in the NotAuthorized element.

8. Click the **Log in to Claims Viewer** button.

9. Provide your credentials and complete the login process.

    The AuthorizeView component is rendering the user's name.

10. Click the **Log out of Claims Viewer** button.

The preceding code sets the value of myClaims to the list of the user's claims. But how does my app get the list of claims? The claims come from the ID token that is sent from Azure AD. We can view the ID token by using the browser's developer tools. The ID token is a **JSON Web Token (JWT)**.

View the JSON Web Token (JWT)

We will view the ID token sent from Azure AD to our web app. The ID token uses JWT to share security information between a server and a client. We do this as follows:

1. Press *F12* to open the browser's developer tools.

2. Select the **Network** tab.

3. Click the **Log in to Claims Viewer** button.

4. Provide your credentials and complete the login process.

5. Click on **token** and select the **Preview** tab, as shown in the following screenshot:

Figure 10.14: Sample Token

6. Copy the value of id_token to the clipboard.

   Navigate to https://jwt.ms/.

7. Paste the contents of the clipboard into the empty text area.

   After you paste the contents of your token, the decoded token is rendered. This is the information that will be displayed on our **WhoAmI** page. Next to the **Decoded Token** tab is the **Claims** tab.

8. Click on the **Claims** tab to learn more about each of the claims in the token.

9. Close the browser.

Now that we know what to expect on our **WhoAmI** page, let's finish it.

Add an authentication policy

We want to limit access to the list of users' claims to only users who are members of the ViewAll group in Azure AD. To do that, we will add an authentication policy. We do this as follows:

1. Return to Visual Studio.

2. Open the Program.cs file.

3. Add the following code above the last line in the file:

```
builder.Services.AddAuthorizationCore(options =>
{
    options.AddPolicy("view-all", policy =>
        policy.RequireAssertion(context =>
        context.User.HasClaim(c =>
            c.Type == "groups" &&
            c.Value.Contains("{Object ID}")))));
});
```

4. Open the Pages/Secure.razor page.

5. Add the **view-all** policy to the Authorize attribute as shown below:

```
@attribute [Authorize(Policy = "view-all")]
```

The preceding code will prevent users who do not meet all the requirements of the view-all policy from viewing the page.

6. Open the Pages/WhoAmI.razor page.

7. Add the following markup below the existing AuthorizeView component:

```
<h2>My Claims</h2>

<AuthorizeView Policy="view-all">
    <NotAuthorized>
        <div>
            <b>WARNING: You are not authorized!</b>
            You must be a member of the ViewAll
            group in Azure AD.
        </div>
    </NotAuthorized>
    <Authorized>
        <ul>
            @foreach (Claim item in myClaims!)
            {
                <li>@item.Type: @item.Value</li>
            }
        </ul>
    </Authorized>
</AuthorizeView>
```

The preceding code will prevent users who do not meet all the requirements of the view-all policy from viewing the list of claims.

8. Press *Ctrl+F5* to start the application without debugging.

9. Click the **Log in to Claims Viewer** button.

10. Click the **Secure Page** link.

   You are not authorized to see this page because the user does not meet the requirements of the policy. This message is coming from the App component.

11. Click the **Who Am I?** link.

   You are not authorized to view your claims. This message is coming directly from the WhoAmI component.

12. Return to Visual Studio.

13. Open the Program.cs file.

14. Replace the {Object ID} placeholder with the value of the **Object ID** for the **ViewAll** group in Azure AD.

> **IMPORTANT NOTE**
>
> You saved the value of the group's **Object ID** after you added the **ViewAll** group during the **Add a user and group to Azure AD** step.

15. Select **Build Solution** from the **Build** menu.

16. Return to the browser.

   Since the user now meets the requirements of the policy, you are now able to view the list of their claims.

17. Click the **Secure Page** link.

   Likewise, since the user now meets all of the requirements of the policy, you are now able to view the **Secure** page.

We have created a secure application that allows authenticated users who are members of the ViewAll group to view the claims provided by the ID token from Azure AD.

Summary

You should now be able to render the list of an authenticated user's claims by delegating identity management to Azure AD.

In this chapter, we learned the difference between authentication and authorization. We also learned how to work with the authentication components. Finally, we learned how to control the user interface by using the `Authorize` attribute and the `AuthorizeView` component.

After that, we used the **Blazor WebAssembly App Empty** project template to create a new project. Next, we used the Azure Portal to configure our Azure AD tenant to add a new application. Then we added a group to our new application and added a user to that group. We used the Client ID and the Tenant ID from Azure AD to update the `appsettings.json` file in our project. We added the required NuGet packages and finished configuring our application to use authentication. We added the `Authentication`, `LoginDisplay`, `Secure`, and `WhoAmI` components. Finally, we used a policy to restrict access to the list of claims.

In the next chapter, we will use SQL Server to build a task manager using the ASP.NET Web API.

Questions

The following questions are provided for your consideration:

1. What is the difference between authentication and authorization?
2. If you add a `Secure` component to the `Home` page, will the user need to be authenticated to render it?
3. How can you secure a Blazor WebAssembly app without using the `Authorize` attribute on every routable component?
4. What are some of the claims that are included in a **JSON Web Token (JWT)**?

Further reading

The following resources provide more information concerning the topics covered in this chapter:

- For more information on the current authentication state, refer to `https://learn.microsoft.com/en-us/dotnet/api/microsoft.aspnetcore.components.authorization`.
- For more information on the `ClaimsPrincipal` class, refer to `https://learn.microsoft.com/en-us/dotnet/api/system.security.claims.claimsprincipal`.

- For more information on the Microsoft identity platform, refer to `https://learn.microsoft.com/en-us/azure/active-directory/develop`.

- For the `RemoteAuthenticatorViewCore` source code in GitHub, refer to `https://github.com/dotnet/aspnetcore/blob/600eb9aa53c052ec7327e2399744215d be493a89/src/Components/WebAssembly/WebAssembly.Authentication/src/ RemoteAuthenticatorViewCore.cs`.

- To decode a **JSON Web Token (JWT)**, refer to `https://jwt.ms`.

Join our community on Discord

Join our community's Discord space for discussions with the author and other readers:

`https://packt.link/BlazorWASM2e`

11

Building a Task Manager Using ASP.NET Web API

Most websites are not islands standing alone. They need a server. They rely on a server for both data access and security, among other services.

In this chapter, we will learn how to create a hosted Blazor WebAssembly app. We will learn how to use the **HttpClient** service to call web APIs, and we will also learn how to use **JSON helper methods** to make requests to a web API to read, add, edit, and delete data.

The project that we create in this chapter will be a **task manager**. We will use a multi-project architecture to separate the Blazor WebAssembly app from the ASP.NET Web API endpoints. The hosted Blazor WebAssembly app will use JSON helper methods to read, add, edit, and delete tasks that are stored in a SQL Server database. An ASP.NET core project will host the Blazor WebAssembly app and provide the ASP.NET Web API endpoints. A third project will be used to define the classes that are shared by the other two projects.

Islands stand alone.

Most websites are not islands -

they need a server.

In this chapter, we will cover the following topics:

- Understanding hosted applications
- Using the `HttpClient` service
- Using JSON helper methods
- Creating the task manager project

Technical requirements

To complete this project, you need to have Visual Studio 2022 installed on your PC. For instructions on how to install the free Community Edition of Visual Studio 2022, refer to *Chapter 1, Introduction to Blazor WebAssembly*. You will also need access to a version of SQL Server. For instructions on how to install the free edition of SQL Server 2022, refer to *Chapter 1, Introduction to Blazor WebAssembly*.

The source code for this chapter is available in the following GitHub repository: `https://github.com/PacktPublishing/Blazor-WebAssembly-by-Example-Second-Edition/tree/main/Chapter11`.

The Code in Action video is available here: `https://packt.link/Ch11`.

Understanding hosted applications

When we create a new Blazor WebAssembly project by using Microsoft's **Blazor WebAssembly App Empty** project template, we have the option to create a hosted Blazor WebAssembly app by checking the **ASP.NET Core Hosted** checkbox.

The following screenshot highlights the **ASP.NET Core Hosted** checkbox:

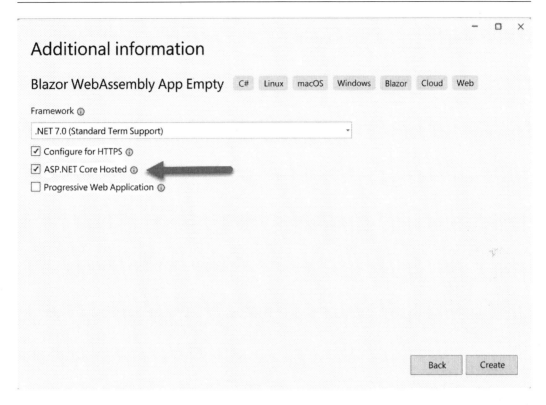

Figure 11.1: Blazor WebAssembly App Empty project template

The hosted Blazor WebAssembly app, created by the **Blazor WebAssembly App Empty** project template, includes the following three projects:

- Client project
- Server project
- Shared project

Client project

The client project is a client-side Blazor WebAssembly project. It is almost identical to the stand-alone Blazor WebAssembly app we created in *Chapter 2, Building Your First Blazor WebAssembly Application*. The only big difference is in how the data is accessed. In the client project, the sample data is accessed from the server project using Web API endpoints instead of a static file. Since the server project is both hosting the client project and serving the data via ASP.NET Web API, it won't have any CORS problems.

Server project

The server project is an ASP.NET Core project. This project is responsible for serving the client application. In addition to hosting the client app, the server project provides the Web API endpoints.

IMPORTANT NOTE

In this scenario, since the ASP.NET Core project is serving the Blazor WebAssembly app, it must be set as the startup project in the solution.

Shared project

The shared project is also an ASP.NET Core project. It contains application logic that is shared between the other two projects. In the past, we had to write validation code on both the client and the server. We had to write JavaScript validation code for the client and C# validation code for the server. Not surprisingly, sometimes the two validation models did not match. The shared project solves that problem since all the validation code is maintained in a single location using a single language.

By using a multi-project solution, we can create a more robust application. The shared project defines the classes, and the client project uses the HttpClient service to make requests for data from the server project.

Using the HttpClient service

HTTP is not just for serving web pages – it can also be used for serving data. These are the HTTP methods that we will be using in this chapter:

- GET: This method is used to request one or more resources.
- POST: This method is used to create a new resource.

- PUT: This method is used to update the specified resource.
- DELETE: This method is used to delete the specified resource.

The HttpClient service is a preconfigured service for making HTTP requests from a Blazor WebAssembly app to a server. It is configured in the Client/Program.cs file. The following code is used to configure it:

```
builder.Services.AddScoped(sp => new HttpClient {
    BaseAddress = new Uri(builder.HostEnvironment.BaseAddress) });
```

The HttpClient service is added to a page using **dependency injection (DI)**. To use the HttpClient service in a component, you must inject it by either using the @inject directive or the Inject attribute. For more information on DI, see *Chapter 7, Building a Shopping Cart Using Application State*.

The following code demonstrates the two different ways to inject the HttpClient service into a component:

```
@inject HttpClient Http[Inject]
public HttpClient Http { get; set; }
```

The first example is used in .razor files while the second example is used in .razor.cs files. After we have injected the HttpClient service into a component, we can use the JSON helper methods to send requests to a Web API.

Using JSON helper methods

There are three JSON helper methods. There is one for reading data, one for adding data, and one for updating data. Since there is not one for deleting data, we will use the HttpClient.DeleteAsync method to delete data.

The following table shows the relationship between the JSON helper methods and the HTTP methods:

JSON Helper Method	HTTP Method	Action
GetFromJsonAsync	GET	Read
PostAsJsonAsync	POST	Create
PutAsJsonAsync	PUT	Update
HttpClient.DeleteAsync	DELETE	Delete

Table 11.1: Relationship between the HTTP methods and the JSON helper methods

In the following code examples, we will be referring to the `TaskItem` class. This is the `TaskItem` class:

```
public class TaskItem
{
    public int TaskItemId { get; set; }
    public string? TaskName { get; set; }
    public bool IsComplete { get; set; }
}
```

GetFromJsonAsync

The `GetFromJsonAsync` method is used to read data. It does the following:

- Sends an `HTTP GET` request to the indicated URI.
- Deserializes the JSON response body to create the indicated object.

The following code uses the `GetFromJsonAsync` method to return a collection of `TaskItem` objects:

```
IList<TaskItem>? tasks;
string requestUri = "api/TaskItems";


tasks = await Http.GetFromJsonAsync<IList<TaskItem>>(requestUri);
```

In the preceding code, the type of object returned by the `GetFromJsonAsync` method is `IList<TaskItem>`.

We can also use the `GetFromJsonAsync` method to get an individual object. The following code uses the `GetFromJsonAsync` method to return a single `TaskItem` object where id is the unique identifier of the object:

```
TaskItem? task;
string requestUri = "api/TaskItems/{id}";


task = await Http.GetFromJsonAsync<TaskItem>(requestUri);
```

In the preceding code, the type of object returned by the GetFromJsonAsync method is TaskItem.

PostAsJsonAsync

The PostAsJsonAsync method is used to add data. It does the following:

- Sends an HTTP POST request to the indicated URI. The request includes the JSON-encoded content used to create the new data.
- Returns an HttpResponseMessage instance that includes both a status code and data.

The following code creates a new TaskItem object by using the PostAsJsonAsync method:

```
TaskItem newTaskItem = new() { TaskName = "Buy Milk"};
string requestUri = "api/TaskItems";

var response =
    await Http.PostAsJsonAsync(requestUri, newTaskItem);

if (response.IsSuccessStatusCode)
{
    var task =
        await response.Content.ReadFromJsonAsync<TaskItem>();
}
else
{
    // handle error
};
```

In the preceding code, the new TaskItem is deserialized from the response using the ReadFromJsonAsync method if the HTTP response returns a success status code.

TIP

The ReadFromJsonAsync method returns deserialized content. It is included in the System.Text.Json library provided by Microsoft. The System.Text.Json library includes high-performance, low-allocating methods for serializing and deserializing JSON text to and from objects.

PutAsJsonAsync

The `PutAsJsonAsync` method is used to update data. It does the following:

- Sends an `HTTP PUT` request to the indicated URI. The request includes the JSON-encoded content used to update the data.

- Returns an `HttpResponseMessage` instance that includes both a status code and data.

The following code updates an existing `TaskItem` object by using the `PutAsJsonAsync` method:

```
string requestUri = $"api/TaskItems/{updatedTaskItem.TaskItemId}";


var response =
    await Http.PutAsJsonAsync<TaskItem>
        (requestUri, updatedTaskItem);


if (response.IsSuccessStatusCode)
{
    var task =
        await response.Content.ReadFromJsonAsync<TaskItem>();
}
else
{
    // handle error
};
```

In the preceding code, the updated `TaskItem` is deserialized from the response using the `ReadFromJsonAsync` method if the HTTP response returns a success status code.

HttpClient.DeleteAsync

The `HttpClient.DeleteAsync` method is used to delete data. It does the following:

- Sends an `HTTP DELETE` request to the indicated URI.

- Returns an `HttpResponseMessage` instance that includes both a status code and data.

The following code deletes an existing `TaskItem` object by using the `Http.DeleteAsync` method:

```
string requestUri = $"api/TaskItems/{taskItem.TaskItemId}";


var response = await Http.DeleteAsync(requestUri);
```

```
if (!response.IsSuccessStatusCode)
{
    // handle error
};
```

In the preceding code, the TaskItem with the indicated TaskItemId is deleted.

The JSON helper methods make it easy to consume web APIs. We use them to read, create, and update data. We use HttpClient.DeleteAsync to delete data.

Now, let's get a quick overview of the project that we are going to build in this chapter.

Creating the TaskManager project

In this chapter, we will build a hosted Blazor WebAssembly app to manage tasks. We will be able to view, add, edit, and delete tasks. The tasks will be stored in a SQL Server database.

This is a screenshot of the completed application:

Figure 11.2: TaskManager project

The build time for this project is approximately 60 minutes.

Project overview

The TaskManager project will be created by using Microsoft's **Blazor WebAssembly App Empty** project template to create a hosted Blazor WebAssembly project. First, we will add both a TaskItem class and a TaskItemsController class. Next, we will use Entity Framework migrations to create a database in SQL Server. We will add Bootstrap and Bootstrap icons to our project to style our UI. Finally, we will demonstrate how to read data, update data, delete data, and add data using the HttpClient service.

Create the TaskManager project

We need to create a new hosted Blazor WebAssembly app. We do this as follows:

1. Open Visual Studio 2022.

2. Click the **Create a new project** button.

3. Press *Alt+S* to enter the **Search for templates** textbox.

4. Enter Blazor and press the *Enter* key.

    The following screenshot shows the **Blazor WebAssembly App Empty** project template:

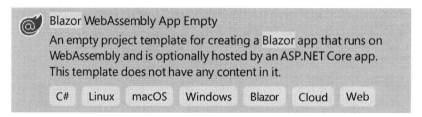

Figure 11.3: Blazor WebAssembly App Empty project template

5. Select the **Blazor WebAssembly App Empty** project template and click the **Next** button.

6. Enter TaskManager in the **Project name** textbox and click the **Next** button.

    This is a screenshot of the dialog used to configure our new project:

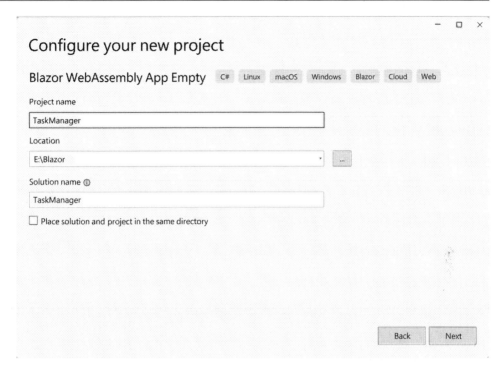

Figure 11.4: Configure your new project dialog

TIP

In the preceding example, we placed the TaskManager project into the E:/ Blazor folder. However, the location of this project is not important.

7. Select **.NET 7.0** as the version of the Framework to use.

8. Check the **Configure for HTTPS** checkbox.

9. Check the **ASP.NET Core Hosted** checkbox.

10. Uncheck the **Progressive Web Application** checkbox.

This is a screenshot of the dialog used to collect additional information about our new project:

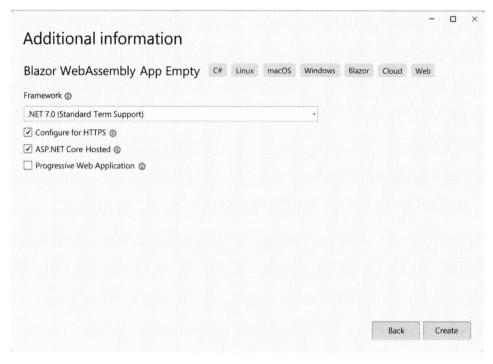

Figure 11.5: Additional information dialog

11. Click the **Create** button.

We have created a hosted **TaskManager** Blazor WebAssembly project.

The **TaskManager** solution comprises three different projects. The following screenshot of Visual Studio's **Solution Explorer** shows the three projects that are in the solution:

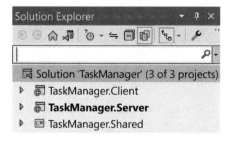

Figure 11.6: Solution Explorer

12. Right-click the **TaskManager.Server** project and select the **Set as Startup Project** option from the menu.

We have created the **TaskManager** solution and set the **TaskManager.Server** project as the startup project. Now we need to add a shared class to the **TaskManager.Shared** project.

Adding the TaskItem class

We need to add the TaskItem class. We do this as follows:

1. Right-click the **TaskManager.Shared** project and select the **Add, Class** option from the menu.

2. Name the new class TaskItem.

3. Click the **Add** button.

4. Make the class public by adding the public modifier:

   ```
   public class TaskItem
   ```

5. Add the following properties to the TaskItem class:

   ```
   public int TaskItemId { get; set; }
   public string? TaskName { get; set; }
   public bool IsComplete { get; set; }
   ```

6. From the **Build** menu, select the **Build Solution** option.

We have added the TaskItem class. Next, we need to add an API controller for the TaskItem class. The API Controller will handle incoming HTTP requests from the Blazor WebAssembly client and will send responses back to it.

Adding the TaskItem API controller

We need to add a TaskItemsController class. We do this as follows:

1. Right-click the **TaskManager.Server** project and select the **Add, New Folder** option from the menu.

2. Name the new folder Controllers.

3. Right-click the TaskManager.Server.Contollers folder and select the **Add, Controller** option from the menu.

4. Select the **API Controller with actions, using Entity Framework** option:

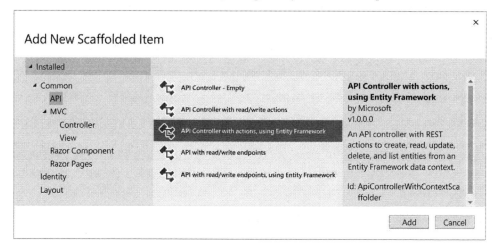

Figure 11.7: Add New Scaffolded Item dialog

5. Click the **Add** button.

6. Set **Model class** to **TaskItem (TaskManager.Shared)**.

7. Click the **Add data context** button to open the **Add Data Context** dialog:

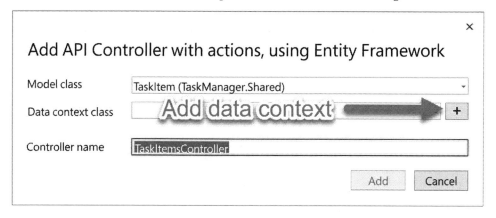

Figure 11.8: Add API Controller with actions, using Entity Framework dialog

8. Click the **Add** button to accept the default values.

Figure 11.9: Add Data Context dialog

9. Click the **Add** button on the **Add API Controller with actions, using Entity Framework** dialog.

We have created the TaskItemsController class. Now we need to set up SQL Server.

Setting up SQL Server

We need to create a new database on SQL Server and add a table to contain the tasks. We do this as follows:

1. Open the TaskManager.Server/appsettings.json file.

2. Update the connection string to the following:

```
"ConnectionStrings": {
  "TaskManagerServerContext": "Server={Server name};
Database=TaskManager; Trusted_Connection=True; Encrypt=False;"
}
```

3. Replace the {Server name} placeholder with the name of your SQL Server.

IMPORTANT NOTE

Although we are using SQL Server 2022 Express, it does not matter what version of SQL Server you use for this project.

4. From the **Tools** menu, select the **NuGet Package Manager, Package Manager Console** option.

5. In **Package Manager Console**, use the drop-down list to change **Default project** to **Task-Manager.Server**.

6. Execute the following commands in **Package Manager Console**:

```
Add-Migration Init
Update-Database
```

The preceding commands use Entity Framework migrations to update SQL Server.

7. From the **View** menu, select **SQL Server Object Explorer**.

8. If you do not see the SQL Server instance that you are using for this project, click the **Add SQL Server** button to connect it:

Figure 11.10: SQL Server Object Explorer

9. Navigate to the **TaskManager** database.

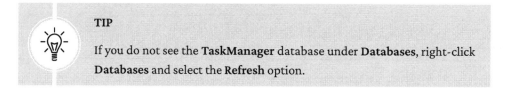

> **TIP**
>
> If you do not see the **TaskManager** database under **Databases**, right-click **Databases** and select the **Refresh** option.

10. Navigate to **TaskManager**, **Tables**, **dbo.TaskItem**:

Figure 11.11: TaskManager database

11. Right-click **dbo.TaskItem** and select the **View Data** option.

12. Enter a couple of tasks by completing the **TaskName** field and setting the **IsComplete** field to **False**:

	TaskItemId	TaskName	IsComplete
	1	Buy Milk	False
▶	2	Read Email	*False*
*	NULL	NULL	NULL

Figure 11.12: Sample data

13. Press *Ctrl+F5* to start the application without debugging.

14. Add /api/taskitems to the address bar and press *Enter*.

The following screenshot shows the JSON that is returned by TaskItemsController:

```
←  →  C      🔒 localhost:7167/api/taskitems

▼ [
    ▼ {
            "taskItemId": 1,
            "taskName": "Buy Milk",
            "isComplete": false
      },
    ▼ {
            "taskItemId": 2,
            "taskName": "Read Email",
            "isComplete": false
      }
  ]
```

Figure 11.13: JSON returned by the TaskItem API controller

15. Close the browser.

We have demonstrated that TaskItemsController works. Now we can start working on the TaskManager.Client project. We will use Bootstrap to style our UI and Bootstrap icons to provide the trashcan image on the delete button.

Install Bootstrap

We need to install Bootstrap and Bootstrap icons in our web app. We do this as follows:

1. Return to Visual Studio.

2. Press *Ctrl+Alt+L* to view **Solution Explorer**.

3. Right-click the TaskManager.Client/wwwroot/css folder and select the **Add, Client-Side Library** option from the menu.

4. Enter bootstrap into the **Library** search textbox and press the *Enter* key.

5. Select **Choose specific files**.

6. Select only the **css** files, as shown in the following screenshot:

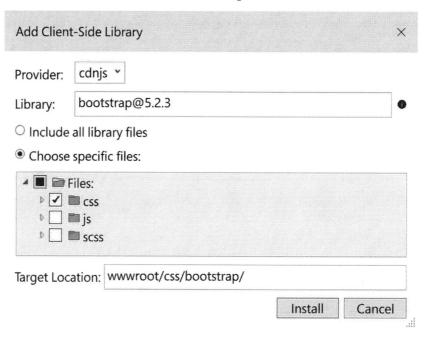

Figure 11.14: Add Client-Side Library dialog

TIP

Although the preceding screenshot has version 5.2.3 of Bootstrap selected, you can use any version of Bootstrap 5 to complete this project.

7. Click the **Install** button.

> **IMPORTANT NOTE**
>
> After you install Bootstrap, a new folder will be added to the wwwroot/css
> folder. This new folder contains all the CSS files needed for Bootstrap. We
> will only be using the bootstrap.min.css file in this project.

8. Open the TaskManager.Client/wwwroot/index.html file.

9. Add the following markup to the head element before the link to the css/app.css
    stylesheet:

    ```
    <link href="css/bootstrap/css/bootstrap.min.css"
          rel="stylesheet" />
    ```

10. Right-click the TaskManager.Client/wwwroot/css folder and select the **Add, Client-Side
    Library** option from the menu.

11. Enter bootstrap-icons into the **Library** search textbox and press the *Enter* key.

12. Select **Choose specific files**.

13. Select only the **font** files as shown in the following screenshot:

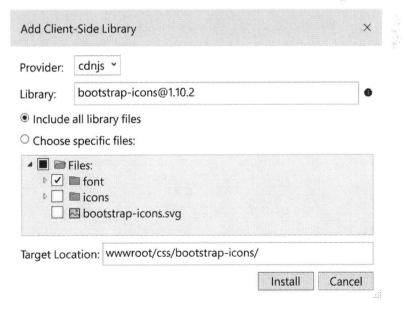

Figure 11.15: Add Client-Side Library dialog

14. Open the `TaskManager.Client/wwwroot/index.html` file.

15. Add the following markup to the head element before the link to the `css/app.css` stylesheet:

```
<link href="css/bootstrap-icons/font/bootstrap-icons.css"
    rel="stylesheet" />
```

We have installed both `Bootstrap` and `Boostrap icons`. Now we will update the **Home** page to display the tasks that are stored in SQL Server.

Displaying the tasks

We need to fetch the list of tasks and display them to the user. We do this as follows:

1. Right-click the `TaskManager.Client.Pages` folder and select the **Add, Class** option from the menu.

2. Name the new class `Index.razor.cs`.

3. Click the **Add** button.

4. Add the partial modifier to the class:

```
public partial class Index
```

5. Add the following using statement:

```
using Microsoft.AspNetCore.Components;
```

6. Add the following property to the `Index` class:

```
[Inject] public HttpClient Http { get; set; }
```

The preceding code injects the `HttpClient` service into the component.

7. Add the following code to the `Index` class:

```
private IList<TaskItem>? tasks;
private string? error;

protected override async Task OnInitializedAsync()
{
    try
    {
        string requestUri = "api/TaskItems";
```

```
        tasks =
            await Http.GetFromJsonAsync<IList<TaskItem>>
            (requestUri);
    }
    catch (Exception)
    {
        error = "Error Encountered";
    };
}
```

The preceding code uses the GetFromJsonAsync method to return the collection of TaskItem objects.

8. Verify that Visual Studio has automatically added the following using statements:

```
using System.Net.Http.Json;
using TaskManager.Shared;
```

9. Open the TaskManager.Client.Pages/Index.razor page.

10. Remove the h1 element.

11. Add the following @if statement:

```
@if (tasks == null)
{
    <p><em>Loading...</em></p>
}
else
{
    @foreach (var taskItem in tasks)
    {

    }
}
```

The preceding markup displays the loading message if the value of tasks is null. Otherwise, it loops through the collection of TaskItem objects in tasks.

12. Add the following markup to the @foreach loop:

```
<div class="d-flex col-md-6 mx-auto border-bottom"
    @key="taskItem">
    <div class="p-2 flex-fill">
        <input type="checkbox"
            checked="@taskItem.IsComplete" />
        <span>
            @taskItem.TaskName
        </span>
    </div>
    <div class="p-1">
        <button type="button"
                class="btn btn-outline-danger btn-sm"
                title="Delete task">
            <span class="bi bi-trash"></span>
        </button>
    </div>
</div>
```

The preceding markup displays a checkbox, the TaskName field, and a delete button for each TaskItem class.

13. Press *Ctrl+F5* to start the application without debugging.

The following is a screenshot of the **Home** page:

Figure 11.16: List of tasks

We have added a list of tasks to the **Home** page, but nothing happens when we click either the checkbox or the **delete** button. Next, we need to allow the user to mark a task as complete.

Completing the tasks

We will allow the user to mark a task as complete by clicking the checkbox next to the name of the task. We do this as follows:

1. Return to Visual Studio.

2. Right-click the TaskManager.Client/Pages folder and select the **Add, New Item** option from the menu.

3. Enter css in the **Search** box.

4. Select **Style Sheet**.

5. Name the file Index.razor.css.

6. Click the **Add** button.

7. Replace the default text with the following style:

```css
.completed-task {
    text-decoration: line-through;
}
```

The preceding style will render a line through the tasks that are in the completed-task class.

8. Open the TaskManager.Client/wwwroot/index.html file.

9. Uncomment the following link element:

```html
<link href="TaskManager.Client.styles.css"
    rel="stylesheet" />
```

10. Open the Index.razor file.

11. Update the span element used to display the task's name to the following:

```html
<span
    class="@((taskItem.IsComplete? "completed-task" : ""))">
    @taskItem.TaskName
</span>
```

The preceding markup will set the class of the span element to completed-task when the task is completed by checking the checkbox associated with the task.

12. Add the following markup to the input element of type checkbox:

```
@onchange="@(()=>CheckboxChecked(taskItem))"
```

13. Open the TaskManager.Client.Pages/Index.razor.cs file.

14. Add the following CheckboxChecked method:

```csharp
private async Task CheckboxChecked(TaskItem task)
{
    task.IsComplete = !task.IsComplete;
```

```
        string requestUri = $"api/TaskItems/{task.TaskItemId}";

        var response =
            await Http.PutAsJsonAsync<TaskItem>
            (requestUri, task);

        if (!response.IsSuccessStatusCode)
        {
            error = response.ReasonPhrase;
        };
    }
```

The preceding code uses the `PutAsJsonAsync` method to update the indicated `TaskItem` class.

15. Press *Ctrl+F5* to start the application without debugging.

16. Mark one of the tasks as complete by clicking the checkbox next to it.

    The following screenshot shows a task that has been completed:

Figure 11.17: Completed task

17. Return to Visual Studio.

18. Select the **dbo.TaskItem [Data]** tab.

19. Click *Shift+Alt+R* to refresh the data.

20. Verify that the **IsComplete** field has been updated to **True** for the `TaskItem` that you marked as complete.

When a user checks the checkbox next to a task, the UI is updated, and the SQL Server database is updated. Next, we need to add the ability to delete tasks.

Deleting tasks

We need to allow users to delete tasks. We do this as follows:

1. Open the `Index.razor` file.

2. Update the `button` element to the following by adding the highlighted code:

```
<button type="button"
        class="btn btn-outline-danger btn-sm"
        title="Delete task"
        @onclick="@(()=>DeleteTask(taskItem))">
    <span class="bi bi-trash"></span>
</button>
```

3. Open the `TaskManager.Client.Pages/Index.razor.cs` file.

4. Add the following `DeleteTask` method:

```
private async Task DeleteTask(TaskItem taskItem)
{
    tasks!.Remove(taskItem);
    StateHasChanged();
    string requestUri =
        $"api/TaskItems/{taskItem.TaskItemId}";

    var response = await Http.DeleteAsync(requestUri);

    if (!response.IsSuccessStatusCode)
    {
        error = response.ReasonPhrase;
    };
}
```

The preceding code uses the `Http.DeleteAsync` method to delete the indicated `TaskItem` class.

5. Press *Ctrl+F5* to start the application without debugging.

6. Click the button with the garbage can icon to delete one of the tasks.

7. Return to Visual Studio.

8. Select the **dbo.TaskItem [Data]** tab.

9. Click *Shift+Alt+R* to refresh the data.

10. Verify that the `TaskItem` has been deleted.

We have added the ability to delete tasks. Now we need to add the ability to add new tasks.

Adding new tasks

We need to provide a way for users to add new tasks. We do this as follows:

1. Open the Index.razor file.

2. Add the following markup before the @foreach loop:

```
<div class="d-flex col-md-6 mx-auto py-2">
    <input type="text"
            class="form-control m-1"
            placeholder="Enter Task" @bind="newTask" />
    <button type="button" class="btn btn-success"
        @onclick="AddTask">
        Add
    </button>
</div>
```

3. Open the TaskManager.Client.Pages/Index.razor.cs file.

4. Add the following field:

```
private string? newTask;
```

5. Add the following AddTask method:

```
private async Task AddTask()
{
    if (!string.IsNullOrWhiteSpace(newTask))
    {
        TaskItem newTaskItem = new TaskItem
        {
            TaskName = newTask,
            IsComplete = false
        };

        tasks!.Add(newTaskItem);

        string requestUri = "api/TaskItems";

        var response =
            await Http.PostAsJsonAsync
```

```
                (requestUri, newTaskItem);

        if (response.IsSuccessStatusCode)
        {
            newTask = string.Empty;
        }
        else
        {
            error = response.ReasonPhrase;
        };
    };
}
```

The preceding code uses the PostAsJsonAsync method to create a new TaskItem class.

6. Press *Ctrl+F5* to start the application without debugging.

7. Add a few new tasks.

8. Return to Visual Studio.

9. Select the **dbo.TaskItem [Data]** tab.

10. Click *Shift+Alt+R* to refresh the data.

11. Verify that the new tasks have been added to the SQL Server database.

We have added the ability for users to add new tasks.

Summary

You should now be able to create a hosted Blazor WebAssembly app that uses ASP.NET Web API to update data in a SQL Server database.

In this chapter, we introduced hosted Blazor WebAssembly apps, the HttpClient service, and the JSON helper methods used to read, create, and update data. We also demonstrated how to delete data using the HttpClient.DeleteAsync method.

After that, we used Microsoft's **Blazor WebAssembly App Empty** project template to create a hosted Blazor WebAssembly app. We added a TaskItem class to the TaskManager.Shared project and a TaskItem API controller to the TaskManager.Server project. Next, we configured SQL Server by updating the connection string to the database and using Entity Framework migrations. To enhance the UI, we added Bootstrap and Bootstrap icons. Finally, we used the HttpClient service to read the list of tasks, update a task, delete a task, and add new tasks.

We can apply our new skills to create a hosted Blazor WebAssembly app that is part of a multi-project solution and use ASP.NET Web API to read, create, update, and delete data.

In the next chapter, we will build an expense tracker using the EditForm component.

Questions

The following questions are provided for your consideration:

1. What are the benefits of using a hosted Blazor WebAssembly project versus a standalone Blazor WebAssembly project?

2. What is the difference between HTTP GET, HTTP POST, and HTTP PUT?

3. In our project, how would we obtain the TaskItemId of a TaskItem that was created using the PostAsJsonAsync method?

4. Can you add, edit, and delete data in a SQL Server database directly from Visual Studio?

Further reading

The following resources provide more information concerning the topics covered in this chapter:

- For more information on the HttpClient class, refer to https://learn.microsoft.com/en-us/dotnet/api/system.net.http.httpclient.

- For more information on calling a web API from Blazor WebAssembly, refer to https://learn.microsoft.com/en-us/aspnet/core/blazor/call-web-api.

- For more information on the extension methods that perform serialization and deserialization using System.Text.Json, refer to https://learn.microsoft.com/en-us/dotnet/api/system.text.json.

- For more information on Entity Framework, refer to https://learn.microsoft.com/en-us/ef.

- For more information on Bootstrap, refer to https://getbootstrap.com.

12

Building an Expense Tracker Using the EditForm Component

Most applications require some data input by the user. The Blazor WebAssembly framework includes a component that makes it easy to create data input forms and validate the data on those forms.

In this chapter, we will learn how to use the **EditForm** component and the various built-in input components. We will also learn how to use the built-in input validation components in conjunction with **Data Annotations** to validate the data on the form. Finally, we will learn how to use the **NavigationLock** component to prevent users from losing their edits if they navigate away from the form before they have saved their updates.

The project that we'll create in this chapter will be a travel expense tracker. We will use a multi-project architecture to separate the Blazor WebAssembly app from the ASP.NET Web API endpoints. The page used to add and edit expenses will use the EditForm component as well as many of the built-in input components. It will also use the built-in validation components to validate the data on the form. Finally, we will add a NavigationLock component to remind the user to save their data before navigating to another page.

Editing data?

The EditForm component

makes it effortless!

In this chapter, we will cover the following topics:

- Creating a data entry form
- Using the built-in input components
- Using the validation components
- Locking navigation
- Creating the expense tracker project

Technical requirements

To complete this project, you need to have Visual Studio 2022 installed on your PC. For instructions on how to install the free Community Edition of Visual Studio 2022, refer to *Chapter 1, Introduction to Blazor WebAssembly*. You will also need access to a version of SQL Server. For instructions on how to install the free edition of SQL Server 2022, refer to *Chapter 1, Introduction to Blazor WebAssembly*.

The source code for this chapter is available in the following GitHub repository: `https://github.com/PacktPublishing/Blazor-WebAssembly-by-Example-Second-Edition/tree/main/Chapter12`.

The Code in Action video is available here: `https://packt.link/Ch12`.

Creating a data entry form

In the previous chapters of this book, we used the standard HTML `form` element to collect user input. However, the Blazor WebAssembly framework provides an enhanced version of the standard HTML `form` element called the `EditForm` component.

The `EditForm` component not only manages forms but also coordinates both validation and submission events. The following code shows a simple `EditForm` element:

```
<EditForm Model="expense" OnValidSubmit="@HandleValidSubmit">
    Vendor <InputText @bind-Value="expense.Vendor"
                      placeholder="Enter Vendor"/>
    <button type="submit">
        Save
    </button>
</EditForm>

@code {
    private Expense expense = new();
}
```

This is the HTML that is rendered by the proceeding `EditForm` component:

```
<form>
    Vendor <input placeholder="Enter Vendor"
                  class="valid" _bl_2="">
      <button type="submit">
          Save
      </button>
</form>
```

In the preceding `EditForm` component, the `Model` property specifies the top-level model object for the form. The `OnValidSubmit` property specifies the callback that will be invoked when the form is submitted without any validation errors.

Binding a form

The `EditContext` property of the `EditForm` class is used to track the metadata about the editing process. The metadata includes the fields that have been modified and the current validation messages. There are two ways to assign the `EditContext` property:

- Assign the `Model` property of the `EditForm` class. If we use the `Model` property, the edit context will be automatically constructed using the model.

- Assign the `EditContext` property of the `EditForm` class.

The following code shows how to render the preceding `EditForm` component using the `EditContext` property instead of the `Model` property:

```
<EditForm EditContext="editContext"
          OnValidSubmit="@HandleValidSubmit">
    Vendor <InputText @bind-Value="expense.Vendor" />
    <button type="submit">
        Save
    </button>
</EditForm>

@code {
    private Expense expense = new();
    private EditContext? editContext;

    protected override void OnInitialized()
```

```
    {
        editContext = new(expense);
    }
}
```

IMPORTANT NOTE

If we attempt to assign both the Model property and the EditContext property of an EditForm component, a runtime error will be generated.

Submitting a form

There are three properties of the EditForm component that are involved with form submission:

- OnValidSubmit: The callback that is invoked when the form is submitted and the EditContext property is valid.

- OnInvalidSubmit: The callback that is invoked when the form is submitted and the EditContext property is invalid.

- OnSubmit: The callback that is invoked when the form is submitted. When we use this property, we need to manually trigger validation by using the Validate method of the EditContext property of the EditForm.

We can use the OnValidSubmit and OnInvalidSubmit callbacks together or separately, or we can use the OnSubmit callback by itself. If we use the OnSubmit callback, we are responsible for performing the form validation. Otherwise, the form validation is performed by the EditForm component.

IMPORTANT NOTE

If we set an OnSubmit callback, any callbacks set using OnValidSubmit or OnInvalidSubmit are ignored.

There are quite a few built-in input components that we can use in conjunction with the EditForm component.

Using the built-in input components

The following table lists the built-in input components along with the HTML that they render:

Input Component	HTML Rendered
InputCheckbox	`<input type="checkbox">`
InputDate<TValue>	`<input type="date">`
InputFile	`<input type="file">`
InputNumber<TValue>	`<input type="number">`
InputRadio<TValue>	`<input type="radio">`
InputRadioGroup<TValue>	Group of child InputRadio<TValue>
InputSelect<TValue>	`<select>`
InputText	`<input>`
InputTextArea	`<textarea>`

Table 12.1: Built-in input components

All the built-in input components can receive and validate user inputs when placed within an EditForm element. The EditForm cascades its EditContext to its descendants. Also, all of the built-in input components support arbitrary attributes. Therefore, any attribute that does not match a component parameter is added to the HTML element that is rendered by the component.

InputCheckbox

The InputCheckbox component is for editing Boolean values. It does not allow binding to a nullable property.

InputDate

The InputDate component is for editing date values. The supported date types are DateTime and DateTimeOffset. If a datatype that is not supported is entered into this component, the framework will create a validation error.

InputFile

The InputFile component is for uploading files.

TIP

The project in this chapter does not use the InputFile component. For more information on using the InputFile component, refer to *Chapter 9, Uploading and Reading an Excel File.*

InputNumber

The InputNumber component is for editing numeric values. The supported numeric types are Int32, Int64, Single, Double, and Decimal. If a datatype that is not supported is entered into this component, the framework will create a validation error unless the target property is nullable. In that case, the invalid input will be considered null and the text in the input will be cleared.

InputRadio

The InputRadio component is for selecting a value from a group of choices.

InputRadioGroup

The InputRadioGroup component is for grouping InputRadio components.

InputSelect

The InputSelect component is for rendering a dropdown selection. The InputSelect component includes a ChildContent property for rendering the content inside of the select element.

If the option you select does not have a value attribute since its value is null, the text content is treated as the value. This is standard HTML. However, when using two-way binding with Blazor, you must provide a string.Empty as the value for null values to prevent the value of the text from being returned.

InputText

The InputText component is for editing string values. The InputText component does not specify a type. This allows you to use any of the available input types for the HTML input element, such as password, tel, or color.

The default type for an HTML input element is text.

InputTextArea

The InputTextArea component is for editing string values using multiline input.

By using the various built-in input components in conjunction with their parent EditForm, we can easily add an input form to a Blazor WebAssembly app.

The input data is validated both when the form is submitted and when the data is changed. To communicate the validation status of the input form, we can use the built-in validation components.

Using the validation components

Input validation is an important aspect of every application since it prevents users from entering invalid data. The Blazor WebAssembly framework uses data annotations for input validation. There are over 30 built-in Data Annotation attributes. This is a list of the ones that we will be using in this project:

- Required: This attribute specifies that a value is required.
- Display: This attribute specifies the string to display in error messages.
- MaxLength: This attribute specifies the maximum string length allowed.
- Range: This attribute specifies the maximum and minimum values.

The following code demonstrates the use of a few data annotations:

```
[Required]
public DateTime? Date { get; set; }

[Required]
[Range(0, 500, ErrorMessage = "The Amount must be <= $500")]
public decimal? Amount { get; set; }
```

In the preceding example, both the Date field and the Amount field are required. Also, the Amount field must be a value between 0 and 500 inclusive, or the indicated error message is displayed.

There are two built-in validation components:

- ValidationMessage: This component displays all the validation messages for the indicated field within the EditContext.
- ValidationSummary: This component displays all the validation messages for all the fields within the EditContext. It provides a summary of the validation messages.

The location of the validation component within the page determines where it will be rendered. In the following example, the ValidationMessage is placed after each related input component and the ValidationSummary is placed after the **Save** button.

This is a sample `ValidationMessage` component:

```
<ValidationMessage For="() => expense.Date" />
```

This is a sample `ValidationSummary` component:

```
<ValidationSummary />
```

An `EditForm` component can include both types of validation components. However, to use either type of validation component, we must add `DataAnnotationsValidator` to the `EditForm` component.

The following screenshot shows the results of both a `ValidationSummary` component and individual `ValidationMesssage` components:

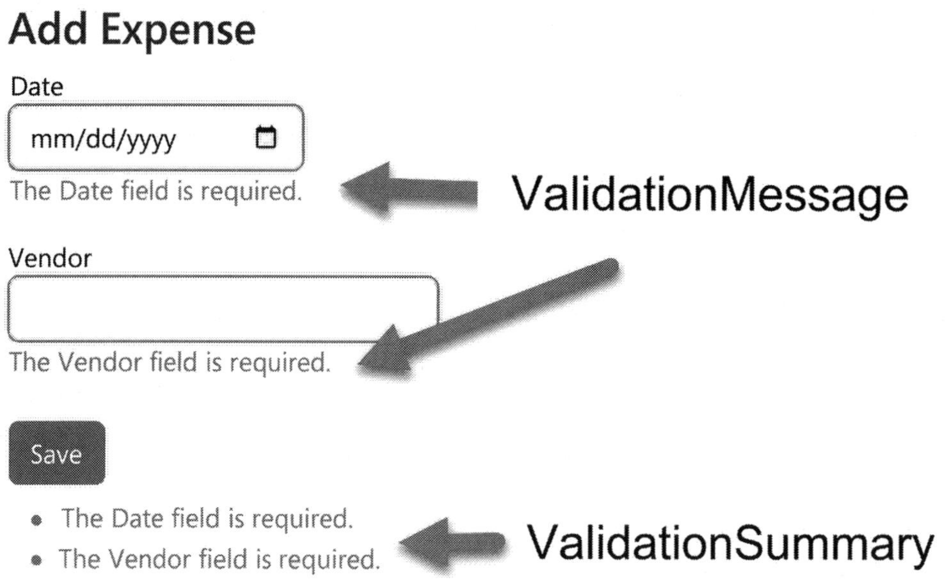

Figure 12.1: Validation components

The validation components make it easy to add validation to a Blazor WebAssembly app.

Locking navigation

How many times have you completed a form and forgotten to save it before navigating to another page? It happens to everyone. The `NavigationLock` component can be used to notify the user that they are about to navigate away from the current page and allow them to cancel that action. It does that by intercepting navigation events.

This is a sample `NavigationLock`:

```
<NavigationLock ConfirmExternalNavigation="true"
    OnBeforeInternalNavigation="HandleBeforeInternalNav" />
```

The `NavigationLock` class includes two properties:

- `ConfirmExternalNavigation` – gets or sets whether the user should be asked to confirm external navigations. The default value is `false`.

- `OnBeforeInternalNavigation` – gets or sets the callback that is invoked when an internal navigation event occurs.

This is a sample method that is invoked from the `OnBeforeInternalNavigation` property:

```
private async Task HandleBeforeInternalNav
    (LocationChangingContext context)
{
    if (context.IsNavigationIntercepted)
    {
        var confirm = await JS.InvokeAsync<bool>("confirm",
                "Are you sure you are ready to leave?");

        if (!confirm)
        {
            context.PreventNavigation();
        }
    }
}
```

In the preceding code, the `IsNavigationIntercepted` method is used to determine whether the navigation was intercepted from a link. If it was intercepted from a link, a JavaScript `confirm` dialog is displayed. If the user does not confirm that they want to leave the page, the `PreventNavigation` method prevents the navigation from occurring.

TIP

For more information on invoking JavaScript functions from .NET methods, refer to *Chapter 5, Building a Local Storage Service Using JavaScript Interoperability (JS Interop)*.

Now let's get a quick overview of the project that we are going to build in this chapter.

Creating the expense tracker project

In this chapter, we will build a project to track travel expenses. We will be able to view, add, and edit expenses. The expenses will be stored in a Microsoft SQL Server database.

This is a screenshot of the Home page from the completed application:

Figure 12.2: Home page of the expenses tracker

This is a screenshot of the Add Expense page from the completed application:

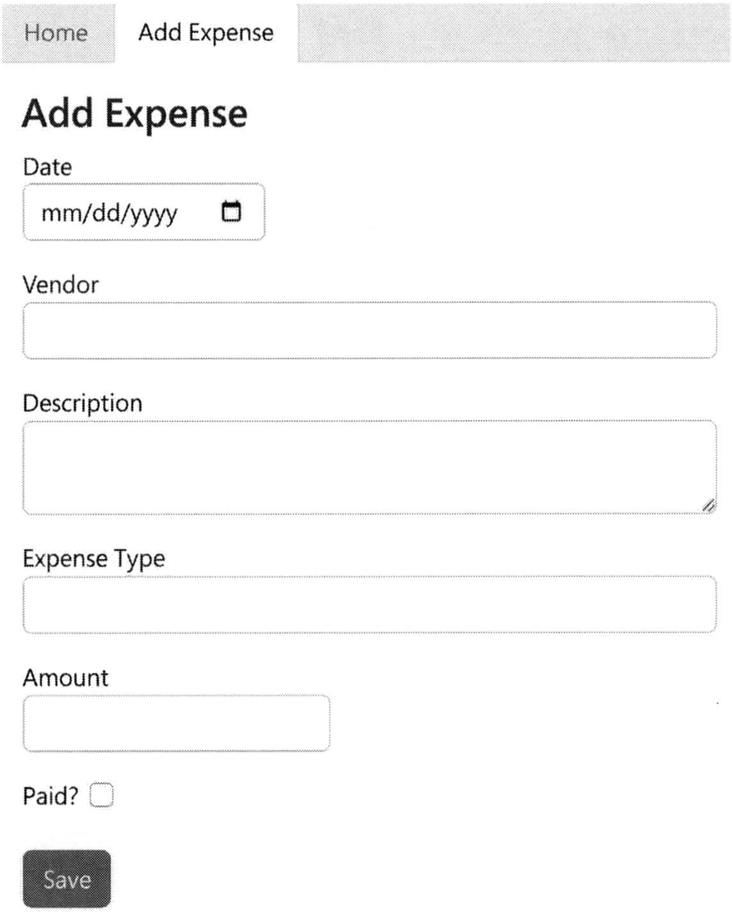

Figure 12.3: Add Expense page of expense tracker

The build time for this project is approximately 60 minutes.

Project overview

The ExpenseTracker project will be created by using Microsoft's **Blazor WebAssembly App Empty** project template to create a hosted Blazor WebAssembly project. First, we will add Bootstrap and a tabbed menu. Then, we will add the classes and API controllers needed for our project. We will add a table to the Home page to display the current list of expenses. We will use the EditForm component in conjunction with many of the built-in input components to add and edit the expenses. Finally, we will add a NavigationLock component to prevent the user from losing their edits by navigating to another page.

Create the expense tracker project

We need to create a new Blazor WebAssembly app. We do this as follows:

1. Open Visual Studio 2022.

2. Click the **Create a new project** button.

3. Press *Alt+S* to enter the search for templates textbox.

4. Enter Blazor and press the *Enter* key.

    The following screenshot shows the **Blazor WebAssembly App Empty** project template:

Figure 12.4: Blazor WebAssembly App Empty project template

5. Select the **Blazor WebAssembly App Empty** project template and click the **Next** button.

6. Enter ExpenseTracker in the **Project name** textbox and click the **Next** button.

This is a screenshot of the dialog used to configure our new project:

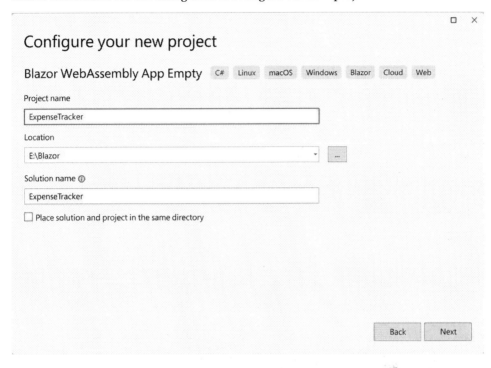

Figure 12.5: Configure your new project dialog

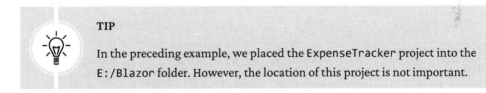

TIP

In the preceding example, we placed the ExpenseTracker project into the E:/Blazor folder. However, the location of this project is not important.

7. Select **.NET 7.0** as the version of the Framework to use.

8. Check the **Configure for HTTPS** checkbox.

9. Check the **ASP.NET Core Hosted** checkbox.

10. Uncheck the **Progressive Web Application** checkbox.

This is a screenshot of the dialog used to collect additional information about our new project:

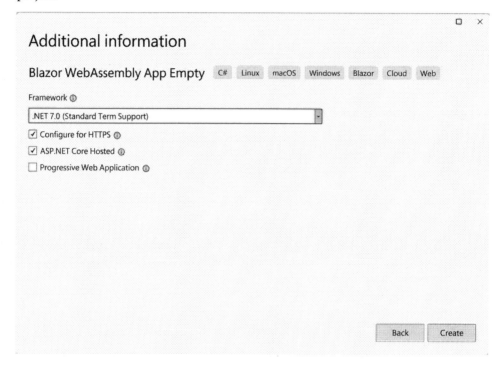

Figure 12.6: Additional Information Dialog

11.   Click the **Create** button.

We have now created a hosted **ExpenseTracker** Blazor WebAssembly project.

The **ExpenseTracker** solution comprises three different projects. The following screenshot of Visual Studio's **Solution Explorer** shows the three projects that are in the solution:

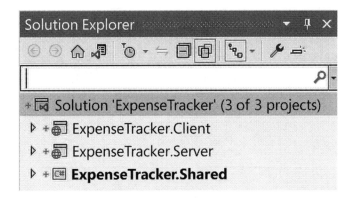

Figure 12.7: Solution Explorer

12. Right-click the **ExpenseTracker.Server** project and select the **Set as Startup Project** option from the menu.

We have created the **ExpenseTracker** solution and set the **ExpenseTracker.Server** project as the startup project. Now we need to work on our UI. We will use Bootstrap to style our controls.

Install Bootstrap

We need to install Bootstrap into our web app. We do this as follows:

1. Right-click the ExpenseTracker.Client/wwwroot/css folder and select the **Add, Client-Side Library** option from the menu.

2. Enter bootstrap into the **Library** search textbox and press the *Enter* key.

3. Select **Choose specific files**.

4. Select only the **css** files, as shown in the following screenshot:

Add Client-Side Library	✕

Provider: cdnjs ⌄

Library: bootstrap@5.2.3   ⓘ

○ Include all library files

◉ Choose specific files:

▲ ■ 📁 Files:
  ▷ ✓ 📁 css
  ▷ ☐ 📁 js
  ▷ ☐ 📁 scss

Target Location: wwwroot/css/bootstrap/

[Install]   [Cancel]

Figure 12.8: Add Client-Side Library dialog

TIP

Although the preceding screenshot has version 5.2.3 of Bootstrap selected, you can use any version of Bootstrap 5 to complete this project.

5. Click the **Install** button.

IMPORTANT NOTE

After you install `Bootstrap`, a new folder will be added to the `wwwroot/css` folder. This new folder contains all the CSS files needed for `Bootstrap`. We will only be using the `bootstrap.min.css` file in this project.

6. Open the `ExpenseTracker.Client/wwwroot/index.html` file.

7. Add the following markup to the head element before the link to the `css/app.css` stylesheet:

```
<link href="css/bootstrap/css/bootstrap.min.css"
      rel="stylesheet" />
```

We have installed `Bootstrap`. Now we will add the classes to store the expense information.

Add the classes

We need to add both an `ExpenseType` class and an `Expense` class. We do this as follows:

1. Right-click the `ExpenseTracker.Shared` folder and select the **Add, Class** option from the menu.
2. Name the new class `ExpenseType`.
3. Click the **Add** button.
4. Make the class public by adding the `public` modifier:

```
public class ExpenseType
```

5. Add the following properties to the `ExpenseType` class:

```
public int Id { get; set; }
public string? Type { get; set; }
```

6. Right-click the `ExpenseTracker.Shared` folder and select the **Add, Class** option from the menu.
7. Name the new class `Expense`.
8. Click the **Add** button.
9. Make the class public by adding the `public` modifier:

```
public class Expense
```

10. Add the following using statement:

```
using System.ComponentModel.DataAnnotations;
```

11. Add the following properties to the `Expense` class:

```
public int Id { get; set; }

[Required]
```

```
public DateTime? Date { get; set; }

[Required]
[MaxLength(100)]
public string? Vendor { get; set; }

public string? Description { get; set; }

[Required]
[Display(Name = "Expense Type")]
public int? ExpenseTypeId { get; set; }

[Required]
[Range(0,
       500,
       ErrorMessage = "The {0} field must be <= {2}")]
public decimal? Amount { get; set; }

public bool Paid { get; set; }
```

In the preceding code, we have used data annotations to add some simple data validation. Date, Vendor, ExpenseTypeId, and Amount are all required. The maximum length of Vendor is 100 characters. The display name for ExpenseTypeId is ExpenseType. The Amount of the expense is capped at 500.

12. From the **Build** menu, select the **Build Solution** option.

We have now added both the ExpenseType class and the Expense class and built our application. Now we need to configure the ASP.NET Web API endpoints.

Add the API controllers

We need to add an API controller for each of the new classes. We do this as follows:

1. Right-click the ExpenseTracker.Server project and select the **Add, New Folder** option from the menu.

2. Name the new folder Controllers.

3. Right-click the ExpenseTracker.Server.Contollers folder and select the **Add, Controller** option from the menu.

4. Select the **API Controller with actions, using Entity Framework** option.

   The following screenshot of the **Add New Scaffolded Item** dialog has the **API Controller with actions, using Entity Framework** option highlighted:

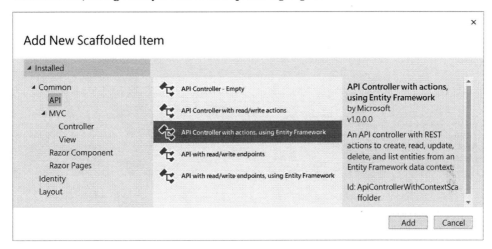

Figure 12.9: Add New Scaffolded Item dialog

5. Click the **Add** button.

6. Set **Model class** to **ExpenseType (ExpenseTracker.Shared)**.

7. Click the **Add data context** button to open the **Add Data Context** dialog:

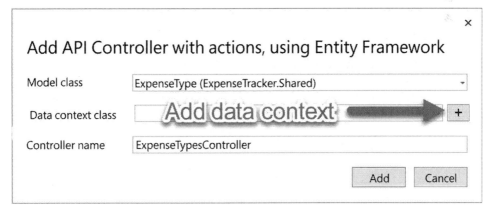

Figure 12.10: Add API Controller with actions, using the Entity Framework dialog

8.   Click the **Add** button to accept the default values.

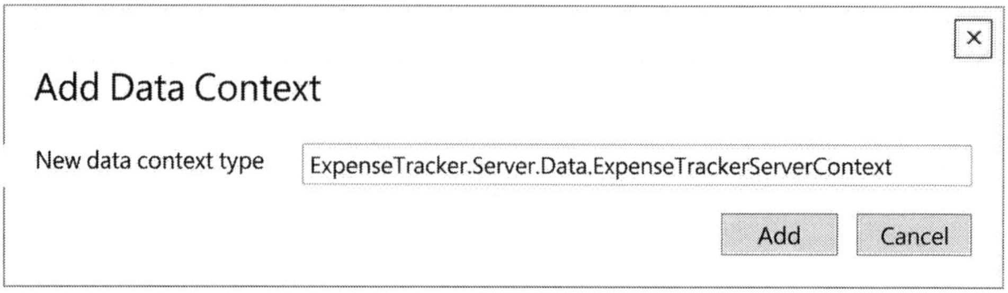

Figure 12.11: Add Data Context dialog

9.   Click the **Add** button on the **Add API Controller with actions, using Entity Framework** dialog.

We have created the ExpenseTypeController class. Now we need to repeat the preceding steps to create the ExpenseController class.

10. Right-click the ExpenseTracker.Server.Controllers folder and select the **Add, Controller** option from the menu.

11. Select the **API Controller with actions, using Entity Framework** option.

12. Click the **Add** button.

13. Set **Model class** to **Expense (ExpenseTracker.Shared)**.

14. Click the **Add** button.

We have added two new controllers to provide the API endpoints that our application will use. For more information on using ASP.NET Web API, refer to *Chapter 11, Building a Task Manager Using ASP.NET Web API*.

Next, we need to create the SQL Server database.

Create the SQL Server database

We need to create the SQL Server database and add a table for the expenses and a table for the expense types. We do this as follows:

1.   Open the ExpenseTracker.Server/appsettings.json file.

2. Update the connection string to the following:

```
"ConnectionStrings": {
  "ExpenseTrackerServerContext": "Server={Server name};
Database=ExpenseTracker; Trusted_Connection=True; Encrypt=False;"
}
```

3. Replace the {Server name} placeholder with the name of your SQL Server.

IMPORTANT NOTE

Although we are using SQL Server Express 2022, it does not matter what version of SQL Server you use for this project.

4. Open the ExpenseTracker.Server.Data/ExpenseTrackerServerContext.cs file.

5. Add the following OnModelCreating method:

```
protected override void OnModelCreating
    (ModelBuilder modelBuilder)
{
    modelBuilder.Entity<ExpenseType>().HasData(
    new ExpenseType { Type = "Airfare", Id = 1 },
    new ExpenseType { Type = "Lodging", Id = 2 },
    new ExpenseType { Type = "Meal", Id = 3 },
    new ExpenseType { Type = "Other", Id = 4 }
    );
}
```

The preceding code will seed the ExpenseType table.

6. From the **Tools** menu, select the **NuGet Package Manager**, **Package Manager Console** option.

7. In the **Package Manager Console**, verify that the **Default project** is set to **ExpenseTracker. Server**.

8. Execute the following commands in the **Package Manager Console**:

```
Add-Migration Init
Update-Database
```

The preceding commands use `Entity Framework migrations` to update SQL Server.

9. Press *Ctrl+F5* to start the application without debugging.

10. Add `/api/expensetypes` to the address bar and press *Enter*.

The following screenshot shows the JSON that is returned by `ExpenseTypesController`:

```
▼ [
    ▼ {
          "id": 1,
          "type": "Airfare"
      },
    ▼ {
          "id": 2,
          "type": "Lodging"
      },
    ▼ {
          "id": 3,
          "type": "Meal"
      },
    ▼ {
          "id": 4,
          "type": "Other"
      }
  ]
```

Figure 12.12: JSON returned by the ExpenseTypes API controller

11. Close the browser.

We have created a new database on SQL Server, added two tables, and populated one of the tables with seed data. After we finished setting up SQL Server, we tested that `ExpenseTypesController` works. Finally, we are ready to create a component to display the expenses that are stored in SQL Server.

View the expenses

We need to add a table to the **Home** page to display the list of expenses. We do this as follows:

1. Return to Visual Studio.

2. Open the `ExpenseTracker.Client.Pages/Index.razor` page.

3. Remove the h1 element.

4. Add the following code:

```
@using ExpenseTracker.Shared
@inject HttpClient Http


<h2>Expenses</h2>

@if (expenses == null)
{
    <p><em>Loading...</em></p>
}
else if (expenses.Count == 0)
{
    <div>None Found</div>
}
else
{
}

@code {
    List<Expense>? expenses;
}
```

The preceding code defines expenses as a `List<Expense>` and checks to see if it is null or empty. If it is null, it renders the loading message, and if it is empty, it renders the **None Found** message.

5. Add the following `OnInitializedAsync` method to the code block:

```
protected override async Task OnInitializedAsync()
{
    expenses = await Http.GetFromJsonAsync
        <List<Expense>>("api/expenses");
}
```

The preceding code populates the expenses object by using the GetFromJsonAsync method of the HttpClient. For more information on the HttpClient refer to *Chapter 11, Building a Task Manager User ASP.NET Web API.*

6. Add the following table element to the else statement:

```
<table class="table">
</table>
```

7. Add the following thead element to the table element:

```
<thead>
    <tr>
        <th></th>
        <th>#</th>
        <th>Date</th>
        <th>Vendor</th>
        <th class="text-right">Amount</th>
    </tr>
</thead>
```

8. Add the following tbody element to the table element after the thead element:

```
<tbody>
    @foreach (var item in expenses)
    {
        <tr class="@(item.Paid ? "" : "table-danger")">
            <td>
                <a href="/expense/@item.Id">Edit</a>
            </td>
            <td>@item.Id</td>
            <td>@item.Date!.Value.ToShortDateString()</td>
            <td>@item.Vendor</td>
            <td class="text-right">@item.Amount</td>
        </tr>
    }
</tbody>
```

The preceding code loops through each of the Expense objects in the collection and displays them as rows in a table. If the expense is not yet paid, the row is highlighted in red by using the table-danger class.

9.   Press *Ctrl+F5* to start the application without debugging.

This is a screenshot of our application:

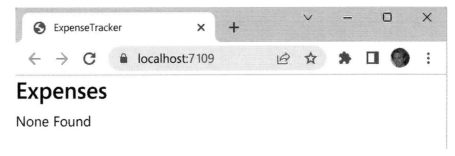

Figure 12.13: Home page of the ExpenseTracker

10.   Close the browser window.

We have added the ability to display the expenses in a table on the Home page. Next, we need to add the ability to add expenses.

Add the edit expense component

We need to add a component to enable us to add and edit expenses. We do this as follows:

1.   Return to Visual Studio.

2.   Open the `ExpenseTracker.Client.MainLayout.razor` page.

3.   Add the following markup before the `main` element:

```
<ul class="nav nav-tabs bg-secondary bg-opacity-10">
    <li class="nav-item">
        <NavLink class="nav-link"
                 href=""
                 Match="NavLinkMatch.All">
            Home
        </NavLink>
    </li>
    <li class="nav-item">
        <NavLink class="nav-link" href="expense">
            Add Expense
        </NavLink>
    </li>
</ul>
```

4. The preceding markup uses Bootstrap to render a tabbed interface with two options: **Home** and **Add Expense**.

5. Update the main element to the following to add some padding to the rendered element:

```
<main class="p-3">
    @Body
</main>
```

6. Right-click the ExpenseTracker.Client.Pages folder and select the **Add**, **Razor Component** option from the menu.

7. Name the new component ExpenseEdit.

8. Click the **Add** button.

9. Update the markup to the following:

```
@page "/expense"
@page "/expense/{id:int}"

@using ExpenseTracker.Shared
@using Microsoft.AspNetCore.Components.Forms

@inject HttpClient Http
@inject NavigationManager Nav

@if (id == 0)
{
    <h2>Add Expense</h2>
}
else
{
    <h2>Edit Expense</h2>
}

@if (!ready)
{
    <p><em>Loading...</em></p>
}
else
{
    <EditForm Model="expense"
```

```
                    OnValidSubmit="HandleValidSubmit">
        </EditForm>
        <div>@error</div>
    }

    @code {

    }
```

The preceding code displays EditForm if the component is ready. It uses the value of the id parameter to determine if the form is performing an add or an edit.

10. Add the following code to the code block:

```
[Parameter] public int id { get; set; }

private bool ready;
private string? error;
private Expense? expense = new();
private List<ExpenseType>? types;
```

11. Add the following OnInitializedAsync method to the code block:

```
protected override async Task OnInitializedAsync()
{
    types = await Http.GetFromJsonAsync<List<ExpenseType>>
      ("api/ExpenseTypes");

    if (id > 0)
    {
        try
        {

        }
        catch (Exception)
        {
            Nav.NavigateTo("/");
        }
    }
    ready = true;
}
```

The preceding code initializes both the types object and the expense object. Once they have both been initialized, the value of ready is set to true.

12. Add the following code to the try block:

```
var result = await Http.GetFromJsonAsync<Expense>
    ($"api/Expenses/{id}");

if (result != null)
{
    expense = result;
}
```

The preceding code initializes the expense object.

13. Add the following HandleValidSubmit method to the code block:

```
private async Task HandleValidSubmit()
{
    HttpResponseMessage response;
    if (expense!.Id == 0)
    {
        response = await Http.PostAsJsonAsync
            ("api/Expenses", expense);
    }
    else
    {
        string requestUri = $"api/Expenses/{expense.Id}";
        response = await Http.PutAsJsonAsync
            (requestUri, expense);
    };
    if (response.IsSuccessStatusCode)
    {
        Nav.NavigateTo("/");
    }
    else
    {
        error = response.ReasonPhrase;
    };
}
```

The preceding code adds new expenses by using the PostAsJsonAsync method and updates existing expenses by using the PutAsJsonAsync method. If the relevant method is successful, the user is returned to the **Home** page. Otherwise, an error message is displayed.

We have completed the code for this component, but EditForm is still empty. We now need to add some markup to EditForm.

Add the input components

We need to add input components to the EditForm element. We do this as follows:

1. Add the following markup to EditForm to input the Date property:

```
<div class="row mb-3">
    <label>
        Date
        <InputDate @bind-Value="expense.Date"
                   class="form-control" />
    </label>
</div>
```

2. Add the following markup to EditForm to input the Vendor property:

```
<div class="row mb-3">
    <label>
        Vendor
        <InputText @bind-Value="expense.Vendor"
                   class="form-control" />
    </label>
</div>
```

3. Add the following markup to EditForm to input the Description property:

```
<div class="row mb-3">
    <label>
        Description
        <InputTextArea @bind-Value="expense.Description"
                       class="form-control" />      </label>
</div>
```

4. Add the following markup to `EditForm` to input the `ExpenseTypeId` property:

```
<div class="row mb-3">
    <label>
        Expense Type
        <InputSelect @bind-Value="expense.ExpenseTypeId"
                     class="form-control">
            <option value=""></option>
            @foreach (var item in types!)
            {
                <option value="@item.Id">
                    @item.Type
                </option>
            }
        </InputSelect>
    </label>
</div>
```

5. Add the following markup to `EditForm` to input the `Amount` property:

```
<div class="row mb-3">
    <label>
        Amount
        <InputNumber @bind-Value="expense.Amount"
                     class="form-control" />
    </label>
</div>
```

6. Add the following markup to `EditForm` to input the `Paid` property:

```
<div class="row mb-3">
    <label>
        Paid?
        <InputCheckbox @bind-Value="expense.Paid"
                       class="form-check-input mx-1" />
    </label>
</div>
```

7. Add the following markup to EditForm for the Submit button:

```
<div class="pt-2 pb-2">
    <button type="submit"
        class="btn btn-primary mr-auto">
        Save
    </button>
</div>
```

8. Add the following markup to EditForm to add the validation summary:

```
<DataAnnotationsValidator />
<ValidationSummary />
```

9. Open the ExpenseTracker.Client.wwroot/css/app.css file.

10. Add the following styles:

```
.invalid {
    outline: 1px solid red;
}

.validation-message {
    color: red;
}

h2 {
    color: darkblue;
}
```

The preceding styles provide validation styling for the related elements and change the color of the h2 elements to dark blue.

11. Press *Ctrl+F5* to start the application without debugging.

12. Select the **Add Expense** link.

13. Click the **Save** button.

The following screenshot shows the validation errors:

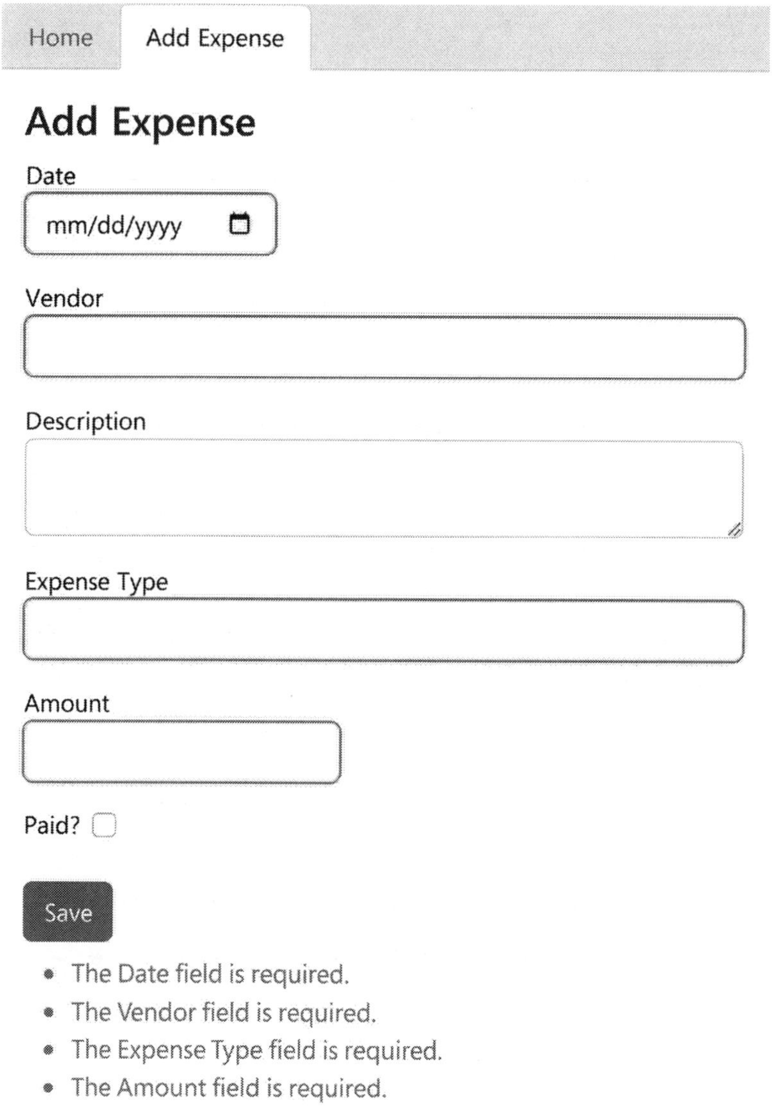

Figure 12.14: Data validation for the ExpenseEdit component

Test the edit expense component

1. Add a valid expense.
2. Click the **Save** button.

If the expense is valid, clicking the **Save** button will save the expense to the SQL Server database and return the user to the **Home** page.

3. Click the **Edit** link next to the new expense.

4. Modify the expense.

5. Click the **Save** button.

6. Click the **Add Expense** link.

7. Add another valid expense.

8. Click the **Save** button.

9. Click the **Add Expense** link.

10. Add another valid expense but do not click the **Save** button.

11. Click the **Home** link.

12. Click the **Add Expense** link.

The valid expense is gone.

If the user enters data and navigates away from the page before they click the **Save** button, all their data entry is lost. To help prevent this from happening, we can lock their navigation by using the NavigationLock component.

Lock navigation

We need to add a NavigationLock component. We do this as follows:

1. Return to Visual Studio.

2. Open the ExpenseTracker.Client.Pages/ExpenseEdit.razor page.

3. Add the following @inject directive:

```
@inject IJSRuntime JS
```

4. Add the following NavigationLock below the @inject directives:

```
<NavigationLock ConfirmExternalNavigation="true"
    OnBeforeInternalNavigation="HandleBeforeInternalNav" />
```

5. Add the following code to the code block:

```
private async Task HandleBeforeInternalNav
    (LocationChangingContext context)
{
```

```
if (context.IsNavigationIntercepted)
{
    var confirm = await JS.InvokeAsync<boo>("confirm",
        "Are you sure you are ready to leave?");

    if (!confirm)
    {
        context.PreventNavigation();
    }
}
}
```

The preceding code uses JavaScript to display a confirm dialog when the user uses a link to navigate away from the current page.

6. Press *Ctrl+F5* to start the application without debugging.

7. Select the **Add Expense** link.

8. Add a valid expense.

9. Click the **Home** link.

    The following `confirm` dialog will be displayed:

Figure 12.15: Confirm dialog

10. Click the **Cancel** button to cancel navigation.

We have completed the expense tracker project.

Summary

You should now be able to use the `EditForm` component in conjunction with the built-in input components to create an input data form. You should also be comfortable with the built-in validation components. Finally, you should understand how to lock the navigation.

In this chapter, we introduced the built-in EditForm component, various input components, and the validation components. We also introduced a component that can be used to lock the user's navigation. After that, we used the **Blazor WebAssembly App** project template to create a multi-project solution. We added a couple of classes and a couple of API controllers. Next, we configured SQL Server by updating the connection string to the database and using **Entity Framework** migrations. We updated the Home page to display the list of expenses. We added a new page that included an EditForm component and many of the built-in input components to input, validate, and submit the expenses. Finally, we added a NavigationLock component.

We can apply our new skills to add data input and validation to any Blazor WebAssembly app.

The next step is to start building your own web apps. To stay up to date and learn more about Blazor WebAssembly, visit https://blazor.net, and read the *ASP.NET Blog* at https://devblogs.microsoft.com/dotnet/category/aspnet/.

We hope you enjoyed the book and wish you every success!

Questions

The following questions are provided for your consideration:

1. What are the advantages of using the built-in input components?

2. How would you update the HandleBeforeInternalNav method to only display the confirm dialog if there are unsaved changes?

3. What is the purpose of the EditForm component?

Further reading

The following resources provide more information concerning the topics in this chapter:

- For more information on ASP.NET Core component forms, refer to https://learn.microsoft.com/en-us/dotnet/api/microsoft.aspnetcore.components.forms.

- For more information on data annotations, refer to https://learn.microsoft.com/en-us/dotnet/api/system.componentmodel.dataannotations.

- For more information on routing, refer to https://learn.microsoft.com/en-us/dotnet/api/microsoft.aspnetcore.components.routing.

Join our community on Discord

Join our community's Discord space for discussions with the author and other readers:

`https://packt.link/BlazorWASM2e`

packt.com

Subscribe to our online digital library for full access to over 7,000 books and videos, as well as industry leading tools to help you plan your personal development and advance your career. For more information, please visit our website.

Why subscribe?

- Spend less time learning and more time coding with practical eBooks and Videos from over 4,000 industry professionals

- Improve your learning with Skill Plans built especially for you

- Get a free eBook or video every month

- Fully searchable for easy access to vital information

- Copy and paste, print, and bookmark content

At www.packt.com, you can also read a collection of free technical articles, sign up for a range of free newsletters, and receive exclusive discounts and offers on Packt books and eBooks.

Other Books You May Enjoy

If you enjoyed this book, you may be interested in these other books by Packt:

C# 11 and .NET 7 – Modern Cross-Platform Development Fundamentals, Seventh Edition

Mark J. Price

ISBN: 9781803237800

- Build rich web experiences using Blazor, Razor Pages, the Model-View-Controller (MVC) pattern, and other features of ASP.NET Core
- Write, test, and debug functions
- Query and manipulate data using LINQ
- Integrate and update databases in your apps using Entity Framework Core models
- Build and consume powerful services using the latest technologies, including Web API and Minimal API

Apps and Services with .NET 7

Mark J. Price

ISBN: 9781801813433

- Learn how to build more efficient, secure, and scalable apps and services
- Leverage specialized .NET libraries to improve your applications
- Implement popular third-party libraries like Serilog and FluentValidation
- Build cross-platform apps with .NET MAUI and integrate with native mobile features
- Get familiar with a variety of technologies for implementing services like gRPC and GraphQL
- Explore Blazor WebAssembly and use open-source Blazor component libraries
- Store and manage data locally and in the cloud with SQL Server and Cosmos DB

Web Development with Blazor, Second Edition

Jimmy Engström

ISBN: 9781803241494

- Understand the different technologies that can be used with Blazor, such as Blazor Server, Blazor WebAssembly, and Blazor Hybrid
- Find out how to build simple and advanced Blazor components
- Explore the differences between Blazor Server and Blazor WebAssembly projects
- Discover how Minimal APIs work and build your own API
- Explore existing JavaScript libraries in Blazor and JavaScript interoperability
- Learn techniques to debug your Blazor Server and Blazor WebAssembly applications
- Test Blazor components using bUnit

Packt is searching for authors like you

If you're interested in becoming an author for Packt, please visit authors.packtpub.com and apply today. We have worked with thousands of developers and tech professionals, just like you, to help them share their insight with the global tech community. You can make a general application, apply for a specific hot topic that we are recruiting an author for, or submit your own idea.

Share your thoughts

Now you've finished *Blazor WebAssembly By Example, Second Edition*, we'd love to hear your thoughts! Scan the QR code below to go straight to the Amazon review page for this book and share your feedback or leave a review on the site that you purchased it from.

https://packt.link/r/1803241853

Your review is important to us and the tech community and will help us make sure we're delivering excellent quality content.

Index

Download a free PDF copy of this book

Thanks for purchasing this book!

Do you like to read on the go but are unable to carry your print books everywhere? Is your eBook purchase not compatible with the device of your choice?

Don't worry, now with every Packt book you get a DRM-free PDF version of that book at no cost.

Read anywhere, any place, on any device. Search, copy, and paste code from your favorite technical books directly into your application.

The perks don't stop there, you can get exclusive access to discounts, newsletters, and great free content in your inbox daily

Follow these simple steps to get the benefits:

1. Scan the QR code or visit the link below

https://packt.link/free-ebook/9781803241852

2. Submit your proof of purchase
3. That's it! We'll send your free PDF and other benefits to your email directly

Made in the USA
Monee, IL
09 February 2024